The Effects of Commuting on Pilot Fatigue

Committee on the Effects of Commuting on Pilot Fatigue

Board on Human-Systems Integration

Division of Behavioral and Social Sciences and Education

Transportation Research Board

NATIONAL RESEARCH COUNCIL
OF THE NATIONAL ACADEMIES

THE NATIONAL ACADEMIES PRESS
Washington, D.C.
www.nap.edu

THE NATIONAL ACADEMIES PRESS 500 Fifth Street, N.W. Washington, DC 20001

NOTICE: The project that is the subject of this report was approved by the Governing Board of the National Research Council, whose members are drawn from the councils of the National Academy of Sciences, the National Academy of Engineering, and the Institute of Medicine. The members of the committee responsible for the report were chosen for their special competences and with regard for appropriate balance.

This study was supported by Grant No. DTFAWA-10-C-00115 between the National Academy of Sciences and the Federal Aviation Administration. Any opinions, findings, conclusions, or recommendations expressed in this publication are those of the author(s) and do not necessarily reflect the views of the organizations or agencies that provided support for the project.

International Standard Book Number-13: 978-0-309-21696-8
International Standard Book Number-10: 0-309-21696-6

Additional copies of this report are available from the National Academies Press, 500 Fifth Street, N.W., Lockbox 285, Washington, DC 20055; (800) 624-6242 or (202) 334-3313 (in the Washington metropolitan area); Internet, http://www.nap.edu

Printed in the United States of America

Suggested citation: National Research Council. (2011). *The Effects of Commuting on Pilot Fatigue.* Committee on the Effects of Commuting on Pilot Fatigue, Board on Human-Systems Integration. Division of Behavioral and Social Sciences and Education. Washington, DC: The National Academies Press.

THE NATIONAL ACADEMIES

Advisers to the Nation on Science, Engineering, and Medicine

The **National Academy of Sciences** is a private, nonprofit, self-perpetuating society of distinguished scholars engaged in scientific and engineering research, dedicated to the furtherance of science and technology and to their use for the general welfare. Upon the authority of the charter granted to it by the Congress in 1863, the Academy has a mandate that requires it to advise the federal government on scientific and technical matters. Dr. Ralph J. Cicerone is president of the National Academy of Sciences.

The **National Academy of Engineering** was established in 1964, under the charter of the National Academy of Sciences, as a parallel organization of outstanding engineers. It is autonomous in its administration and in the selection of its members, sharing with the National Academy of Sciences the responsibility for advising the federal government. The National Academy of Engineering also sponsors engineering programs aimed at meeting national needs, encourages education and research, and recognizes the superior achievements of engineers. Dr. Charles M. Vest is president of the National Academy of Engineering.

The **Institute of Medicine** was established in 1970 by the National Academy of Sciences to secure the services of eminent members of appropriate professions in the examination of policy matters pertaining to the health of the public. The Institute acts under the responsibility given to the National Academy of Sciences by its congressional charter to be an adviser to the federal government and, upon its own initiative, to identify issues of medical care, research, and education. Dr. Harvey V. Fineberg is president of the Institute of Medicine.

The **National Research Council** was organized by the National Academy of Sciences in 1916 to associate the broad community of science and technology with the Academy's purposes of furthering knowledge and advising the federal government. Functioning in accordance with general policies determined by the Academy, the Council has become the principal operating agency of both the National Academy of Sciences and the National Academy of Engineering in providing services to the government, the public, and the scientific and engineering communities. The Council is administered jointly by both Academies and the Institute of Medicine. Dr. Ralph J. Cicerone and Dr. Charles M. Vest are chair and vice chair, respectively, of the National Research Council.

www.national-academies.org

COMMITTEE ON THE EFFECTS OF COMMUTING ON PILOT FATIGUE

Clinton V. Oster, Jr. (*Chair*), School of Public and Environmental Affairs, Indiana University
Benjamin A. Berman, Senior Research Associate, Ames Research Center, U.S. National Aeronautics and Space Administration
J. Lynn Caldwell, Senior Research Psychologist, Wright-Patterson Air Force Base, OH
David F. Dinges, Department of Psychiatry, Perelman School of Medicine, University of Pennsylvania
R. Curtis Graeber, The Graeber Group, Kirkland, WA
John K. Lauber,[1] Independent Consultant, Vaughn, WA
David E. Meyer, Department of Psychology, University of Michigan
Matthew Rizzo, Department of Neurology, Mechanical and Industrial Engineering, and the Public Policy Center, University of Iowa
David J. Schroeder, Independent Consultant
J. Frank Yates, Department of Psychology, University of Michigan

Toby Warden, *Study Director*
Julie Schuck, *Senior Program Associate*
Eric Chen, *Senior Project Assistant*
Stephen Godwin, *Liaison,* Studies and Special Programs, Transportation Research Board

[1]Resigned from the committee in February 2011.

BOARD ON HUMAN-SYSTEMS INTEGRATION
2010-2011

Acknowledgments

This report is the work of the Committee on the Effects of Commuting on Pilot Fatigue, a project of the National Research Council's (NRC's) Division of Behavioral and Social Sciences and Education, overseen by the Board on Human-Systems Integration. The expertise and hard work of the committee were advanced by the support of our sponsor, the contributions of able consultants and staff, and the input of stakeholders. This study was congressionally mandated and sponsored by the Federal Aviation Administration, and the support of their staff Jodi Baker, John Duncan, Dale E. Roberts, Kevin West, and Larry Youngblut were much appreciated.

The committee also benefited from presentations by Lori Brown, faculty specialist, Western Michigan University College of Aviation; Bob Coffman, Coalition of Airline Pilots Association; Captain William McDonald, FedEx; Captain Bill Mims, retired; Jeff Moller, assistant vice president, Operations Systems and Practices, Association of American Railroads; Thomas Nesthus, Civil Aerospace Medical Institute, Federal Aviation Administration; Jessica Nowinski, National Aeronautics and Space Administration (NASA) Ames Research Center; pilot Charlotte O'Connell; George Paul, director, Technical Services, National Air Carriers Association; Mark Rosekind, member, National Transportation Safety Board; Steven Sargent, Compass Airlines; Jeff Skiles, U.S. Airline Pilots Association; Captain Bill Soer; and Irving Statler, NASA Ames Research Center. Comments at committee meetings provided by other stakeholders and guests in attendance were also valuable.

Additionally, the committee wishes to thank the 33 airlines who provided information in response to the committee's request for input (see Appendix B) and the following aviation-related associations who also provided input: Cargo Airline Association, Coalition of Airline Pilots Associations, National Air Carriers Association, and U.S. Airline Pilots Association. This input was critical in allowing the committee to better understand pilot commuting.

To the NRC staff, special thanks are due to Barbara Wanchisen and Mary Ellen O'Connell of the Board on Human-Systems Integration and Stephen Godwin of the Transportation Research Board who provided oversight and support of the study. Thanks also to senior project assistant Eric Chen who provided administrative and logistical support over the course of the study as well as preliminary analysis for the zip code data. We also thank Daniel Cork, senior program officer with the Committee on National Statistics, for his additional statistical analyses; Julie Schuck, senior program associate, for her support with editing and writing; and Cherie Chauvin, program officer, for her help with editing and graphics.

We also thank Jessica Scheer for her assistance with the committee's analysis of the Notice of Proposed Rulemaking comments and Susan Van Hemel for her assistance with fact checking and editing. And finally we thank the executive office reports staff of the Division of Behavioral and Social Sciences and Education, especially Eugenia Grohman, who provided valuable help with the editing and production of the report, and Kirsten Sampson Snyder, who managed the report review process. We would also like to thank Tony Klausing of Indiana University for his assistance with the analysis of the aircraft departure data.

John Lauber, who resigned from the committee in February 2011, provided additional unpaid consultation on the report; we were fortunate to continue to benefit from his expertise after his resignation.

This report has been reviewed in draft form by individuals chosen for their diverse perspectives and technical expertise, in accordance with procedures approved by the NRC's Report Review Committee. The purpose of this independent review is to provide candid and critical comments that will assist the institution in making its published report as sound as possible and to ensure that the report meets institutional standards for objectivity, evidence, and responsiveness to the study charge. The review comments and draft manuscript remain confidential to protect the integrity of the deliberative process.

We wish to thank the following individuals for their review of this report: Evan Byrne, Human Performance and Survival Factors Division, National Transportation Safety Board; Paul Fischbeck, Department of Engineering and Public Policy and Department of Social and Decision Sciences, Center for the Study and Improvement of Regulation, Carnegie Mellon University; R. John Hansman, T. Wilson Professor of Aeronautics & Astronautics, MIT International Center for Air Transportation, Massachusetts Institute of Technology; John Marshall, aviation consultant,

Atlanta, GA; James C. Miller, human factors consultant, San Antonio, TX; John O'Brien, aviation consultant, VA; Joseph P. Ornato, Department of Emergency Medicine, Virginia Commonwealth University, Richmond, VA; Barbara Phillips, Department of Internal Medicine, University of Kentucky; Nicholas Sabatini, aviation consultant, Alexandria, VA; and Nita Lewis Shattuck, Human Systems Integration Program, Operations Research Department, Naval Postgraduate School, Monterey, CA.

Although the reviewers listed above have provided many constructive comments and suggestions, they were not asked to endorse the conclusions or recommendations nor did they see the final draft of the report before its release. The review of this report was overseen by Richard W. Pew, principal scientist, Raytheon BBN Technologies, Cambridge, MA, as coordinator and and Floyd E. Bloom, Molecular and Integrative Neuroscience Department, The Scripps Research Institute, as review monitor. Appointed by the NRC, they were responsible for making certain that an independent examination of this report was carried out in accordance with institutional procedures and that all review comments were carefully considered. Responsibility for the final content of this report rests entirely with the authoring committee and the institution.

Clinton V. Oster, Jr., *Chair*
Toby Warden, *Study Director*
Committee on the Effects of Commuting on Pilot Fatigue

Contents

Figures, Tables, and Boxes

FIGURES

TABLES

BOXES

Summary

The airline industry operates 24 hours a day, 7 days a week, delivering passengers and cargo to locations worldwide. The pilots who fly the airplanes rely on their own expertise and judgment, that of their fellow crew members, the safety features of the airplane, and characteristics of the aviation system to ensure that the flights arrive safely. Fatigue is a widely acknowledged potential safety risk factor that can contribute to less effective pilot performance. Although the number and timing of hours worked and hours slept can contribute to fatigue, the federal regulations that govern pilot flight and duty time have not been revised in decades.

In summer 2010 the U.S. Congress directed the Federal Aviation Administration (FAA) to update these regulations, taking into account recent research related to sleep and fatigue. A Notice of Proposed Rulemaking (NPRM) was released September 14, 2010. As part of their directive, Congress also instructed FAA to have the National Academy of Sciences conduct a study on the effects of commuting on pilot fatigue. The study was designed to review research and other information related to the prevalence and characteristics of commuting; to the science of sleep, fatigue, and circadian rhythms; to airline and regulatory oversight policies; and to pilot and airline practices.[1] It was intended to inform the commuting-specific component of the final regulations. This report describes the results of that study.

Pilots live in diverse geographic regions. They commute between where they live and the airports where their duty assignment begins (i.e., their

[1]This study was restricted to airlines operating under 14 CFR 121, which includes most passenger and cargo airlines that fly transport-category aircraft with 10 or more seats.

domicile). The committee considers pilot "commuting" to be the period of time and the activity required of pilots from leaving home to arriving at the domicile (airport—in the crew room, dispatch room, or designated location at the airport) and from leaving the domicile to returning back to home. Pilot commuting takes place during off-duty hours. Pilot commuting differs from the commuting of other workers in terms of frequency and variability, distance, transport modes, and time of day.

Most pilots work for four main types of airlines: mainline airlines that predominately operate scheduled service in jet aircraft with more than 90 seats and often provide intercontinental service; regional airlines that predominately operate scheduled service in aircraft, both jet and turboprop, with 90 or fewer seats; cargo airlines that deliver goods all over the world; and charter airlines that provide nonscheduled passenger flights. Flight scheduling, commuting provisions, seniority systems, and length of duty time vary across these segments of the industry.

For most airline pilots, decisions about where to live and when and how to commute are their own to make. Generally, given the nature of flight scheduling, pilots do not commute on a daily basis; in fact, in some cases, they commute only two or three times a month. However, there are no comprehensive data on the frequency of pilot commuting, the lengths of commutes, or such trip characteristics as the transportation modes used in commuting. There are also no systematic data on the timing, duration, or quality of pilots' sleep before or during their commutes. Furthermore, changes in airports to which the pilots' report for the start of their duty (their domicile) may alter commuting patterns, but the committee was unable to obtain any systematic information about how frequently individual pilots experience domicile changes or how such changes affect pilot commuting behavior.

The committee's analysis of home-to-domicile distances, calculated from zip codes of 17,519 mainline pilots and 7,553 regional airline pilots, provided by 15 airlines, showed that roughly one-half have home-to-domicile distances of less than 150 miles. Less than one-fourth have home-to-domicile distances of more than 750 miles. The distributions are similar for mainline and regional pilots even though these two segments of the industry differ. The proportion of pilots who have long coast-to-coast or international home-to-domicile distances is about 2 percent for mainline pilots and 1 percent for regional pilots. The committee also analyzed the home-to-domicile distances of 4,488 airline pilots from four cargo airlines and 631 airline pilots from five charter airlines, but many of those airlines have different basing policies so the data from their pilots are not directly comparable to mainline and regional airlines.

These home-to-domicile distances are only suggestive of commuting patterns for several reasons. First, the pilots' residence zip codes were for their homes of record (i.e., those designated by the pilots on IRS forms and for the receipt of official notices from the airlines). Some pilots may have more than one home, and some may commute to work from temporary or seasonal residences that are not frequent origination points for their commutes. Second, pilots may arrange for rest facilities and obtain sleep at or near their domiciles (or at an en route location for a multistop commute) between leaving home and arriving at the domicile. Third, commutes may have varying degrees of circuity, particularly those involving multiple connecting flights, so that the actual distances traveled are likely to be longer and may be much longer than the straight-line distances. Fourth, these data are for one point in time and provide no insight into how commuting patterns might change in response to a pilot's career progression or from changes in the patterns of airline operations that result from mergers, bankruptcies, and changing economic or competitive conditions. Finally, the committee does not know the extent to which the sample of pilots in this analysis is representative of the larger pilot population. We caution the reader not to assume that the distance pilots live from the airport reflects their likely commute times. There is remarkably little data to evaluate this assumption.

In all four segments of the industry, a breakdown of the home-to-domicile distances by airline suggests that there is considerable variation across individual airlines. Similarly, an analysis of changes in aircraft departures from the principal cities served by each of 30 mainline, regional, and cargo airlines also found large differences in changes in flight patterns across airlines. Overall, the airline industry is heterogeneous, with great variability across the entire industry, in each segment of the industry, and for individual airlines, as well as among individual pilots.

Commuting is one of many activities that usually take place during a pilot's off-duty time. If decisions about how and when to commute result in a pilot's not having adequate sleep, or if unanticipated circumstances prevent adequate sleep, there is the clear potential that the pilot will arrive to work fatigued and be forced to make the decision about being fit to fly. Similarly, if sleep is inadequate as a result of commuting time and the pilot does not decline the flight assignment on grounds of fatigue, the pilot may experience fatigue during the flight and duty period. A pilot's decision about fitness for duty is likely made within the context of the flight schedule, the airline's relevant policies and their implications for pay (i.e., whether or not the pilot will get paid if he or she calls in fatigued or sick), and knowledge about the specifics of the airplane and flight. Most jet airplanes are highly automated, with the periods of greatest pilot activity for most flights occurring during takeoff and landing. Most turboprop regional airplanes are less automated.

There have been few aviation accidents in which fatigue was cited as a probable cause or contributing factor by the National Transportation Safety

Board (NTSB), the agency responsible for investigating all U.S. airline (and other transportation) accidents.[2] Of the NTSB reports for the 863 relevant accidents that occurred between 1982 and 2010, only nine of the accidents for which the investigation was complete mentioned fatigue as a probable cause or contributing factor.[3] None mentioned commuting as either a probable cause or contributing factor. However, it can be difficult during an accident investigation to determine the extent to which fatigue might have played a role in the accident as well as the extent to which commuting might have contributed to fatigue.

Based on the available information on (1) the commuting practices of pilots and commuting policies of airlines, (2) aviation accident reports, (3) the range of distances pilots live from their work domiciles, and (4) scientific information on fatigue that results from inadequate sleep, prolonged time awake and circadian timing, the committee concludes the following.

CONCLUSION: There is potential for pilots to become fatigued from commuting. However, there is insufficient evidence to determine the extent to which pilot commuting has been a safety risk in part because little is known about specific pilot commuting practices and in part because the safety checks, balances, and redundancies in the aviation system may mitigate the consequences of pilot fatigue.

Given that there is some potential for commuting to contribute to fatigue and clear evidence that fatigue can decrease performance, the committee believes it is important to reduce the likelihood that commuting could contribute to pilot fatigue during duty. At the same time, the safety risk posed by commuting-induced fatigue is unknown. There is a need to understand the extent to which the risk posed by fatigue resulting from some commutes may be mitigated by individual, airplane (e.g., flight deck systems), or aviation system (e.g., crew resource management) characteristics.

Furthermore, there is tremendous variability across individual pilot commuting practices and day-to-day experiences. Attempting to determine

[2]An aircraft accident is defined in Title 49 Section 830.2 as "an occurrence associated with the operation of an aircraft which takes place between the time any person boards the aircraft with the intention of flight and all such persons have disembarked, and in which any person suffers death or serious injury, or in which the aircraft receives substantial damage" (Code of Federal Regulations, 2009).

[3]"The NTSB determines the probable cause or causes of accidents. The objective of this determination is to discern the cause-and-effect relationships in the accident sequence. This could be described as why the accident happened. In determining probable cause, the NTSB considers all facts, conditions, and circumstances associated with the accident. Within each accident occurrence, any information that helps explain why that event happened is designated as either a 'cause' or 'factor.' The term 'factor' is used to describe situations or circumstances that contribute to the accident cause" (National Transportation Safety Board, 2010a, p. 52).

a one-size-fits-all delineation on what constitutes a fatiguing commute based on either time or distance is difficult because the length of the commute, measured either by distance or time spent commuting, does not necessarily determine whether or not the pilot reports fit for duty and well rested. In addition, regulations specific to commuting could inadvertently lead to increased safety problems and additional loss of lives due to the unintended and unanticipated consequences. Consequently, although action is warranted to reduce the likelihood that commuting will present a safety risk, there is a lack of evidence to support the basis for issuance of regulations pertaining to commuting.

> **CONCLUSION: There are inadequate data to specify or determine the effectiveness of regulations regarding pilot commuting. Additional information is needed to determine if a regulatory approach ultimately would be appropriate.**

At the same time, there is extensive scientific evidence on the negative effects of fatigue on performance of many cognitive tasks, including those essential for safely operating a commercial aircraft. These include adverse effects of fatigue induced by sleep loss on maintaining wakefulness and alertness, vigilance and selective attention, psychomotor and cognitive speed, accuracy of performing a wide range of cognitive tasks, working and executive memory, and on higher cognitive functions such as decision making, detection of safety threats, and problem solving, as well as communication and mood. Fatigue is not, however, a binary condition in which one is either rested with no negative effects on performance or fatigued with severe negative effects on performance. There are degrees of fatigue and degrees of the negative effects of fatigue on performance. Moreover, the effects of fatigue on performance can vary substantially from one pilot to the next without any untoward effects on the safety of flight.

The scientific literature shows fatigue as a risk to performance that can result from (1) being awake continuously for more than approximately 16 hours, or (2) sleeping too little (especially less than 6 hours on the day prior to work), or (3) when undertaking work at a time when the body is biologically programmed to be asleep (i.e., an individual's habitual nocturnal sleep period), which for most people is between 10:00 p.m. and 7:00 a.m. Evidence that cognitive performance is adversely affected when sleep per 24 hours is cumulatively less than approximately 6 hours of sleep suggests that pilots should seek to obtain sufficient bed time to ensure they are fit for duty. The detrimental effects of fatigue on performance may be exacerbated by a tendency for individuals to have reduced awareness of the cognitive performance deficits that result.

Pilots are currently required to report fit for duty. Judging whether a pilot is fit for duty is an individual pilot decision that should take into account the amount of sleep received prior to duty.

RECOMMENDATION 1: Pilots should avoid planning commutes or other preduty activities that result in being awake beyond approximately 16 hours before the scheduled end of duty, endeavor to sleep at least 6 hours[4] prior to reporting for duty, and obtain more than 6 hours sleep per day whenever possible to prevent cumulative fatigue from chronic sleep restriction. Pilots should also consider the amount of sleep and time awake in their decision making relative to when to inform their supervisors that they should not fly due to fatigue.

Although there are currently no agreed-on objective standards in the aviation industry to determine whether a pilot is reporting to duty fatigued, there are provisions in the proposed NPRM—Section 117.5—for assessment by others of whether a pilot is fatigued. The validity and reliability of such assessments are unknown, as is the likelihood that they can result in either false positives or false negatives. Consequently it is uncertain whether they can result in effective prevention of fatigue.

CONCLUSION: With regard to the proposed provisions in Section 117.5, there are no valid and reliable tools and techniques feasible to reach the goals of detecting fatigue and fitness for duty in pilots in an operational setting. To achieve these goals, further research would be needed to scientifically validate the tools and techniques, demonstrate that they are technically feasible in an operational environment, and evaluate their relationship to operational safety and the extent to which they can be integrated into an operational context.

Potential fatigue is an inherent component of a system that functions 24 hours a day, 7 days a week. Recognizing this, the international aviation industry has been developing an approach through fatigue risk management systems (FRMS) to better understand when fatigue is a concern and how to best mitigate that risk. Airlines develop FRMS specific to their operational environment. To date, commuting has not been a major consideration in these systems. Incorporating data on commuting in relation to pilots' duty hours and sleep prior to duty would help inform these systems and allow airlines to consider mitigation strategies specific to their operations.

[4]This refers to at least 6 hours of physiological sleep. Since physiological sleep is typically 85 to 95 percent of total bed time in healthy adults, time in bed for sleep will have to be 6.5 to 7 hours to ensure at least 6 hours of physiological sleep are acquired.

RECOMMENDATION 2: The potential effects of commuting on pilot fatigue should be addressed as part of an airline's strategies to manage fatigue risk. If airlines develop fatigue risk management systems (FRMSs), they should gather information about preduty sleep and wake time relative to commuting practices and duty cycle. FRMSs should provide a mechanism for identifying problematic patterns and addressing them. FRMSs can offer both the airline and the Federal Aviation Administration an improved assessment of crew alertness during normal operations and thereby provide some information on the contribution of commuting to fatigue and whether fatigue is or is not within an acceptable level of risk.

Fatigue risk management plans (FRMPs) are the airline carriers' management plans outlining policies and procedures reducing the risk of flight crew member fatigue and improving flight crew member alertness. Public Law 111-216 requires each U.S. carrier operating under Part 121 (most passenger and cargo airlines that fly transport-category aircraft with 10 or more seats) to submit to the FAA their draft FRMPs for review and acceptance. Provided in the FAA's guidance on the development of an FRMP is a requirement for a fatigue education and awareness training program element, one of the subtasks of this element is the effects of commuting on fatigue.

This requirement reflects the perspective that managing the effects of commuting on fatigue is a joint responsibility of airlines and pilots, a position with which the committee agrees. Although the FRMP approach is not as rigorous as the FRMS process, it is required of all Part 121 airlines and therefore presents an opportunity to reach a wider audience than FRMSs.

RECOMMENDATION 3: The committee supports fatigue education and awareness training as part of an airline's fatigue risk management plan. Training relative to commuting should include guidelines regarding the effects of inadequate or disturbed sleep or prolonged wakefulness on fatigue and performance. Fatigue education and awareness training should be annually updated with particular attention to incorporating relevant new developments in sleep science.

As part of its data collection, the committee requested that airlines submit information on their pilot commuting, sick leave, and fatigue policies, if available. Although only a small proportion of airlines responded (39 percent), it is clear from the information submitted and from comments provided in public that there is considerable diversity in these policies. In addition, not all airlines have commuting or fatigue policies, with pilots relying instead on sick leave availability to address potential fatigue. Airlines should consider policies that would help pilots plan predictable commutes that do not promote fatigue on duty and policies that minimize the negative consequences when unanticipated events alter their commuting plans and lead to fatigue. The effects of these policies on pilot behavior are currently not well understood.

RECOMMENDATION 4: The Federal Aviation Administration should convene a joint industry, labor, and government working group, under the auspices of an independent organization (such as the Flight Safety Foundation), to assess industry policies on pilot commuting, sick leave, attendance/reliability, and fatigue and to develop industry best practices. The output of this joint working group should inform the development and updating of airline's fatigue risk management plans and should be validated periodically.

Pilots make decisions about commuting in the context of other factors in their lives, the specifics of their flights, the policies in place at their airlines, including sick leave and commuting policies, and other environmental factors. It is unclear to what extent pilots are aware of the findings from current decision science or consider this information in their decision making. Decision-making strategies informed by this science could be incorporated into FRMP training and considered in the development of industry best practices.

RECOMMENDATION 5: The Federal Aviation Administration should commission efforts to develop protocols and materials for training pilots to make decisions regarding commuting easily and effectively and to ensure that they are informed by current decision science.

As noted above, little is known about pilots' commuting patterns and the extent to which their commuting patterns may affect the amount or quality of sleep or the amount of time awake prior to duty. A better understanding of the relationship of commuting to primary risk factors for fatigue would represent a first step in increasing understanding of the relationship between commuting and fatigue. This information, combined with information that is recommended for inclusion in fatigue risk management plans, or in fatigue risk management systems when such systems are required, will provide input needed to inform further research and industry policies.

RECOMMENDATION 6: To inform the development of industry best practices and policies relative to commuting, the Federal Aviation Administration should fund a study to determine the relationships

between distance from domicile and five primary fatigue risk factors: (1) sleep quantity in the 48 hours prior to the end of duty on each day of the trip; (2) sleep quality in the 48 hours prior to the end of duty on each day of the trip; (3) time awake in the 48 hours prior to the end of duty on each day of the trip; (4) cumulative sleep time in the 72 hours prior to the end of a duty period; and (5) circadian phase at which sleep is obtained and at which duty is undertaken. In order to be maximally useful, the study should include a large random sample of pilots from multiple companies representing the major industry segments. The study should provide objective data on fatigue risk antecedents by using a well-validated technology that provides reliable information on sleep and wake periods, such as wrist actigraphy, as well as sleep-wake diaries.

Collecting data on a 48- to 72-hour period is needed to fully understand pilots' commuting experiences in the context of the many factors that affect their lives and work. The results of the study can help to identify situations that may warrant specific attention or additional research.

1

Introduction

Nearly everyone experiences fatigue, but some professions, such as aviation, medicine, and the military, demand alert, precise, rapid, and well-informed decision making and communication with little margin for error. Recognizing this, the National Transportation Safety Board (NTSB) added "Reduce Accidents and Incidents Caused by Human Fatigue in the Aviation Industry" to its list of most wanted aviation safety improvements two decades ago. Specifically, the NTSB called for research, education, and revisions to regulations related to work and duty hours. Although regulatory change has received attention in the form of at least two rounds of rule-making activity, there have been no actual changes to relevant regulations since 1985 despite a significantly expanded research base on sleep, fatigue, and circadian rhythms.[1]

The potential for fatigue to negatively affect human performance is well established. Concern about this potential in the aviation context extends back decades, with both airlines and pilots agreeing that fatigue is a safety concern. A more recent consideration is whether and how pilot commuting, conducted in a pilot's off-duty time, may affect fatigue during flight duty.

It is important to note, however, that fatigue is not a binary condition in which one is either rested with no negative effects on performance or

[1]A Notice of Proposed Rulemaking (NPRM) with revised regulations on this topic was promulgated in 1995, but it was withdrawn in 2009 with the acknowledgment that changes since 1995 in both the world of commercial aviation and the scientific understanding of fatigue had rendered it out of date. A new rule-making activity was started that resulted in a new NPRM issued in 2010. The committee discusses this FAA rule-making activity related to flight crew fatigue in Chapter 6.

fatigued with severe negative effects on performance. There are degrees of fatigue and degrees of the negative effects of fatigue on performance. Moreover, fatigue is highly variable and is influenced by a number of factors, including amount of sleep, time awake, workload, time on task, and time of day.

STUDY BACKGROUND AND COMMITTEE CHARGE

Concern about the potential contribution to fatigue from time spent commuting to a duty station—known as a pilot's domicile—increased following a fatal Colgan Air crash in Buffalo, New York, on February 12, 2009. The crash, and the first officer's cross-country commute, received substantial media attention. The NTSB determined that the probable cause of the accident was "the captain's inappropriate response" to a low speed condition (National Transportation Safety Board, 2010b, p. 155). The NTSB report identified multiple contributing factors related to flight crew and corporate responsibilities. That report did not list fatigue or commuting as a probable cause or contributing factor in the accident report. Instead, the Board concluded that "the pilots' performance was likely impaired because of fatigue, but the extent of their impairment and the degree to which it contributed to the performance deficiencies that occurred during the flight cannot be conclusively determined" (National Transportation Safety Board, 2010b, p. 108).

Against this backdrop, in September 2010, Congress, through the Airline Safety and Federal Aviation Administration Extension Act of 2010 (P.L. 111-216), directed the Federal Aviation Administration (FAA) to revise its regulations related to work and duty hours to reflect current research. The law also directed the FAA to contract with the National Academy of Sciences, through the National Research Council, to conduct a study of the effects of pilot commuting on fatigue. The Committee on the Effects of Commuting on Pilot Fatigue was constituted to carry out the mandated study, which is intended to inform the development of the commuting-related aspects of the FAA regulations also specified in the act.

The committee was directed to review information in seven specified areas. These areas were (1) the prevalence of pilots commuting in the commercial air carrier industry, including the number and percentage of pilots who commute greater than 2 hours each way to work; (2) characteristics of commuting by pilots, including distances traveled, time zones crossed, time spent, and methods used; (3) the impact of commuting on pilot fatigue, sleep, and circadian rhythms; (4) commuting policies of commercial air carriers (including passenger and all-cargo air carriers), including pilot check-in requirements and sick leave and fatigue policies; (5) post-conference materials from the FAA's June 2008 symposium titled "Aviation Fatigue

BOX 1-1
Committee Statement of Task

Statement of Task:

Under the oversight of the National Research Council's Board on Human-Systems Integration (BOHSI), an ad hoc multidisciplinary committee has been appointed to review the effects of commuting on pilot fatigue. The committee will review available information related to the prevalence and characteristics of commuting, literature related to sleep, fatigue, and circadian rhythms, airline and regulatory oversight policies, and pilot and airline practices.

Based on this review, the committee will

- define "commuting" in the context of pilot alertness and fatigue;
- discuss the relationship between the available science on alertness, fatigue, sleep and circadian rhythms, cognitive and physiological performance, and safety;
- discuss the policy, economic, and regulatory issues that affect pilot commuting;
- discuss the commuting policies of commercial air carriers and to the extent possible, identify practices that are supported by the available research; and
- outline potential next steps, including to the extent possible, recommendations for regulatory or administrative actions, or further research, by the Federal Aviation Administration (FAA).

Management Symposium: Partnerships for Solutions;" (6) FAA and international policies and guidance regarding commuting; and (7) to the extent possible, airline and pilot commuting practices.

On the basis of that review, the committee was charged to discuss relevant issues with the goal of identifying potential next steps, including possible recommendations related to regulatory or administrative actions or further research that can be taken by the FAA: see Box 1-1 for the committee's specific Statement of Task.

The FAA issued a Notice of Proposed Rulemaking (NPRM) on September 14, 2010—with a broad scope encompassing all aspects of pilot flight, duty, and rest requirements—inviting public comment that would be considered in issuing final regulations (Federal Aviation Administration, 2010c).[2] This study is intended to inform the component of those final regulations that are relevant to pilot commuting.

[2]The full text of the NPRM is provided at the following link: http://www.gpo.gov/fdsys/pkg/FR-2010-09-14/pdf/2010-22626.pdf [June 2011].

This report describes pilot commuting and the relevant aspects of the aviation industry; reviews current and proposed regulations and nonregulatory approaches to reducing the risk from fatigue; presents the committee's analyses of input from stakeholders; reviews the scientific literature on fatigue in relation to time awake, time asleep, and time of day; and presents the committee's findings, conclusions, and recommendations based on the information available during the course of the committee's deliberations.

The committee produced an interim report, *Issues in Commuting and Pilot Fatigue: An Interim Report* (National Research Council, 2011). That report described the committee's work to that date, mapped out the approach to information collection for the final report, and provided a review of the relevant scientific literature and regulatory documents. This report incorporates much of the interim report as background information.[3]

INFORMATION COLLECTION

There is extensive research—including research specific to the aviation industry—on alertness, fatigue, sleep, and circadian rhythms; cognitive and physiological performance; and safety. However, there is very little information specifically on pilot commuting, including commuting practices or airline policies and practices related to commuting. To help address this gap, the committee issued a call for input that was sent to pilot and airline associations and passenger groups and was posted on the project website: see Box 1-2. That call included an invitation to respond to a set of questions specific to the types of information the committee was asked to review: see Box 1-3.

The committee also requested information from 84 passenger and cargo airlines listed as Part 121 carriers by the FAA.[4] The airlines were invited to provide input to the study on the relevant topics. The airlines provided a variety of information, including general responses to questions the committee posed, as well as zip code data on pilots' residences and domiciles (their place of work). In the interests of confidentiality, the companies that responded have been de-identified for data presentations in the report. The committee received written input from 37 airlines, associations, and groups: see Appendix A.

In addition, the committee received input from organizations and individuals interested in providing information, both in writing and in presentations to the committee. All parties who wished to talk with us were included

[3]A copy of the report is available for free download from the National Academies Press at http://www.nap.edu/catalog.php?record_id=13097 [June 2011].

[4]Part 121 applies to most passenger and cargo airlines that fly transport-category aircraft with 10 or more seats.

BOX 1-2
Organizations Contacted for Input

PILOT ASSOCIATIONS AND UNIONS

- Air Line Pilots Association
- Coalition of Airline Pilots Associations
- Allied Pilots Association (American Airlines pilots)
- Independent Pilots Association (UPS pilots)
- Southwest Airlines Pilots Association
- Teamsters Local 1224 (Horizon Air, Southern Air, ABX Air, Atlas Air Worldwide [Atlas and Polar Air Cargo], Kalitta Air, Cape Air, Miami Air, Gulfstream Air, Omni Air and USA 3000 pilots)
- U.S. Airline Pilots Association (US Airways pilots)
- International Federation of Airline Pilots Association

AIRLINE-RELATED ASSOCIATIONS

- Air Transport Association
- Cargo Airline Association
- International Air Transport Association
- National Air Carrier Association
- National Air Transport Association
- National Business Aviation Association
- Regional Air Cargo Carriers Association
- Regional Airline Association

INDEPENDENT SAFETY-RELATED ORGANIZATIONS

- Air Travelers Association
- Flight Safety Foundation

at open meetings held in November and December 2010 and February 2011: see Appendix B for the public meeting agendas.

The committee also considered information from the following sources:

- a review of NTSB reports on aviation accidents to identify available information related to the contribution of commuting to flight crew fatigue;
- a review of confidential reports that mentioned commuting or fatigue that were submitted to the aviation safety reporting system (ASRS), a voluntary pilot reporting system;[5]

[5]ASRS is funded by the FAA and hosted by the U.S. National Aeronautics and Space Administration.

BOX 1-3
Topics Posed in Call for Public Input

Interested organizations or individuals were invited to provide comments on their perspective in the following areas, as relevant to their work and experience:

A. the prevalence of pilots commuting in the commercial air carrier industry, including the number and percentage of pilots who commute greater than 2 hours each way to work;
B. the characteristics of commuting by pilots, including distances traveled, time zones crossed, time spent, and methods used;
C. the impact of commuting on pilot fatigue;
D. whether and, if so, how the commuting policies and/or practices of commercial air carriers (including passenger and all-cargo air carriers), including pilot check-in requirements and sick leave and fatigue policies, ensure that pilots are fit to fly and maximize public safety;
E. whether and, if so, how pilot commuting practices ensure that they are fit to fly and maximize public safety;
F. how "commuting" should be defined in the context of the commercial air carrier industry; and
g. how FAA regulations *related to commuting* could or should be amended to ensure that pilots arrive for duty fit to fly and to maximize public safety.

- a review of the comments related to commuting or fitness for duty submitted in response to the NPRM;
- a review of available information on relevant airline policies and practices in the international arena;
- analysis of data requested from airlines on pilot residence (zip code) and duty location/domicile (zip code) to enable an approximation of linear distance between home and domicile; and
- a review of the relevant scientific literature.

OPERATIONAL DEFINITIONS

For the purposes of this report, the committee used or adopted working operational definitions for three key issues: pilot fatigue, pilot domicile and home, and pilot commuting.

Pilot Fatigue

There is very strong evidence that fatigue can result in deteriorated performance (see Chapter 4). The Institute of Medicine defines fatigue as "an unsafe condition that can occur relative to the timing and duration of work and sleep opportunities" (Institute of Medicine, 2009, p. 218). Reported failings from fatigued pilots "have included procedural errors, unstable approaches, lining up with the wrong runway, and landing without clearances" (Federal Aviation Administration, 2010c, p. 55,855). Although it is recognized that fatigue can contribute to aircraft accidents, there is no agreed upon objective measure of fatigue post accident. Therefore, conclusions that fatigue likely contributed to accidents are most often inferred from evaluating sleep-wake history relative to scientific evidence on the causes and consequences of fatigue and, where possible, from review of the cockpit voice recorder. For this study, the committee focused on fatigue that would result from or be mitigated by off-duty activities, particularly those activities related to commuting (e.g., frequency and duration of commutes and opportunities for sleep).

Pilot Domicile and Home

The committee considers a pilot's "domicile" to be the airport where a pilot begins and ends a duty assignment. This term is distinguished from a "hub," which is a focus for the routing of aircraft and passengers. A pilot's domicile may be at one of the airline's hubs, but it may also be at an airport that does not serve as a hub for that airline.

The committee considers a pilot's "home" to be the pilot's residence: it is important to note that it is not necessarily the place where the pilot had the most recent opportunity for his or her customary sleep period prior to duty. The pilot may have access to a hotel room, apartment, or other sleep accommodation near his or her domicile for rest before starting an assignment.

Pilot Commuting

The committee considers pilot "commuting" to be the period of time and the activity required of pilots from leaving home to arriving at the domicile (airport—in the crew room, dispatch room, or designated location at the airport) and from leaving the domicile to returning back to home. Pilot commuting takes place during off-duty hours. Pilot commuting differs from the commuting of other workers in terms of frequency and variability, distance, transport modes, and time of day.

Figure 1-1 depicts pilot commuting in relation to a pilot's off-duty and on-duty periods. The figure illustrates the complexity of factors that affect a pilot's commuting choices including opportunities for rest and sleep. There is the potential for tremendous variability across individual pilot commuting practices and day-to-day experiences. This variability results from many influences, not only the duration or distance of the commute. In addition, commuting practices may be subject to further variation when pilots are

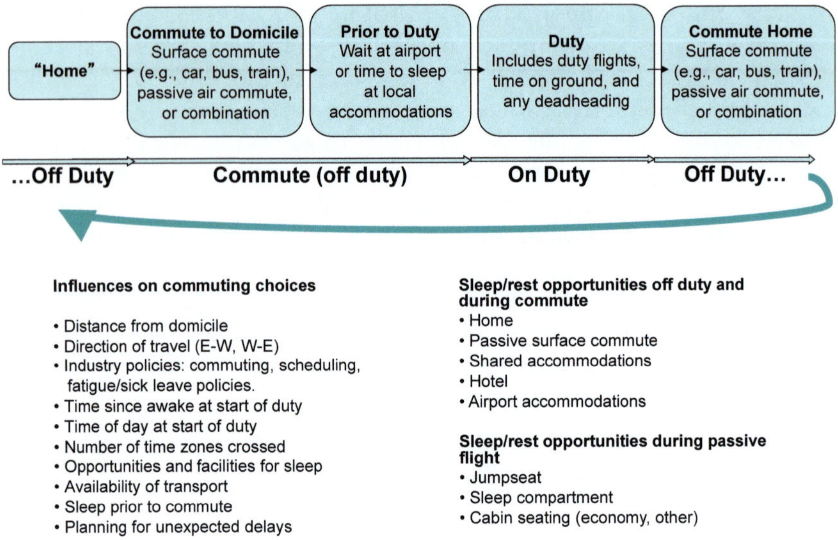

FIGURE 1-1 Commuting in relation to duty.
NOTE: The figure maps a pilot's commuting and duty cycle along a timeline of variable start time and duration, noting the opportunities for rest and sleep and the many influences on commuting. Commuting can be active (driving oneself) or passive (allowing opportunities for rest or sleep). Deadheading (which involves passive traveling by air while on duty) counts toward work time and is not part of commuting.

reassigned to different domiciles with seasonal or economic fluctuations in the industry. In planning a commute, a pilot must consider many things in order to arrive fit for duty such as time of day and time zone at start of duty, availability of seats on commuting flights, affordability and availability of sleep facilities, airline policies, and possible delays. These and other influences on pilots' commuting decisions are discussed further throughout the report.

The airline industry, the FAA, and other stakeholders have not adopted a uniform definition of pilot "commuting." Airlines vary in their definitions and some airlines that provided commuting policies to the committee do not formally define it, although these policies are generally intended for pilots who live far enough away that they have to fly to their domicile to begin duty.

The NPRM notes a reference from the British aviation safety agency (the United Kingdom Civil Agency Authority) to commuting being more than 1.5 hours. In contrast, the FAA advisory circular, on Fitness for Duty, AC-120 FIT, sets a 2-hour threshold (Federal Aviation Administration, 2010c; U.S. Department of Transportation, 2010b). These dividing lines are arbitrary. Distinguishing or characterizing a commute solely on the basis of the duration or distance of commute, or modality of commuting, is overly simplistic. Such an approach may be desired for operational applications, but current thresholds for defining commuting based on time lack evidence-based underpinnings. Commuting matters insofar as it may interfere with fitness for duty. These determinations must be guided by scientific evidence on sleep and fatigue, in both laboratory and operational environments (see Chapter 4).

All commutes, even commutes involving the same amount of time, may not have the same potential to influence fatigue. Some commutes may not be cognitively or physically demanding (e.g., seated as a passenger on a train, bus, or plane), even to the point of permitting sleep to be obtained, while other commutes may entail more physical (e.g., standing) or cognitive (e.g., driving) demands. Also, long distance air commutes that cross time zones have the potential to exacerbate fatigue for a commuting pilot by disrupting the sleep-wake cycle, depending on the time of day, direction of travel, and other characteristics of the flights operated after the commute. Yet, in some situations, the crossing of time zones potentially can mitigate the fatigue from a combined commute and flight duty period.

Pilot Fatigue Management Decision Making

Decision making is central to pilots' efforts to avoid flying aircraft while they are fatigued. There are three major circumstances in which such decision making has special significance: (1) when the pilot is developing plans for commuting to his or her duty station; (2) when the pilot must make adjustments in plans necessitated by arising contingencies (e.g., bad weather); and (3) when the pilot has to decide whether and how to cancel a duty assignment because of (anticipated) fatigue. The decisions in all such situations are highly challenging. For instance, they typically involve multiple, often conflicting considerations, numerous stakeholders with competing interests (e.g., family members, colleagues, and supervisors), and the need to be informed by nonobvious and sometimes counterintuitive facts about the biology of fatigue and rest.

GUIDE TO THE REPORT

The structure of this report corresponds to aspects of the committee's charge. Chapter 2 provides background information on commuting in general followed by an overview of the unique characteristics of pilot commuting. The chapter also includes a review of stakeholder comments that were either provided to the committee or obtained through an analysis of public comments submitted to the FAA on the NPRM. The chapter concludes with a discussion of aviation industry characteristics that are relevant to the effects of commuting on pilot fatigue, including airline pilot hiring policies; airline crew schedules and pilot work patterns; airline route networks and crew basing; and competitive and external factors.

Chapter 3 provides background information on aviation safety, including sources of safety improvement, followed by an analysis of information on fatigue-related aviation accidents from reports by the NTSB. The chapter concludes with a discussion and analysis of pilot commuting patterns that exist today.

Chapter 4 provides an overview of the relevant science related to sleep, circadian rhythms, and fatigue. Chapter 5 includes a discussion, followed by illustrative examples, of aspects of pilot commuting that contribute to the risk of fatigue.

The concluding Chapter 6 discusses ways to reduce the risk from fatigue caused by commuting. The chapter begins with background information on the current regulatory context followed by a discussion of fatigue risk management strategies for airlines. The committee's recommendations are presented at the end of Chapters 5 and 6.

Following the list of references, a glossary and an acronym list are provided. Additional background information, data sources, and analyses are included in the seven appendices. Appendix A identifies the airlines, associations, and groups that submitted documents for the committee's review. Appendix B provides the agendas for the committee's open meetings, which list the organizations and individuals that presented before the committee and responded to its questions. The committee conducted a thorough review of all the documents submitted by airlines, associations, and groups as well as a few individual pilots; a summary of its review is included in Appendix C. In addition, the committee examined public comments in response to FAA's NPRM that related to commuting. Appendix D presents a summary of the analysis of that purposeful sample of public comments. An analysis of scheduled aircraft departures for the third quarters of 2000, 2005, and 2010 is discussed in Chapter 2. The data for this analysis in number of aircraft departures by airline and by city are available in Appendix E for mainline airlines and in Appendix F for regional airlines. Also provided in Appendix E is a list of airport codes alongside the corresponding airports and cities. The final appendix (Appendix G) includes the biographical sketches for the committee members and staff.

2

The U.S. Airline Industry and Pilot Commuting

This chapter discusses characteristics of the U.S. airline industry and the policies and practices that are likely to have an effect on pilots' commuting choices. This discussion draws on the expertise of committee members, information from stakeholders who provided comments at committee meetings or through the study website (see Box 1-3 in Chapter 1), a review of the comments related to commuting that were submitted to the Federal Aviation Administration (FAA) in response to the Notice of Proposed Rulemaking (NPRM), and a review of available airline policies.

COMMUTING: BACKGROUND

Commuting is usually defined as travel between home and a work location on a regular basis. A Gallup Poll found that the mean commute in the United States was 45.6 minutes and the median was 30 minutes; overall, about 64 percent of commutes were less than 1 hour while 8 percent were 2 hours or more (Gallup, Inc., 2007). Characterizing a population's commuting routines is complex at best because of the enormous variation between individuals, as well as the variation for individuals from 1 day or week to another (Lyons and Chatterjee, 2008). Most of the research on the effects of commuting and commuting habits has been conducted in the context of daily routines using ground transportation in large urban areas. Although there are some studies of remote or rural geographic areas and of employees in specific industries, such as shift workers, hospital staff, and miners, there is very little research that examines (or even mentions) the commute of pilots or the airplane as a mode of transport.

The nature of commuting has been changing. In one study of commuting over a 10-year period, half of the sample changed their main method of travel at least once, and one-fifth changed three or more times (Dargay and Hanly, 2003). Several studies have looked at the physiological effects of relatively long car drives (Kluger, 1998); self-reported attitudes in high-congestion conditions (Hennessy and Wiesenthal, 1999); and rail commuting (Walsleben et al., 1999; Evans et al., 2002). A common conclusion across many studies is that unpredictability leads to stress. Unpredictability can be due to unanticipated delays because of traffic volume or weather or the unreliability of services. However, the studies do not examine the extent to which fatigue from commuting would affect subsequent job performance. They also do not make comparisons across modes of transport. There is insufficient research as to whether a 90-minute car drive is more fatiguing than a 90-minute train ride or a 90-minute plane ride.

There is a body of literature looking at the positive effects of travel (Mokhtarian and Solomon, 2001; Bull, 2004; Lyons et al., 2007; Jain and Lyons, 2008). These include a physical and cognitive break between activities at home and those at work and time to do other activities. Some activities—such as reading, writing, or rest—are only possible in passive modes of transportation, such as trains, busses, limousines, and airplanes. But even active modes of transportation, such as driving one's own vehicle, can provide time to think, to listen to an audiobook or music, to admire the landscape, and to engage in conversation with companions. The value of these activities depends on individuals' preferences and other demands on their time.

COMMUTING IN AVIATION

Commuting is different in aviation than in most other industries. For many pilots, commuting is not a daily occurrence, as pilot duty assignments often extend over several days and keep pilots away from home for multiple days at a time. As a result, a pilot's commute to work may be undertaken as infrequently as once or twice per month—or more frequently, depending on the flying schedule and commuting arrangements. Pilots sometimes travel to arrive near their domicile (the location of the airport from which they fly) for a period before they are scheduled to fly for logistical reasons or to have a rest opportunity. This rest opportunity may be of a length and quality varying from a nap in a chair to a full night's sleep in a hotel room or apartment.

It is not uncommon for pilots to travel by air to and from their flight assignment. Pilots commute by air to some extent because they can, and to some extent because they want to: like many Americans, pilots' planned commutes depend on a host of personal and professional decisions involving family, economics, and logistics. Commuting by air enables pilots to live a considerable distance from their domicile and travel to work in a relatively short time.

Pilots who provided input for this study told the committee that their commute is influenced by both economic and lifestyle considerations. In the comments the committee received from pilots, half or more of those who addressed the reasons for commuting by air, cited the high cost of living in the area of their domiciles, frequent domicile closings and the future unpredictability of domicile changes, and a desire to maintain family stability. A pilot may choose a community of residence outside of the domicile area because of cost of living near his or her assigned domicile. A home community may be selected based on such quality-of-life factors as a desired geographic region, proximity to a school system, or the existence of a support infrastructure for family while the pilot is on extended flight duty. Commuting by air also enables a pilot to maintain a stable residence if he or she is reassigned to another domicile. One of the respondents to the NPRM expressed similar sentiments:

> Commuting is common in the airline industry, in part because of life-style choices available to pilots by virtue of their being able to fly at no cost to their duty station, but also because of economic reasons associated with protecting seniority on particular aircraft, frequent changes in the flight crew member's home base, and low pay and regular furloughs by some carriers that may require a pilot to live someplace with a relatively low cost of living. (*quote pulled from public comments in response to FAA's NPRM, see Appendix D*)

The key issue for safety is whether a pilot begins the subsequent duty rested and fit to fly regardless of how the pilot commutes to work.

Although some pilots live at or close to their domiciles, other pilots live in a location that has never been a company domicile, maintaining a consistent residence as their assigned domicile changes from one airport to another. Some commutes may be a legacy of previous domicile closings or changes, in which pilots who once lived near their assigned domiciles must then commute in order to maintain roots in their original home communities. A point frequently made to the committee was that commuting choices, including the availability of travel by air, can provide pilots and their families an aspect of certainty and control when facing or considering the likelihood of mergers, domicile changes, furloughs, and the like, even when considering these as potential disruptions in the future. A pilot's domicile may also change as that pilot's career progresses and the pilot flies progressively larger aircraft, first as a first officer and then as a captain.

Flexibility in commuting choices provides benefits for pilots, but it also provides benefits for the airlines. As discussed below, the U.S. airline

BOX 2-1
Benefits of Commuting

Benefits for Pilots
- Stable residence for family
- Family residence selected for quality-of-life factors
- Low cost of living or low tax jurisdiction location
- No need to relocate to progress in career
- No need to relocate for domicile changes for industry competitive reasons

Benefits for Airlines
- Ability to adapt quickly to changes in flight patterns because of changes in market
- No need to require pilots to live near domicile
- No need to pay relocation expenses for pilots for domicile change
- No need to pay cost-of-living adjustments for domicile change

Benefits for Passengers/Consumers
- Potential lower cost services and lower prices

industry has undergone changes in structure and in the pattern of flights during the last decade. Having pilots able to commute longer distances to their domiciles rather than requiring them to live nearby may allow the industry to change flight patterns more quickly to respond to changing market demands. Since, for most airlines, pilots are not required to live near their domiciles, the airlines typically do not pay for pilot relocation or for cost-of-living adjustments when pilots move from one domicile to another. Airline passengers may benefit since airline costs are lower and, in a competitive market, lower costs tend to lead to lower prices for consumers. Box 2-1 summarizes the benefits of commuting for pilots, airlines, and consumers.

STAKEHOLDERS' COMMENTS

As described in Chapter 1, requests for input data were sent to a variety of different stakeholders in the airline industry (see Box 1-2 in Chapter 1).

Because of the extremely short turnaround (a few weeks) between the requests and the committee meeting, the response rates were relatively modest. As of March 23, 2011, the committee had received responses from 25 airlines (4 mainline passenger carriers, 8 regional passenger carriers, 9 cargo carriers, and 4 nonscheduled charter carriers), 2 of the airline associations, and 2 of the pilot associations. The committee's review of the responses is summarized below and detailed in Appendix C. (Some airlines responded with written input after this date, and their input was considered for this report, but it is not included in the summary of stakeholder response in Appendix C.) The committee also received written statements from three individual commercial pilots who volunteered their thoughts on issues being addressed by the committee.

The committee also reviewed public comments related to commuting submitted in response to the NPRM. The public comments were purposefully sampled to select those that would be most relevant to definitions of pilot commuting and perceptions of commuting practices. Using the FAA's electronic database (a total of 2,419 submissions), relevant comments were identified using key terms: "commut"; "commute"; and "commuting" (N = 176). From these, a total of 85 comments, representing remarks from 85 different individuals or organization representatives, were deemed relevant and selected for qualitative analysis. In many cases, an individual comment contained multiple viewpoints of relevance (e.g., the commenter's own definition of commuting and an opinion on the prevalence of commuting practices with some suggestions for the NPRM). As a result, more than 400 viewpoints of relevance to the study were considered. Appendix D presents a summary of the analysis of the purposeful sample of public comments submitted in response to the NPRM.

Both of these reviews of stakeholder input have limitations that must be considered in interpreting the findings. Neither of these analyses is based on representative samples. In the case of the stakeholder input requested by the committee, individuals or organizations from targeted groups provided input based on an open-ended set of questions or, in a few cases, offered unsolicited input on the study topic. In the case of the review of public comments to the NPRM, respondents were invited to provide feedback on all aspects of the NPRM, and this analysis took into account a selection of comments that were relevant to commuting. The response sample, in both cases, is self-selected. The reader is urged to remember that the views reflected in these analyses represent those individuals and organizations that were motivated to provide input to the committee or feedback in response to the NPRM. Thus, it is difficult to know, or even estimate, the extent to which different results would have been obtained from a larger and more representative sample of the stakeholder population. For those that responded to the requests, it is difficult to know whether each respondent understood each question or request as intended. The reader should also note that not all respondents responded to every question, issue, or request. In addition to self-selecting whether to respond, respondents self-selected the questions or topics to which they responded.

One important initial finding from both of these reviews is that there is no clear, consistent definition of pilot commuting in the airline industry.

There are reports of difficulties in estimating the number of pilots who commute by air or who commute relatively long distances or durations as well as any other types of commuting patterns.

Respondents did offer a wide range of factors that influence pilots' commuting decisions. In order of reported frequency, from high to low, they included high cost of living near the domicile location; frequent domicile closings and future unpredictability of the airline industry; cost and availability of adjunct sleep accommodations; desire to maintain family stability; low pay, especially for regional carriers; lifestyle preferences (e.g., for good weather and outdoor living); and absence of adequate coverage for costly moving expenses. In the aggregate, respondents acknowledged that commuting is a potentially fatiguing activity, but they also commented that commuting conducted responsibly would not necessarily increase fatigue levels significantly. In regard to policies and regulations that might influence commuting practices, the responses were mixed and diverse, ranging from opinions that current policies and practices are appropriate to suggestions for airline ownership of and FAA regulation of factors relevant to commutes and fatigue (e.g., availability of jumpseats and rest accommodations).

AVIATION INDUSTRY CHARACTERISTICS

Characteristics of the aviation industry that influence pilot commuting include airline pilot hiring practices, crew scheduling practices (at many airlines a joint outcome of management decisions and collective bargaining negotiations); route network and crew basing practices; and competitive and passenger demand factors that can cause pilot staffing requirements to change over time. These characteristics also influence pilots' preferences related to commuting and their decisions about where to maintain their homes. Also, some airline policies and practices can facilitate or impede a pilot's ability to commute, with the potential for affecting not only the pilots' choices of whether and how to commute; but also whether they experience fatigue related to the commute and whether they may operate flights in a fatigued condition.

Airline Pilot Hiring Policies

Pilots compete for positions at airlines in an international market for their services in which the supply of pilots in most years has exceeded the demand from a relatively small number of employers. The sources of trained and qualified pilot candidates (primarily, universities, flight schools, the military, and smaller operators) are geographically diverse. The committee did not have information on the percentages of pilots from each source. In the United States, pilots taking entry-level positions at regional airlines have tended to earn lower wages than pilots at mainline carriers. In many cases, pilots who join a regional carrier hope to change employment to a mainline carrier after they have accumulated additional flight experience. Recent contractions and consolidations among several of the mainline airlines and changes in the mandatory pilot retirement age have arguably reduced the outlook for positions at mainline carriers. The tradition in the U.S. airline industry is for the company not to pay for a newly hired pilot's moving expenses or to require that the pilot live at the domicile. As a result, many newly hired pilots may have both the capability and incentive to begin long-distance commuting. Once established, this pattern may continue through subsequent domicile changes as the pilots attempt to maintain a consistent residence.

Airline Crew Schedules and Pilot Work Patterns

At most airlines, labor agreements between pilots and airlines establish specific policies and practices regarding flight crew scheduling (within limitations for flight and duty time as established in the Code of Federal Regulations). Virtually all of these airlines rely on a bidding process to award monthly schedules (sometimes called lines or blocks) to pilots; selection advantages are given to pilots on the basis of seniority. Typically, a monthly schedule consists of multiple assignments of trips (sometimes called pairings), each of which may consist of several flights over a period lasting 1, 2, or up to more than 6 days. Each of these trips begins and ends at the pilot's domicile (there also may be one or more overnights elsewhere) and thus comprises the basic duty assignment to and from which the pilot commutes.

By federal regulations, airline pilots are limited to fly no more than 1,000 hours per year, or an average of about 83 hours per month. On the basis of this monthly limit, the number of flight hours per trip will determine the number of trips—and thus, potentially, the number of commutes—during the month. For example, if each of a pilot's trips involves 20 hours of flying over 4 days, the pilot will do about four of these trips per month for 80 hours of flight time. There will be one or more days off between each trip during which a pilot may elect to commute home.

Using the seniority-based bidding process, pilots select the desired trips and days worked given their individual preferences, including the nature of their commutes. For example, a pilot who commutes by air from home to the domicile may bid for the monthly line of four, 4-day trips; preferably, trips beginning at the domicile late on the first day (allowing for an inbound commute that morning) and ending back at the domicile relatively early on the fourth day (allowing for a homebound commute that evening). This pilot will make four commutes during the month. In contrast, a pilot who lives near the domicile (e.g., a drive of 45 minutes to the airport) may bid for 10 1-day trips, each of which starts early in the morning and returns to the domicile later that day after 8 hours of flight time. This pilot will make 10 commutes during the month to accumulate 80 hours of flight time. Note that in this example the 1-day trips have more flying time per day, on average, than the 4-day trips in the previous example. The pilot living near the domicile will likely work fewer days to accumulate the 80 flight hours for the month; the pilot with a long distance commute will have more work days and fewer days off to accumulate the same number of flight hours.

Airline Route Networks and Crew Basing

Decisions that airlines make about aircraft routings, crew schedules, and crew basing can affect pilots' commuting incentives. The point from which a pilot begins duty (typically his or her domicile, with the exceptions noted below) is influenced by airline management practices that vary in the industry. For example, many scheduled airlines—those that operate on specific routes at established times—operate a hub-and-spoke route network in which many flights converge on one airport (the hub) at about the same time so that passengers and cargo can connect conveniently to a flight that is going to the ultimate destination (a spoke). Either a hub or a spoke city could be a pilot's domicile.

Basing pilots at a hub can be attractive for airlines from the point of view of scheduling flexibility and for exchanging crews during connecting operations in the midst of an operating day. Even in a hub-and-spoke system, though, many airplanes are positioned at the spoke airports overnight, and basing pilots at a spoke airport can reduce the expenses of providing overnight accommodations ("overnighting") for the pilots who work the originating and terminating flights of the day. In any case, the scheduling and routing of crews does not have to match that of the aircraft. For airlines using domicile basing, whether located at a hub, spoke, or elsewhere, the airlines typically leave the pilots responsible for performing the commute—by whatever modes and means necessary—so as to be at the domicile reliably on time and ready for duty. By requiring its pilots to be ready to fly at any domicile, operators are able to select domiciles that minimize the overall costs of staffing the airline, in addition to other factors.

In contrast to the practices of most major scheduled airlines, other airlines (most commonly those offering nonscheduled service[1]) operate flight patterns in which their airplanes may be routed in a highly variable manner in accordance with customer demand, rarely returning to a specified base. Given this aircraft routing it may be most efficient to dispatch flight crews

[1]Nonscheduled airlines operate on customer demand without a regular schedule.

directly from their homes to wherever the previous crew left the airplane. Many of these airlines, consequently, have no established pilot domiciles. In these cases there may be at least a shared responsibility between the company and pilots for the trip from home to the first flying assignment. In one variant of these practices, home basing, there is effectively no commute because the pilot's on-duty work period begins and ends at his or her home. All of the travel to and from the pilot's operational flying is scheduled by, and the responsibility of, the company. As on-duty travel (as distinct from commuting travel), depending on the timing of the flights and as required by regulations governing flight time, duty time, and rest, the company may be required to provide adequate facilities and time for rest between the positioning flight to the duty location and the pilot's first operational flight. In another variant, gateway basing, the company establishes a number of gateway airport locations and assigns the pilot to the gateway nearest his or her home. Pilots are then responsible for commuting between their homes and the gateway, while the companies are responsible for on-duty travel between the gateway and wherever in the world the pilot's first operational flights will begin and end.

Competitive and External Factors

The dynamic and evolving structure of the airline industry affects the environment in which pilots make commuting decisions. Some airlines' responses to a changing competitive environment have involved establishing new hubs and downsizing or closing existing hubs and starting service to cities they previously did not serve or ending service to some cities. Airline mergers and acquisitions have also led to downsizing or elimination of hubs believed to be redundant in the postmerger route structure. Seasonal scheduling can cause other complications and may result in changes in pilot domiciles to accommodate increased or decreased passenger demand for particular routes.

These changes in flight patterns may lead to domicile expansions, contractions, closings, or openings, with concomitant changes to where a pilot is domiciled. Changes in domiciles are handled, typically, through seniority-based bidding: pilots with relatively less seniority may sometimes be involuntarily displaced to new domiciles in other parts of the United States (or even other parts of the world), or, in the extreme, furloughed from the company. Subsequently, recalls from furloughs in response to increases in travel demand may result in pilots being recalled to a domicile that is different from the one from which they were released. Other major disruptions to pilot employment have occurred as airlines have reorganized their fleets and route systems under bankruptcy protection or even ceased operations and liquidated; other employment opportunities for pilots have developed, often at different domiciles, as new entrant airlines have begun operations.

Changing Service Patterns in the U.S. Airline Industry

Figure 2-1 shows the number of passengers carried by U.S. airlines in both domestic and international service in 2000, 2005, and 2010. International traffic increased throughout the period while domestic traffic increased between 2000 and 2005 then decreased in 2010, largely because of changes in the economy. Aggregate traffic statistics for the U.S. airline industry do not show some of the important changes that have occurred over the last decade in both industry structure and service patterns. Throughout the past three decades following airline deregulation, new airlines have entered the market, some airlines have grown, others have gotten smaller sometimes as part of a bankruptcy restructuring, and still others have ceased operations.

Two kinds of changes in the U.S. airline industry over the past decade are particularly notable in their potential to affect pilot commuting patterns: the rise of regional jet service, and mergers. An important industry change that could affect pilot commuting is the rise of the regional jet industry and the extent to which regional jet service operated under contract to mainline carriers has replaced service in larger jets operated directly by mainline carriers. The rise of the regional jet industry is a relatively recent development (see Oster and Strong, 2006). In 1995, there was no regional

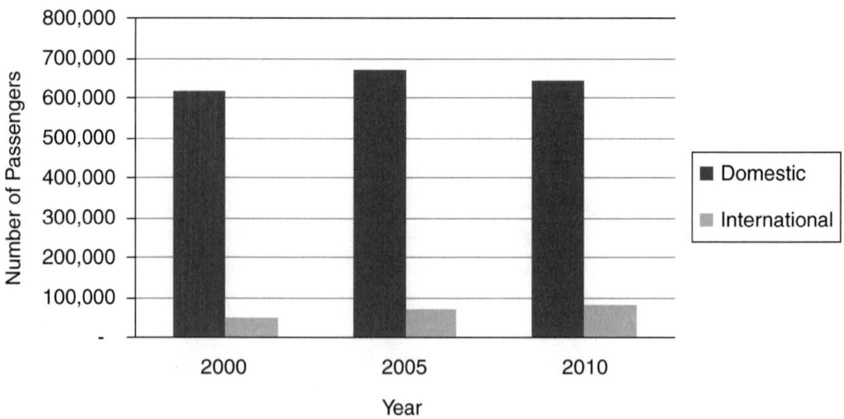

FIGURE 2-1 Passengers carried by U.S. airlines.
SOURCE: Derived from data, used with permission, from Air Transport Association of America, Inc. (2011).

jet service operating from the hub airports of the mainline carriers. By 2000, such service accounted for 16 percent of aircraft departures, and in the next 3 years such service had grown to 38 percent of aircraft departures from hub airports. In that 3-year period, domestic departures from hub airports by mainline carriers declined 18 percent while departures from those hubs by regional airlines under contract to the mainline carriers increased 250 percent, so that combined departures by mainline carriers and regional jets increased by more than 11 percent. Although some of this regional jet service was on routes that had not previously been served by the mainline carriers, much of the service was a replacement of mainline jet service by regional jet service.

The growth of regional airlines at the expense of mainline airlines may change the overall pilot commuting patterns in the airline industry if the commuting patterns of regional pilots are markedly different than those of mainline pilots. Without examining the commuting patterns of pilots in these two industry segments, however, it is not possible to determine even the direction, let alone the magnitude, of such changes. One possibility is that regional pilots might on average commute longer distances than mainline pilots because of the lower salaries regional pilots generally earn, which could make them less able to live close to their domiciles if those domiciles were in areas with a high cost of living. Another possibility is that regional pilots might on average have shorter commutes because the service they provide is more likely to be shorter haul service providing feed to longer mainline flights at the mainline airline's large hub. In a service pattern such as this, a regional pilot is more likely to begin and end the flight sequence each day at the same hub airport, unlike a mainline pilot, particularly a mainline pilot who may have multiday international flight sequences and therefore begin and end days while on assignment at multiple hubs.

Airline mergers were not uncommon prior to airline deregulation in 1978, but the pace of mergers and resulting industry consolidation picked up considerably in the 1980s. Most of those mergers were among relatively small airlines or were the result of large airlines merging with (or acquiring) smaller airlines. However, several of the more recent mergers since 2000 have involved large established carriers. Notable among these was the merger of American and TWA in 2001; the merger of US Airways and America West in 2005; the merger of Delta and Northwest in 2009; and the merger of United and Continental in 2010. As is discussed below, such mergers have the potential to change pilot commuting patterns because they often involve reducing the flight activity at some of the premerger hubs. In addition to the effects of hub expansion and contraction, mergers can bring changes in domicile assignments as pilots from the premerger airlines bid for new opportunities (crew positions and aircraft types) across the changed array of domiciles of the new (merged) airline.

Another recent trend has been mergers and industry consolidation among regional airlines. Notable among these mergers have been the merger of Republic Airways, Shuttle America, and Midwest Airlines in 2005 and 2009; the merger of Skywest, Atlantic Southeast, and ExpressJet Airlines in 2005 and 2009; and the merger of Pinnacle Airlines, Colgan Air, and Mesaba Airlines in 2007 and 2010. Since these regional airlines typically operate under contract with mainline airlines, it remains to be seen how much effect, if any, these regional airline mergers will have on pilot commuting patterns. To the extent that mergers in the regional segment of the industry result in large regional airlines that operate under contract with multiple mainline carriers that operate hubs in different parts of the country, the mergers have the potential to change commuting patterns by regional pilots as pilots assigned to one mainline carrier's hub are assigned to a different mainline carrier's hub.

Departure Changes

Changes in the number of aircraft departures have the potential to affect pilot commuting patterns, particularly when those changes are at the airports most frequently served by an airline and likely to serve as pilot domiciles. If an airline is experiencing growth in departures at an airport, then more pilots are likely to be domiciled there, and pilots who were previously domiciled elsewhere might find their best duty cycle options at that airport. Conversely, if an airline is reducing its departures at an airport, then it is possible that pilots who have less seniority may be furloughed and those more senior pilots who remain might find their best duty cycle options at a different domicile. If pilots perceive that the industry structure and service patterns are likely to continue to evolve and the demand for airline travel likely to continue to be subject to fluctuating economic conditions, they might choose not to relocate their residences each time their domicile changes.

Pilots' Careers

It is important to recognize that there can be pilot domicile changes even when airline service patterns are stable. In many airlines, a pilot's career progression involves moving from smaller to progressively larger aircraft as a first officer and then becoming a captain and again moving from smaller to progressively larger aircraft. In many airlines, the mix of aircraft sizes will differ across their hubs. International service, for example, is typically conducted in large aircraft, so a hub that serves as a base for international service may have a higher proportion of large aircraft than another hub that serves predominately domestic routes. Thus, even in the absence of changes in service patterns, a pilot may change domiciles as part of a normal career progression.

CHANGES IN INDUSTRY PATTERNS

The committee was unable to obtain any systematic information about how frequently pilots experienced domicile changes or how such changes altered pilot commuting behavior. To try to gain some insight into some of the industry changes that might alter commuting behavior, the committee conducted an analysis of changes in the number aircraft departures, by city, by airline, in the cities most frequently served by that airline and thus in the cities most likely to serve as domiciles for pilots.

The data used for this analysis were scheduled aircraft departures taken from the Bureau of Transportation Statistics (n.d.-a). The data were from the third quarters of 2000, 2005, and 2010. All 30 carriers who reported more than 20,000 aircraft departures in the third quarter of 2010 were examined; there were 12 mainline airlines and 18 regional airlines. Two of the airlines were all-cargo airlines, FedEx and UPS, and the rest were passenger airlines. Summary statistics for each mainline airline are presented in Appendix E and for each regional airline in Appendix F. The statistics presented are the total number of aircraft departures in 2000, 2005, and 2010 and the number of aircraft departures for each year by city for each city that was one of the top 10 cities in terms of aircraft departures for that airline in any of the 3 years. For carriers involved in mergers, if the carrier reported data in 2010 as a single carrier, as was the case with Delta, US Airways, and American, the premerger data were combined as if the carriers had been merged in all three time periods. If the carriers involved in the mergers reported data separately in 2010, as was the case with United and Continental, then the carriers were treated separately throughout all three periods.

Rise of Regional Jets

In examining the data, it quickly becomes apparent that the role of affiliated regional carriers has a large impact on mainline service patterns. Three of the mainline carriers, Southwest, Air Tran, and JetBlue, do not use affiliated regional carriers, and all showed growth in departures throughout the period. The remaining mainline airlines, which do use regional affiliated airlines, all showed declines in aircraft departures throughout the period. Both Air Tran and JetBlue are relatively new and small carriers that had comparatively few departures in 2000 and showed strong growth in 2005

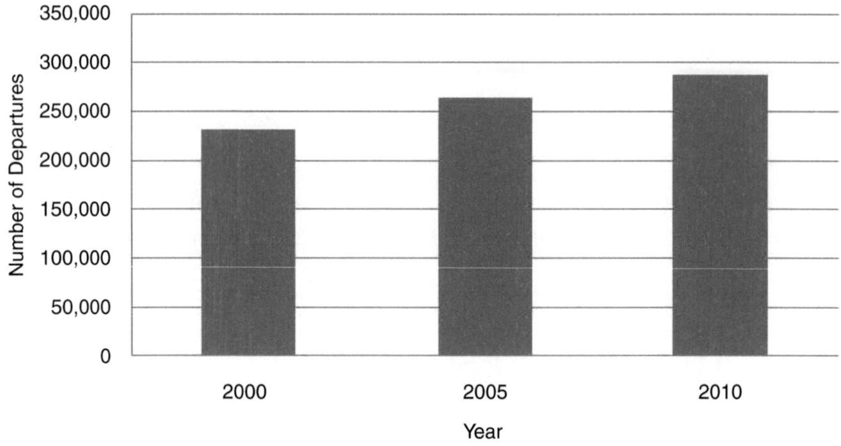

FIGURE 2-2 Southwest total departures.
SOURCE: Data from Bureau of Transportation Statistics (n.d.-a).

and 2010. Both also showed strong growth in departures at their primary hubs, Atlanta for Air Tran and New York's Kennedy Airport for JetBlue.[2]

Southwest is a much more established airline than Air Tran and JetBlue and had the most domestic aircraft departures in 2010 of any U.S. airline. Southwest showed steady increases in departures over the period (see Figure 2-2), and it did not experience sharp decreases in departures at any of its primary cities (see Figure 2-3). There were small drops in several cities and somewhat stronger increases in Las Vegas, Chicago Midway, and Baltimore, as well as significant new service established in Denver. Although these changes in departures reflect changing service patterns, they are not the dramatic changes that have been seen at some of the carriers involved in mergers, as is discussed below.

There is considerable variation in departure changes across the regional carriers. American Eagle, a regional carrier owned by American Airlines, has had a relatively stable pattern of service with its primary airports being the American hubs of Dallas and Chicago: see Figure 2-4. Similarly, Atlantic Southeast, which has been primarily a regional carrier affiliated with Delta, has focused much of its service on Atlanta: see Figure 2-5. When Delta stopped using Dallas and Cincinnati as hubs, Atlantic Southeast also saw

[2]A partial exception to this pattern was Frontier Airlines, which used a regional affiliate, Great Lakes Airlines, to provide some service, and it showed increases in departures over the period. Frontier, however, is something of a hybrid between a mainline and a regional airline in that it operates both larger Airbus aircraft (with more than 90 seats) and smaller regional jets with fewer than 90 seats.

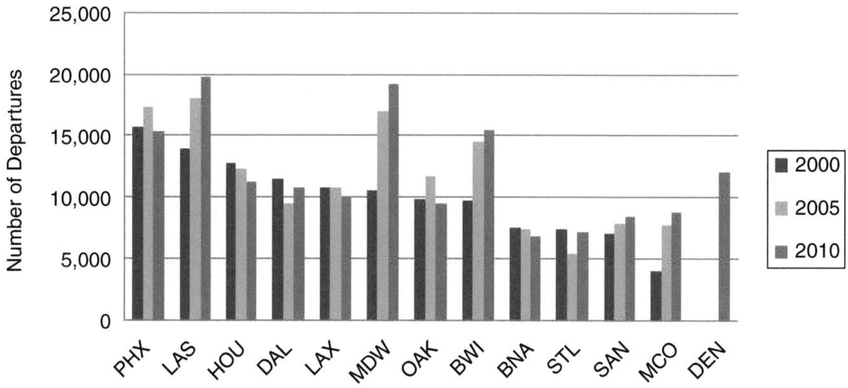

FIGURE 2-3 Southwest departures by city.*
*In all figures for the airline departure analysis, cities are identified by the appropriate airport code. Provided in Appendix E is a list of airport codes alongside the corresponding airports and cities.
SOURCE: Data from Bureau of Transportation Statistics (n.d.-a).

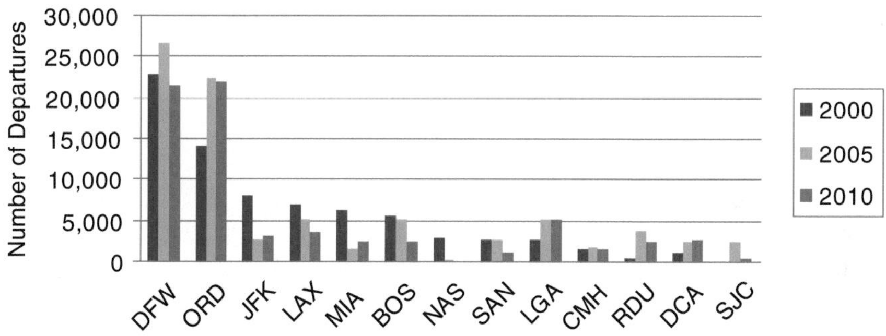

FIGURE 2-4 American Eagle departures by city.
SOURCE: Data from Bureau of Transportation Statistics (n.d.-a).

declines in flights in those cities. Beginning in 2010, Atlantic Southeast has also been providing services associated with United Airlines.

In contrast, Air Wisconsin has experienced greater change in its service patterns: see Figure 2-6. The two principal cities Air Wisconsin served in 2000 were Denver and Chicago, which it served as a United Express carrier. However, in 2010 it became a US Airways Express carrier and switched its primary cities from Denver and Chicago to the US Airways hubs of Philadelphia and Charlotte, both cities it had not served in 2000.

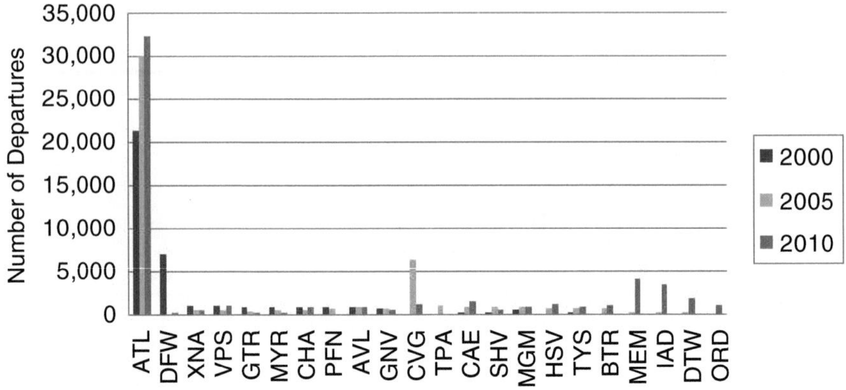

FIGURE 2-5 Atlantic Southeast departures by city.
SOURCE: Data from Bureau of Transportation Statistics (n.d.-a).

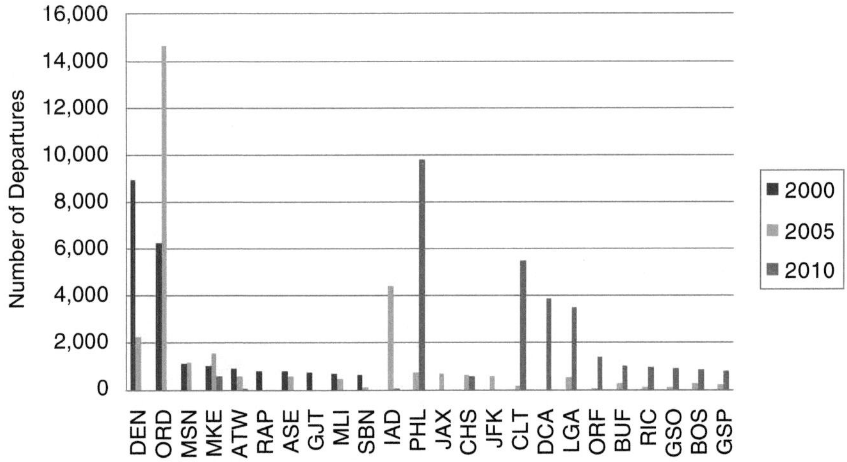

FIGURE 2-6 Air Wisconsin departures by city.
SOURCE: Data from Bureau of Transportation Statistics (n.d.-a).

Indeed, only one of the cities found in Air Wisconsin's top 10 in 2000, Milwaukee, continued to receive Air Wisconsin service in 2010, and none of the cities that were top 10 Air Wisconsin cities in 2010 had been served by Air Wisconsin in 2000.

The Air Wisconsin experience illustrates how changes in contracts between the regional airlines and the mainline airlines can result in large changes in regional operations at specific hub airports, with associated changes in regional pilot domicile assignment. Air Wisconsin effectively moved its entire operation to a different part of the country so that virtually all of its pilots experienced changes in their domiciles.

Mergers

In addition to the rise of affiliated regional airlines, mergers also played an important role in the changing service patterns of the mainline airlines. For example, Delta and Northwest merged at the end of 2009. The merged Delta's total departures are presented in Figure 2-7. Delta experienced steady declines in departures throughout the period.

Delta also experienced some sharp declines at some of their hubs, partly in the wake of the merger and partly for other reasons: see Figure 2-8. While the main Delta hub, Atlanta, experienced only small proportional declines in 2010, the former Northwest hubs of Detroit and Minneapolis/St. Paul experienced sharper declines following the merger. However, not all the declines were necessarily related to the merger. Delta's original Cincinnati hub experienced sharp declines before the merger and even sharper declines following the merger. The even sharper declines in aircraft departures at Dallas/Fort Worth indicate a decision made prior to the merger to no longer operate a hub at that airport. These sorts of sharp declines at airports that had once been hubs may well have placed pressure on pilots to alter their commuting patterns.

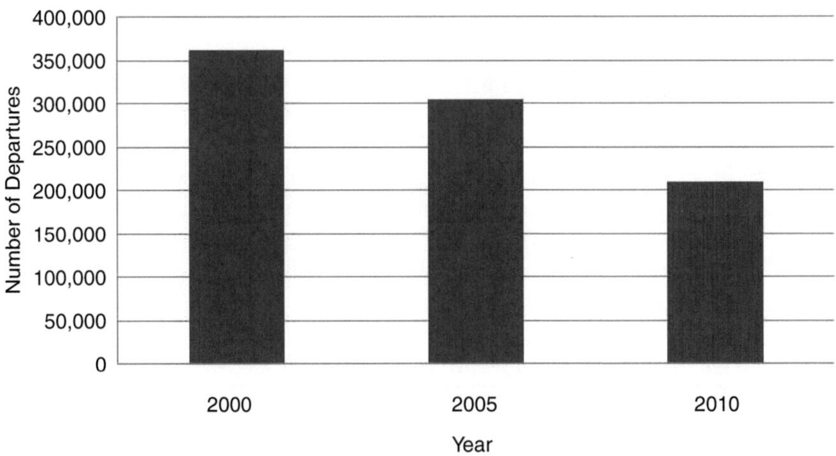

FIGURE 2-7 Delta total departures.
SOURCE: Data from Bureau of Transportation Statistics (n.d.-a).

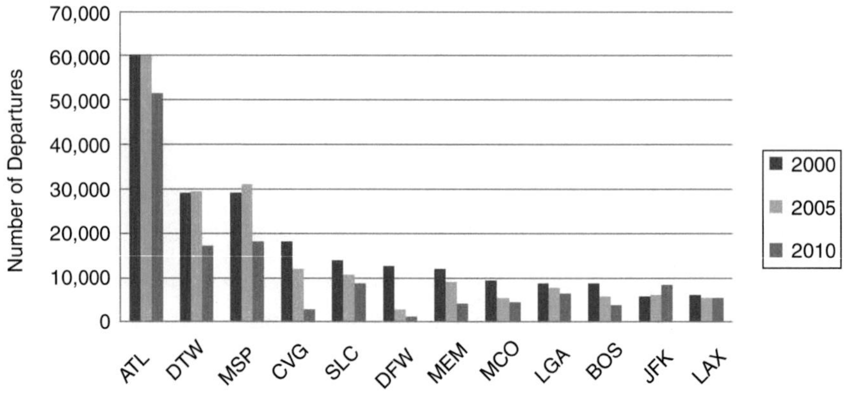

FIGURE 2-8 Delta departures by city.
SOURCE: Data from Bureau of Transportation Statistics (n.d.-a).

After the merger was completed and the Delta and Northwest pilots had integrated their seniority lists, subsequent seniority-based bidding for domiciles and positions may have also resulted in changes to commuting patterns. For example, it is possible that some former Delta pilots who had homes in or near Minneapolis and had been commuting from Minneapolis to Atlanta could now bid to be domiciled at Minneapolis, a former Northwest hub, and have a shorter commute. Such opportunities, however, given the drop in departures in Minneapolis, may have been limited to pilots with relatively high seniority. Another possibility is that former Delta pilots who were both domiciled and living in Atlanta may have found their best postmerger opportunities were in a former Northwest hub and thus may have chosen a longer commute.

As can be seen both with the Delta/Northwest merger noted above and with the other merged carriers shown in Appendix E, mergers often result in decreases in departures at some of the premerger hubs as the merged airline consolidates its operations (as occurred for St. Louis following the American/TWA merger). But airlines have also sharply decreased departures at hubs for reasons not associated with mergers, as was seen in Delta's reducing departures at Dallas/Fort Worth and in Appendix E with US Airways' reducing departures at Pittsburgh. Regardless of the reason that hubs are sharply downsized or eliminated, such actions can put pressure on pilots either to relocate or to alter their commuting patterns. Flight departures are correlated with airline crew staffing requirements. Again, these hub airports are not synonymous with pilot domiciles, but the dynamic nature of hub departure volumes suggests that the staffing of pilots to operate the flights passing through them has been subject to substantial change over at least the past decade. Lacking specific data about pilot commuting patterns, the committee was unable to measure the specific effects of mergers on pilot commuting.

In the absence of opportunities to commute by air, these changes in the airlines' operating pattern could lead to large-scale, sometimes short-term, relocations of pilots and families or inflexibility in the airlines' ability to adjust to changes in flight patterns and thus to staffing needs. Consequently, the availability of commuting by air allows airlines to adjust crew staffing and domiciles quickly in accordance with market demands.

AIRLINE POLICIES AND PRACTICES

Various airline policies and practices may facilitate or hinder pilots' abilities to commute, particularly by air and over long distances. Such policies include access to free or reduced-rate air travel, commuting policies that spell out the consequences of failing to report to the domicile on time because of commuting, and policies related to sick leave (including attendance/reliability) and fatigue. For the most part, these policies are currently unregulated and subject to collective bargaining agreements. The committee requested information from airlines, airline associations, and pilot associations about these policies and practices. Responses were received from 33 airlines including mainline, regional, cargo, and charter carriers. It is important to note that these responses were a collection of heterogeneous submissions. Airlines provided a range of information: some airlines provided basic descriptive statements about their policies while others provided copies of the actual policies. The committee did not request nor receive information as to how these policies were developed, on what scientific research they were based, or on how the policies were implemented.

Access to Air Travel and Rest Facilities

As is the case with many other airline employees, pilots are able to take advantage of free or reduced-rate (nonrevenue) travel, on a standby basis. Nonrevenue travel is available on the pilot's own airline network and, in many cases, also on other airlines. Seating may be available using unsold seats in the passenger cabin or the jumpseat, which is an additional observer seat on the flight deck available to other pilots by courtesy of the captain. Although some airlines allow pilots to reserve the flight deck jumpseat in advance, other carriers require pilots to stand by for the jumpseat until it is awarded to the senior requestor 30 minutes before flight time. Under these procedures, only the most senior pilots would be able to rely on obtaining a jumpseat for their commutes.

Some airlines have adopted additional corporate policies that facilitate pilot commuting by air or reduce the potential for stress and fatigue. For example, FedEx reported to the committee that it allowed pilots to reserve the jumpseat in advance; provided sleeping facilities at both its sorting hubs and outlying stations; and included the time spent in commuting from the pilot's home airport to the domicile in the calculation of duty time with respect to the limits established by the labor contract. (Time spent commuting is not considered in duty time under current FAA regulations.) Similarly, Delta Airlines reported in a submission to the committee that it allows jumpseats to be reserved in advance. Some cargo and charter carriers that engage in home basing reported to the committee that they provided reserved seats for the trip to the pilot's duty location and provided minimum rest periods of 4-9 hours, depending on the carrier, between the arrival of the commuting flight and commencement of preflight activities for a pilot's operational flight.

Although nonrevenue travel dramatically lowers the cost of commuting for pilots, it has the disadvantage of the uncertainty of standing by for open seats, especially given recently experienced record load factors.[3] Figure 2-9 shows the changes in system-wide domestic load factors from 2000 through 2010. By 2010, load factors had increased to over 82 percent. (Load factors on international flights by U.S. carriers were over 81 percent.) During the most popular travel times and on the most popular routes, load factors are even higher. The result is that there are fewer and fewer empty seats available to pilots (or other airline employees) for nonrevenue travel than was the case when load factors were lower.

Adding to uncertainty over commuting arrangements are flight delays and cancellations due to bad weather, air traffic control delays at congested hub airports, and flights delayed or cancelled because of unscheduled maintenance needs. Pilots told the committee in testimony that they experience stress from these uncertainties, with the risk of losing pay and being subject to disciplinary actions if their commute goes badly and they do not arrive at the domicile in a timely manner. Furthermore, they stated that the most common way to mitigate this uncertainty is to begin the commute on an earlier flight from the home airport to the domicile, which takes more time away from home and may reduce sleep opportunities prior to the start of duty.

Although some airlines provide quiet, dark, temperature-controlled sleeping facilities in or near the domicile, most airlines do not. Many pilots arrange for their own sleeping facilities at or near their domiciles. These facilities range from private apartments owned or rented by the pilots to

[3]The passenger load factor is a measure of how much of an airline's passenger carrying capacity is used and is calculated as the ratio of revenue passenger miles to available seat miles.

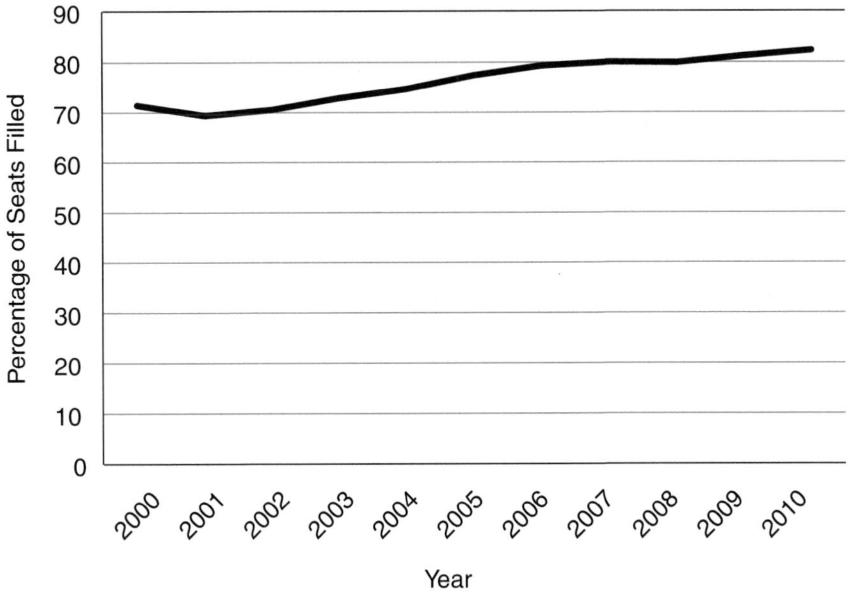

FIGURE 2-9 U.S. carrier domestic load factors.
SOURCE: Data from Bureau of Transportation Statistics (n.d.-b).

hotel rooms rented by the night to temporary living arrangements shared among groups of pilots. The arrangements at shared accommodations (often referred to by pilots as "crash pads") vary from a private bedroom regularly assigned and available to the pilot to a shared room with multiple bunk beds in which the pilot takes a "hot bunk" that is open for the night. Thus, shared accommodations can achieve the ideal of a quiet, dark, temperature-controlled sleeping area, or they can fall well short of the ideal. The quality of sleep obtainable at these locations, whether at hotels, shared apartments, or company provided rest facilities, may vary considerably.

The challenge of obtaining restful sleep in a less-than-ideal facility can further increase the stress of commuting and can contribute to pilots' operating flights in a fatigued state. This outcome is more likely if a pilot commutes to the domicile with the intent of obtaining rest there, is unable to sleep well, anticipates becoming fatigued by the end of the upcoming duty shift, yet declines to call off the trip (desiring not to cause a flight delay or concerned about losing pay from a trip dropped due to fatigue).

Commuting Policies

A pilot who does not report to the domicile on time to prepare for the first operational flight of the trip (usually 1 hour prior to scheduled pushback) must be replaced by a reserve pilot. The flight's departure may well be delayed if a late-arriving pilot does not alert the company about the situation ahead of time. Consequently, pilots who show up late for duty risk disciplinary actions up to and including termination. Airlines recognize that the uncertainties of commuting may be responsible for some late reports or no-shows for duty. It is in the interest of the airline to receive "prenotification" from pilots who are experiencing difficulty with their commute in order to facilitate the call-up of reserve pilots without the cost and disruption of a flight delay. However, it is also in the interest of the airline to maintain consequences for pilots who report late in order to motivate the pilots to arrive for duty reliably on time.

Consistent with these goals, some of the airlines that provided information to the committee reported the establishment of commuting policies that require pilots, for example, to attempt standby travel on two flights that have open seat availability and would arrive at the domicile on time. Pilots who do not clear the standby list for the first flight must then notify a crew scheduler or chief pilot about their situation (providing the airline with the desired advance notification of a possible late report). If these pilots do not clear standby for the second flight, they may be provided a reserved seat on the same flight (possibly bumping a paying passenger) or may be allowed to drop the beginning of their scheduled trip with loss of pay for the missed flight segments, depending on the airline's policy. Under some commuting policies, pilots who provide the specified prenotification may be assured that no disciplinary action will be taken for the late arrival. At other airlines, disciplinary action may be taken for overuse or abuse of the commuting policy, while overuse or abuse may not be well defined. One airline reported to the committee that repeated use of the allowances in the commuting policy might result in the pilot losing the privileges of that policy in the future.

Sick Leave and Attendance/Reliability Policies

Regulations require the individual pilot to assess his or her fitness to fly and require pilots to decline to fly whenever unable to meet medical certification requirements (i.e., they are sick). Most airlines provide sick leave as an employee benefit, with an earned bank of sick or multipurpose leave hours for pilots to use to avoid loss of pay when missing a trip due to illness. Traditionally, 1 hour of the pilot's earned sick leave bank would be used to substitute for each hour of flying time on the missed trip (most pilots are paid by the hour of flight time, or more specifically, block time including taxiing).[4]

The potential relevance of sick leave to commuting, the committee was told informally, is that a pilot who is experiencing difficulty with a commute may choose to call in sick for the upcoming trip in order to maintain pay for the trip (which may be up to one-third of one's monthly earnings, depending on the number of trips per month). Atlantic Southeast Airlines provided, in a submission to the committee, an excerpt from its Flight Operations Manual that "the use of sick leave when commute difficulties are encountered is a violation of Atlantic Southeast policy and could subject the pilot to discipline." Regardless of stated policy, airlines recognize that this use or abuse of sick leave does occur. Perhaps in response (among other reasons), some airlines have established attendance and reliability policies that require pilots who frequently use sick leave to provide documentation of their illness and treatment, submit to interviews by flight managers, or be subject to disciplinary steps that may potentially lead to termination.

Fatigue Policies

Some airlines have established specific policies about flight crew fatigue. Uniformly, under the policies reported to the committee, airlines rely on the pilots to report fit for duty, including being properly rested, and also to notify the airline if they are too fatigued to operate safely at any time during a trip. In what appears to be a typical airline procedural response to a statement of fatigue by a pilot, Ameristar Air Cargo reported to the committee in a submission: "There are no adverse consequences for a pilot to call in fatigued. If a pilot uses the word 'fatigue,' 'tired,' or similar wording that he or she is unfit for flight, that pilot is automatically removed from a flight assignment." Beyond this initial response, there is variation as to whether, as a matter of policy or practice, managers interview or investigate pilots who make such fatigue calls. Reported policies varied as to whether the pilot receives pay for a trip not flown because of fatigue or forfeits the pay that would have been earned from the trip.

Delta Airlines reported to the committee that in its experience ". . . our recent reviews have not shown us a significant amount of absences or missed flights due to commuting. To our knowledge, we only have a few

[4]Under some labor agreements, though, the use of sick leave has been capped on a monthly basis, so a pilot calling in sick for a trip may lose some or all of the pay for that trip. This kind of agreement may provide a different incentive for a pilot who is sick to perhaps report for work and attempt to fly when not medically qualified.

fatigue situations per year that are associated with commuting." However, no systemic, reliable information from any airline was available to the committee about the effects, if any, of commuting on pilots' reliably arriving at their domicile on time for duty or about the effects, if any, of commuting on either fatigue or fatigue calls.

3

Aviation Safety and Pilot Commuting

The concern about the potential effects of pilot commuting on fatigue is rooted in concerns that increased pilot fatigue might increase the risk of an airline accident. As discussed in Chapter 4, there is extensive scientific evidence on the negative effects of fatigue on the performance of many cognitive tasks, including those essential for safely operating a commercial aircraft. This chapter provides the context in which to consider that evidence.

This chapter begins with a review of the airline safety record in the United States and then turns to the sources of improvement in aviation safety. Of particular importance for the focus of this report is a discussion of those features of the aviation system that can mitigate the risk of individual pilot fatigue for flight safety. In the third section the chapter examines investigations of the National Transportation Safety Board (NTSB) for accidents that occurred from 1982 to 2010 in order to determine how often fatigue is found to be a probable cause or contributing factor for an accident and the extent to which there is evidence that commuting might have contributed to that fatigue. Finally, the chapter examines what is known about the current patterns of pilot commuting.

AVIATION SAFETY

Figure 3-1 confirms that airline travel is the safest form of passenger travel in the United States. Measured on the basis of fatalities per 100 million passenger miles, the fatality rate for both buses and trains was about 4 times higher than for airlines while the fatality rate for automobiles was about 75 times higher.

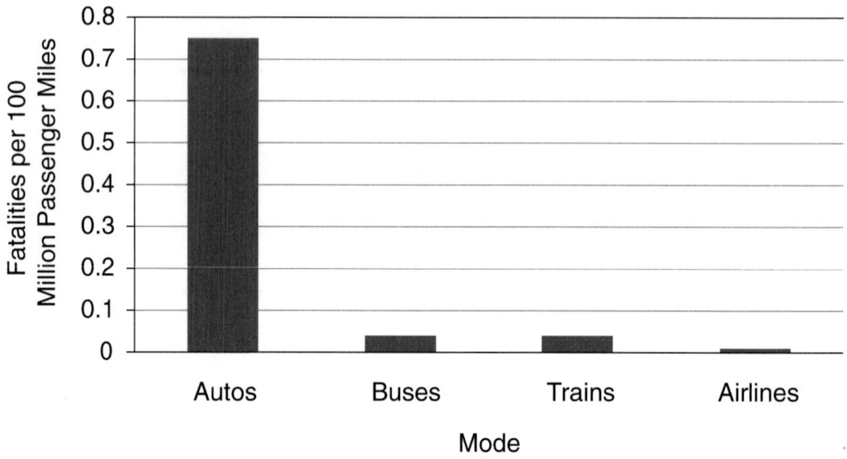

FIGURE 3-1 Safety of travel in the United States: 1989-2007.
SOURCE: Derived from data, used with permission, from Air Transport Association of America, Inc. (n.d.). See http://www.airlines.org/Economics/DataAnalysis/Pages/SafetyRecordofUSAirCarriers.aspx [August 2011]. 1927-1937: AA Statistical Handbook (December 1945). 1938-1971: CAB Handbook of Airline Statistics (1973), Part VIII, Items 19c, d, pp. 595-596; NTSB Safety Studies Division. 1972-1982: FAA Statistical Handbook (1972-1982), Table 9.3, p. 161, citing NTSB for totals; 1983-present: NTSB Aviation Accident Statistics, Table 6. Fatal Accident Rate excludes incidents resulting from illegal acts, consistent with NTSB practice.

Although measuring safety in terms of fatalities per passenger mile is a useful way of comparing safety across different modes of road travel, it is not the most useful way to measure airline safety.[1] For automobile travel, for example, the risk of an accident varies across the types of roads used. Travel on interstate highways is much safer than travel on arterial highways, which in turn are much safer than travel on local roads (National Research Council, 2010, Figure 3-10). Travel on rural roads is more dangerous than travel on urban roads for all highway types. But in all of these categories of highway travel, the risk is roughly proportional to the distance traveled, so that the risk of a fatal accident on a 200-mile trip is about twice the risk on a 100-mile trip. Thus, for highway travel, measuring safety on a passenger-mile basis is a reasonable portrayal of the risk a traveler faces.

[1]Transportation safety is usually measured as the ratio of some adverse outcome, such as an accident or fatality, to a measure of exposure such as the number of trips taken or the distance traveled.

The safety of airline travel is different. With airline flights, the risk of accident is largely confined to the landing and takeoff phases of flight, including the climb, descent, and approach phases.[2] Thus, for airline travel, the risk of an accident on a 1,000-mile flight is virtually the same as on a 500-mile flight since the only difference is the amount of time spent in cruise. When looking at airline travel, either across segments of the industry or over time, it is better to measure safety on a departure basis rather than on a mileage basis.

A common way to do this is to measure fatal accidents per million aircraft departures. One shortcoming of this measure, however, is that a fatal accident is defined as one in which at least one passenger was killed. In this measure, an accident in which one passenger of 200 passengers on board was killed is treated the same as one in which all 200 passengers were killed. So fatal accidents per 1 million departures, although better than a distance-based measure, is still not a good measure of the risk a passenger faces when taking an airline flight. However, this measure is often used when looking at worldwide safety trends because there is often limited information available about enplanements in some countries, some ambiguity about the number of passengers killed in an accident, or the definition of what constitutes a fatality may differ slightly. In the United States and throughout much of the rest of the world a fatality is considered to be from the accident if the passenger dies within 30 days of the accident from injuries suffered in the accident. To reflect the risk to a passenger from taking an airline flight, a commonly used measure is passenger fatalities per million enplanements.

Figure 3-2 shows the aviation safety record from 1959 through 2009 for U.S. and Canadian operators (combined) and for operators in the rest of the world. Canadian operators have generally had comparable safety to U.S. operators, and the two countries are often grouped together.[3] Two things are apparent in the figure. First, the safety record both in the United States and Canada and in the rest of the world has improved considerably since the 1960s and 1970s. Second, the safety record in the United States and Canada has been markedly better than the combined record for the rest of the world. It is important to note, however, that the safety record in the rest of the world varies considerably both by region and by individual airline: consequently, although the combined safety record is worse than for the United States and Canada, there are individual airlines in the rest of the world that have amassed excellent safety records.

---

[2]For commercial jet service between 1999 and 2008, only 10 percent of fatal accidents occurred during the cruise phase of flight according to the Boeing Commercial Airplanes *Statistical Summary of Commercial Jet Airplane Accidents* (Boeing Commercial Airplanes, 2011).

[3]For more discussion of U.S. and Canadian aviation safety, see Oster et al. (1992, Ch. 4).

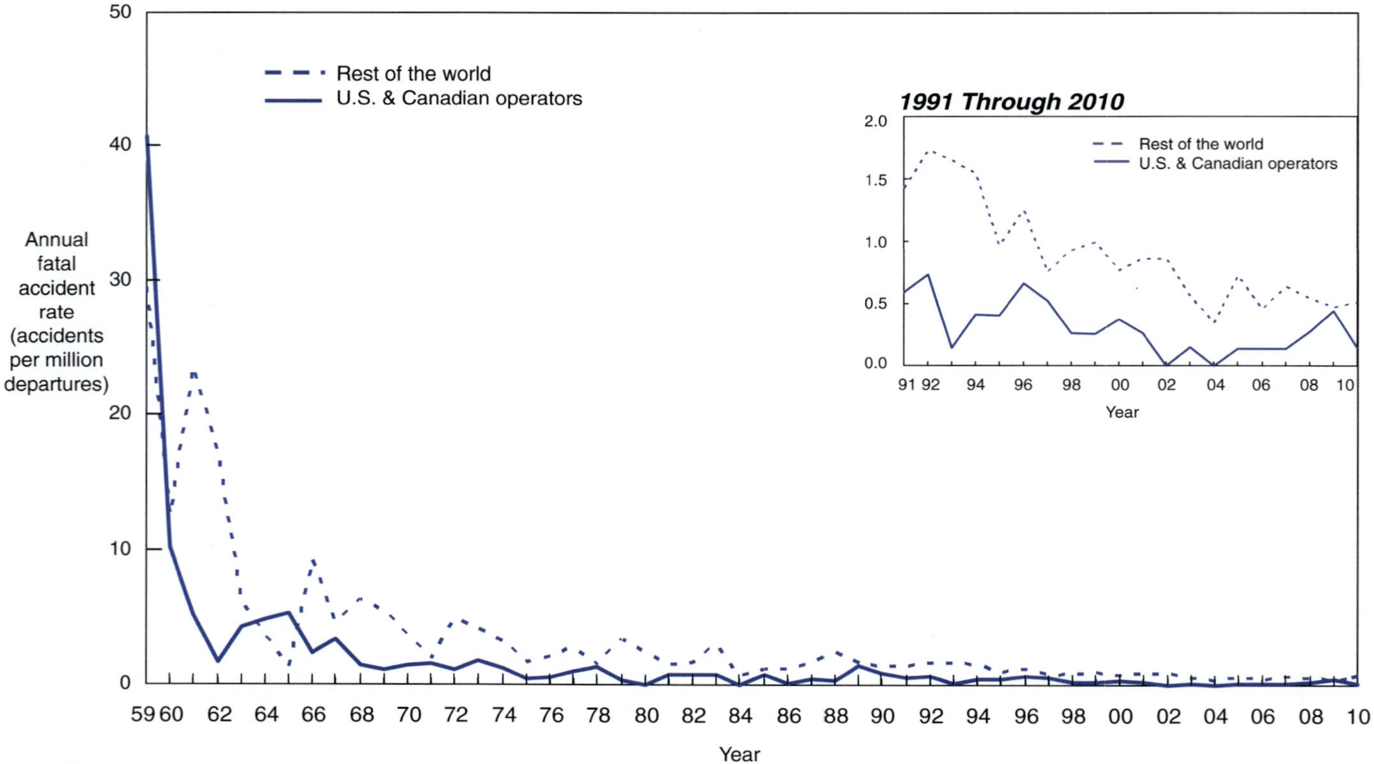

FIGURE 3-2 U.S. and Canadian operators accident rates by year.
SOURCE: Boeing Commercial Airplanes (2011, p. 18). Reprinted with permission.

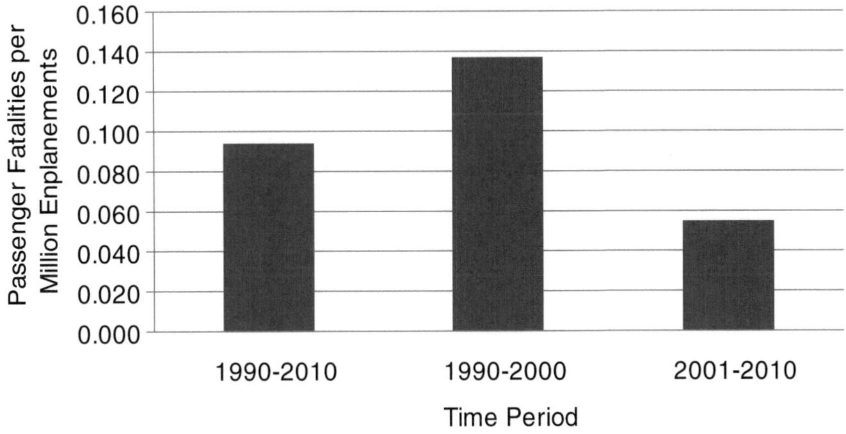

FIGURE 3-3 U.S. air carrier safety record: 1990-2010.
SOURCE: Data on passenger fatalities and enplanements calculated from information from the National Transportation Safety Board (n.d.) and the Bureau of Transportation Statistics (n.d.-a).

Figure 3-3 shows the U.S. Air Carrier Safety record over the 1990 to 2010 period. As can be seen in the figure, the safety record for the second half of this period is notably better than for the first half.[4] However, looking at aviation safety records over time must be done with care. Airline accidents are rare events, but when an accident happens, large numbers of people can be killed, so the passenger fatality rates from year to year show considerable variation. Therefore, one needs to be cautious in drawing inferences about airline safety getting better or worse when looking at only a few years of data.

IMPROVEMENTS IN AVIATION SAFETY

Commercial aviation involves complex interactions and coordination among equipment, information, and people. As a result it is not surprising that the reasons aviation safety has improved over time involve a variety of factors. One source of improvement has been the improved performance and reliability of critical equipment such as aircraft, engines, and avionics. Equipment failures have decreased dramatically and system redundancy has typically enabled safe landings when these failures do occur. Similarly, more accurate air traffic control procedures have improved safety margins

[4]Fatalities from accidents involving illegal acts (sabotage, suicide, and terrorism) have been excluded from this analysis.

both in the air and on the ground. Airline pilot training has benefited from the widespread use of improved training programs and advanced flight simulators in which pilots can learn to manage both normal and non-normal events safely (Helmreich et al., 1999). Many of these and other improvements have resulted from the combined efforts of many people and organizations—including the National Transportation Safety Board, the Federal Aviation Administration, airframe and aircraft component manufacturers, airlines, pilots, and many others—to understand the causes of accidents and to take steps to reduce the risk of future accidents.

A particularly important component of aviation safety improvement for the purpose of the committee's work has been the joint application of procedural, social, and technological systems to identify crew errors on the flight deck and to facilitate their correction or mitigation. Such errors can stem from a variety of human factors including fatigue. One approach known to reduce risks from errors is crew resource management (CRM) (see Helmreich and Foushee, 2010). CRM training is mandated by the Federal Aviation Administration (FAA) for the pilots of all Part 121 operators to facilitate effective crew communication, coordination, and the use of appropriate resources to prevent error. This systematic training is designed to enhance the ability of crews to perform as a team in order to reduce the potential for human error and improve safety on the flight deck. Such training emphasizes the importance of communication and consultation with each other regarding potential safety threats (including crew members' own fatigue state), managing such threats, confirming actions being taken, and cross-checking information from both instruments and external sources. The intention is to improve situational awareness, problem solving, and decision making.

If an individual crew member is fatigued and thus more likely to make errors, CRM can help mitigate the effects of fatigue so that the errors are made less frequently or are caught quickly before they lead to an increased safety risk. Specifically, the practice of CRM requires a crew member to monitor other crew members, aircraft automation, and the overall flight situation and to identify any suspected errors with a verbal challenge that must be acknowledged. Such crew coordination practices have been shown in observational studies to be effective in identifying, trapping, and correcting pilot errors due to fatigue (Foushee et al., 1986; Thomas et al., 2006; Petrilli et al., 2007; Helmreich and Foushee, 2010; Thomas and Ferguson, 2010).

Checklists are another highly reliable error-trapping mechanism (Boorman, 2001; Pronovost et al., 2006) that can help pilots avoid missing key actions for successfully completing important safety-related tasks. Similarly, the use of callouts can help maintain attention both for the person making the callout and the person receiving it. The use of standard operating procedures and the annual training that reinforces their use provides highly structured, routinized processes that can facilitate reliable and repeatable cognitive performance. In addition, social interaction among the crew members can help maintain alertness on the flight deck and, through exchanging relevant information, can help reorient a pilot to focus on task performance. Taken together, these forms of crew interaction can help mitigate fatigue risk in individual pilots as well as fatigued crews. A potential downside is that they may mask a pilot's awareness of his or her actual level of fatigue.

For very long flights of more than 8 hours, crew augmentation, adding one or two additional crew members, can help mitigate fatigue risk particularly when inflight rest facilities such as bunks are provided for crew members to sleep when they are not on duty. Even on shorter flights, research has shown that short, controlled naps are a well-established fatigue-mitigation strategy (Rosekind et al., 1994; Werfelman et al., 2009) that can enhance all cognitive and physiological processes.[5] However, in considering naps, one has to take account of sleep inertia so that recovery time is provided before the crew member has to perform.

Flight deck technologies can also help mitigate the effects of fatigue. Onboard map displays have greatly enhanced crews' cognitive situation awareness regarding airplane navigation (Wiener and Nagel, 1988). A range of systems such as stall and wind shear warnings, Traffic Collision Avoidance Systems, and Ground Proximity Warning Systems (now part of the Terrain Awareness and Warning System) have been shown to be highly effective in helping crews manage safety risks even when tired at the end of a long flight or series of flights (see, e.g., Kuchar and Drumm, 2007). More generally, when designed properly, automation can support and supplement the cognitive capacity crews need to operate safely, while enabling a pilot to transition back to taking over the aircraft manually when necessary. Air traffic control flight monitoring can also trap and help correct errors both by monitoring by human controllers and with automated systems such as Minimum Safe Altitude Warning Systems.

Each of these systems and processes can be effective in mitigating risks to safety from an individual's fatigue but none is completely reliable and some introduce other cognitive loads. Taken together, however, they help mitigate potential safety risks of fatigue.

FATIGUE-RELATED AVIATION ACCIDENTS

A complication in understanding past accidents and in preventing future ones is that airline accidents rarely have a single cause. Rather, accidents are

[5]Napping is discussed further in Chapter 4.

usually the culmination of a sequence of events that involve multiple causes and contributing factors. It is often difficult to determine what happened that led to an accident and what the contributing factors were, particularly when the flight deck crew is killed in the accident and cannot provide input to the investigation. Although there is usually information about what they were saying from the cockpit voice recorder and information about what was happening to the aircraft from the flight data recorder, there can often be some doubt about whether all of the things that may have contributed to the accident were identified and understood.

Assessing the role that pilot fatigue may have played in an accident is a challenge because of other potential contributing factors. In some cases, the cockpit voice recorder may reveal that pilots talked about being fatigued during the flight or there may have been other signs of fatigue from the cockpit voice recorder. In other cases, the record may be clear that a pilot received very little sleep prior to the flight.

Beyond assessing the role of fatigue in an accident, assessing the role that pilot commuting may have played in pilot fatigue may be an even greater challenge. A pilot who lives close to the domicile and has a short commute may not necessarily arrive for duty well rested depending on the pilot's activities prior to the commute. If the pilot did not sleep well the night before reporting for duty or if the pilot engaged in physically tiring activity prior to reporting for duty, then the pilot may be fatigued even if the commute was very short. Conversely, if the pilot commutes to the domicile by air from a distant point, that pilot will not necessarily report for duty fatigued. The pilot may fly to the domicile city the day before the duty cycle begins and get a good night's sleep in a hotel before reporting for duty. It is important to realize that the length of the commute, measured either by distance or time spent commuting, does not necessarily determine whether or not the pilot reports for duty fit and well rested.

As discussed in Chapter 4, fatigue can be exacerbated by cumulative sleep debt, the situation when sleep obtained over multiple days is too short in duration to maintain alertness. If a commute prior to the start of duty contributes to cumulative sleep debt from inadequate sleep throughout a multiday trip, then it is conceivable that commuting may have contributed to fatigue that built during the multiday trip and subsequently contributed to an accident. In the analysis of NTSB accident reports discussed below, the committee was unable to assess whether this might have happened in any of the fatigue-related accidents.

Although there is strong evidence that fatigue can result in deteriorated pilot performance (discussed below), even in such cases, the fact that a pilot is likely to have been fatigued does not necessarily mean that the pilot's fatigue resulted in errors made during the accident sequence or contributed to the cause of the accident. Well-rested pilots have been involved in airplane crashes and fatigued pilots have completed flights without accidents. However, because the contribution of fatigue can be difficult to detect during an accident investigation, it is quite possible that fatigue may have contributed to accidents even when there is no clear evidence of pilot fatigue in the accident record.

Committee's Method of Analysis

Recognizing these challenges, the committee examined NTSB reports of recent accidents[6] to try to assess the roles that pilot fatigue and commuting may have played as risks to aviation safety. Between 1982 and 2010, there were 863 accidents in the Part 121 portion of the industry where the NTSB had determined the probable cause and contributing factors[7] to the accident.

One approach would have been to look at the accident reports for all 863 accidents to determine how often pilot fatigue or commuting might have played a role in the accident. Unfortunately, the committee did not have the time or the resources to conduct such an analysis. Instead, the committee did an electronic search of the NTSB Aviation Accident and Incident Data System, which contains information collected during NTSB investigations of accidents and incidents involving civil aircraft within the United States, its territories and possessions, and in international waters. This system contains both the NTSB "probable cause reports," which provide the NTSB findings as to the probable cause and contributing factors of the accident, and the NTSB "factual reports," which provide descriptions of the sequence of events that culminated in the accident.[8]

One limitation of this analysis is that it provides no information about how often pilots were fatigued during their flights but were not involved in an accident. A second limitation of this approach is that accidents in which

[6]An aircraft accident is defined in Title 49 Section 830.2 as "an occurrence associated with the operation of an aircraft which takes place between the time any person boards the aircraft with the intention of flight and all such persons have disembarked, and in which any person suffers death or serious injury, or in which the aircraft receives substantial damage."

[7]"The NTSB determines the probable cause or causes of accidents. The objective of this determination is to discern the cause-and-effect relationships in the accident sequence. This could be described as why the accident happened. In determining probable cause, the NTSB considers all facts, conditions, and circumstances associated with the accident. Within each accident occurrence, any information that helps explain why that event happened is designated as either a 'cause' or 'factor.' The term 'factor' is used to describe situations or circumstances that contribute to the accident cause" (National Transportation Safety Board, 2010a, p. 52).

[8]The database was accessed through the FAA's Aviation Safety Information Analysis and Sharing System (ASIAS) (see http://www.asias.faa.gov/portal/page/portal/asias_pages/asias_home/datainfo:databases:k-o) [June 2011] by using the NTSB Query Tool. The database can be accessed directly through the NTSB website, but the ASIAS website provides easier and quicker access to the same data.

fatigue may have played some role in the accident but in which the NTSB determined that the role was not sufficient for fatigue to be considered a probable cause or contributing factor will not be included. For example, considerable attention was paid to the first officer's commute and possible fatigue following the 2009 Colgan Air crash in Buffalo, New York. However, this accident was the culmination of a series of events and errors by the flight crew and the NTSB did not find that fatigue was either a probable cause or a contributing factor in that accident, so that accident was not included in our analysis as a fatigue-related accident.

Both fatigue and commuting were discussed in the NTSB report on the Colgan accident. In the wake of that accident, the NTSB made 25 safety recommendations. One of those recommendations was related to fatigue and recommended that the FAA:

> Require all 14 *Code of Federal Regulations* Part 121, 135, and 91K operators to address fatigue risks associated with commuting, including identifying pilots who commute, establishing policy and guidance to mitigate fatigue risks for commuting pilots, using scheduling practices to minimize opportunities for fatigue in commuting pilots, and developing or identifying rest facilities for commuting pilots. (National Transportation Safety Board, 2010b, pp. 112-113)

To carry out its analysis, the committee did an electronic search of the NTSB's online accident database for Part 121 accidents between 1982 and 2010 where the probable cause or contributing factor contained any of the words "fatigue" or "tired" or "sleep" or "commute" or "commuting." Each record found in the search was reviewed to see if the reference was to pilot fatigue. (Many of the references were to component failure due to metal fatigue.)

Table 3-1 shows the number of accidents in each injury category and how many of those accidents had references to pilot fatigue, including the statements on probable cause and contributing factors.[9] Of the 863 Part 121 accidents that occurred during this period, nine of the accidents made some reference to pilot fatigue as a contributing factor.

Table 3-2 lists each of the nine accidents with fatigue as a probable cause or contributing factor. Each accident report was examined individu-

---

[9]The NTSB injury categories are defined as follows: Fatal—Any injury that results in death within 30 days of the accident; Serious—Any injury that (1) requires the individual to be hospitalized for more than 48 hours, commencing within 7 days from the date the injury was received; (2) results in a fracture of any bone (except simple fractures of fingers, toes, or nose); (3) causes severe hemorrhages, nerve, muscle, or tendon damage; (4) involves any internal organ; or (5) involves second- or third-degree burns, or any burns affecting more than 5 percent of the body surface; Minor—Any injury that is neither fatal nor serious; None—No injury (taken from CFR, Title 49, Transportation, Part 830).

TABLE 3-1 Total Accidents and Fatigue Accidents by Injury Category, 1982-2010

Injury Category	Total Accidents	Fatigue Accidents
Part 121 Fatal	95	2
Part 121 Serious	423	4
Part 121 Minor	78	0
Part 121 None	337	3
Total	863	9

SOURCE: National Transportation Safety Board Accident and Incident Data System, accessed through the Federal Aviation Administration's Aviation Safety Information Analysis and Sharing System (ASIAS).

TABLE 3-2 Fatigue-Related Accidents, 1993-2009

Event Date	Operator Name	Category of Operation	Flight Phase	Fatal/ Nonfatal
Aug 18-93	Connie Kalitta Services	Nonscheduled	Approach	Serious
May 8-99	American Eagle	Scheduled	Landing-Roll	Serious
June 1-99	American Airlines	Scheduled	Landing	Fatal
July 26-02	Federal Express Corp	Nonscheduled	Approach	Serious
Oct 19-04	Corporate Airlines	Scheduled	Approach	Fatal
Feb 18-07	Shuttle America Corporation	Scheduled	Landing-Roll	None
Apr 12-07	Pinnacle Airlines	Scheduled	Landing	None
Jan 27-09	Empire Airlines	Nonscheduled	Landing	Serious
May 6-09	World Airways	Nonscheduled	Landing-Flare	Serious

SOURCE: National Transportation Safety Board Accident and Incident Data System, accessed through the Federal Aviation Administration's Aviation Safety Information Analysis and Sharing System (ASIAS).

ally to determine if commuting by the pilots appears to have been a major contributor to that fatigue.

Connie Kalitta Services

The NTSB Aircraft Accident Report provides the following flight history factual information for an uncontrolled collision with terrain on August 18, 1993: "A Douglas DC-8-61 freighter . . . registered to American International Airways (AIA) Inc., [doing business as] Connie Kalitta Services, Inc., and operat[ed] as AIA flight 808, collided with level terrain approximately ¼ mile from the approach end of runway 10, after the captain lost control of the airplane while approaching the Leeward Point Airfield at the U.S. Naval Air Station (NAS), Guantanamo Bay, Cuba. The airplane was destroyed by impact forces and a post-accident fire, and the three flight crew members sustained serious injuries" (National Transportation Safety Board, 1994a, p. 1).

Prior to the accident, on August 16 at 2300 (start of the duty day), the captain and first officer originated their 4-day flight sequence in Atlanta, Georgia (ATL). Their duty day ended at 1200 August 17 at the Dallas/Fort Worth airport, where they were allowed an 11-hour rest period (relieved of flight duty and provided with a hotel room) (National Transportation Safety Board, 1994a). It does not appear to the committee that commuting prior to the start of the flight sequence contributed to the fatigue on the day of the accident.

The NTSB determined "that the probable causes of this accident were the impaired judgment, decision-making, and flying abilities of the captain and flight crew due to the effects of fatigue; the captain's failure to properly assess the conditions for landing and maintaining vigilant situational awareness of the airplane while maneuvering onto final approach; his failure to prevent the loss of airspeed and avoid a stall while in the steep bank turn; and his failure to execute immediate action to recover from a stall.

Additional factors contributing to the cause were the inadequacy of the flight and duty time regulations applied to 14 CFR, Part 121, Supplemental Air Carrier, international operations, and the circumstances that resulted in the extended flight/duty hours and fatigue of the flight crew members. Also contributing were the inadequate crew resource management training and the inadequate training and guidance by American International Airways, Inc., to the flight crew for operations at special airports, such as Guantanamo Bay; and the Navy's failure to provide a system that would assure that the local tower controller was aware of the inoperative strobe light so as to provide the flight crew with such information" (National Transportation Safety Board, 1994a, p. 78).

American Eagle

The FAA's Aviation Safety Information Analysis and Sharing (ASIAS) Brief Report, based on information from the NTSB Aviation Accident/Incident Database, provides the following flight history on a runway overrun and collision on May 8, 1999: "A Saab 340B . . . sustained substantial damage during landing at John F. Kennedy International Airport (JFK), Jamaica, New York. The airplane was owned by AMR Leasing Corporation, and operated by American Eagle Airlines Inc. as flight 4925. There were no injuries to 3 crew members [two pilots and the flight attendant] and 26 passengers, while 1 passenger sustained a serious injury [while exiting the airplane]" (National Transportation Safety Board, 1999, p. 4).

The report describes the flight crew's sleep and duty time prior to the accident: "The flight crew was working a continuous duty overnight schedule. The previous day, they both awoke during the morning hours, did not sleep during the day, and reported for duty about 2200 for a flight scheduled at 2246. The flight was delayed, and arrived at Baltimore/Washington International Airport (BWI) about 0100. They were asleep about 0130, and awoke about 0445 for the accident flight, which was scheduled to depart at 0610" (National Transportation Safety Board, 1999, p. 10). The accident report does not contain any information on pilot's commutes prior the start of the flight sequence, but it does not appear to the committee that commuting was the primary contributor to fatigue on the accident flight.

The NTSB determined that the probable cause of this accident was the "pilot-in-command's failure to perform a missed approach as required by his company procedures. Factors [contributing to the accident] were the pilot-in-command's improper in-flight decisions, the pilot-in-command's failure to comply with FAA regulations and company procedures, inadequate crew coordination, and fatigue" (National Transportation Safety Board, 1999, p. 10).

American Airlines

The NTSB describes the flight history of a June 1, 1999, aircraft accident: "American Airlines flight 1420, a McDonnell Douglas DC-9-82 (MD-82), . . . crashed after it overran the end of runway 4R during landing at Little Rock National Airport in Little Rock, Arkansas. . . . The captain and 10 passengers were killed; the first officer, the flight attendants, and 105 passengers received serious or minor injuries" (National Transportation Safety Board, 2001, p. 1).

The report goes on to describe the flight crew's commute and sleep patterns prior to the accident: "Flight 1420 was the third and final leg of the first day of a 3-day sequence for the flight crew. The flight sequence began at O'Hare International Airport, Chicago, Illinois [where the captain was domiciled]" (p. 1). "On May 30, 1999, the first officer traveled from his home outside Los Angeles, California, to Chicago. The first officer indicated that he had been commuting from his home to the Chicago-O'Hare base for about 3 months and that, as a result, he was adjusted to the central time zone. The first officer indicated that he was involved in routine activities while in the Chicago area" (p. 11). "The captain and the first officer reportedly received a normal amount of sleep the night before the accident; both went to sleep about 2200 and awoke about 0730. Also, there was no evidence that either pilot had experienced cumulative sleep loss in the days before the accident" (pp. 143-144). Thus, it doesn't appear to the committee that commuting was a contributing factor to the fatigue the pilots experienced on the accident flight.

The NTSB determined "that the probable causes of this accident were the flight crew's failure to discontinue the approach when severe thunderstorms and their associated hazards to flight operations had moved into the airport area and the crew's failure to ensure that the spoilers had extended after touchdown.

Contributing to the accident were the flight crew's (1) impaired performance resulting from fatigue and the situational stress associated with the intent to land under the circumstances, (2) continuation of the approach to a landing when the company's maximum crosswind component was exceeded, and (3) use of reverse thrust greater than 1.3 engine pressure ratio after landing" (National Transportation Safety Board, 2001, pp. 169-170).

Federal Express

The NTSB describes the flight history of a July 26, 2002, aircraft accident: "Federal Express (FedEx) flight 1478, a Boeing 727-232F (727), . . . struck trees on short final approach and crashed short of runway 9 at the Tallahassee Regional Airport (TLH), Tallahassee, Florida. . . . The captain, first officer, and flight engineer were seriously injured, and the airplane was destroyed by impact and resulting fire" (National Transportation Safety Board, 2004, p. 1). The captain lived in Memphis, Tennessee, and the first officer stayed in an apartment in Memphis on July 23 and 24 and a hotel in Winnipeg, Manitoba, Canada, on July 25. The flight engineer commuted from Albany, New York, to Memphis on July 24. He spent the night of July 25 in a hotel in Ottawa, Ontario, Canada, while on another flight sequence. It does not appear to the committee that commuting played a role in the fatigue that contributed to the accident.

The NTSB determined "that the probable cause of the accident was the captain's and first officer's failure to establish and maintain a proper glidepath during the night visual approach to landing. Contributing to the accident was a combination of the captain's and first officer's fatigue, the captain's and first officer's failure to adhere to company flight procedures, the captain's and flight engineer's failure to monitor the approach, and the first officer's color vision deficiency" (National Transportation Safety Board, 2004, p. 68).

Corporate Airlines

The NTSB describes the flight history of an October 19, 2004, aircraft accident: "Corporate Airlines (doing business as American Connection) flight 5966, a BAE Systems BAE-J3201, . . . struck trees on final approach and crashed short of runway 36 at Kirksville Regional Airport (IRK), Kirksville, Missouri. . . . The captain, first officer, and 11 of the 13 passengers were fatally injured, and 2 passengers received serious injuries" (National Transportation Safety Board, 2006, p. 1).

"The flight crew was on a regularly scheduled 4-day sequence that began on Sunday, October 17, 2004. The accident occurred on the last flight of the third day, which departed from STL [St. Louis, Missouri] about 1842" (National Transportation Safety Board, 2006, p. 1). Because the accident occurred on the third day of the trip sequence, it does not appear to the committee that the commutes the pilots experienced prior to the start of the trip sequence contributed to their fatigue on the accident flight.

The NTSB determined "that the probable cause of the accident was the pilots' failure to follow established procedures and properly conduct a nonprecision instrument approach at night in instrument meteorological conditions, including their descent below the minimum descent altitude (MDA) before required visual cues were available (which continued unmoderated until the airplane struck the trees) and their failure to adhere to the established division of duties between the flying and nonflying (monitoring) pilot.

Contributing to the accident were the pilots' failure to make standard callouts and the current Federal Aviation Regulations that allow pilots to descend below the MDA into a region in which safe obstacle clearance is not assured based upon seeing only the airport approach lights. The pilots' failure to establish and maintain a professional demeanor during the flight and their fatigue likely contributed to their degraded performance" (National Transportation Safety Board, 2006, p. 58).

Shuttle America

The NTSB describes the flight history of a February 18, 2007, runway overrun and subsequent collision: "Delta Connection flight 6448, an Embraer ERJ-170, . . . operated by Shuttle America, Inc., was landing on runway 28 at Cleveland Hopkins International Airport (CLE), Cleveland, Ohio, during snow conditions when it overran the end of the runway, contacted an instrument landing system (ILS) antenna, and struck an airport perimeter fence. The airplane's nose gear collapsed during the overrun. Of the 2 flight crew members, 2 flight attendants, and 71 passengers on board, 3 passengers received minor injuries" (National Transportation Safety Board, 2008b, p. 1).

During the first two flights of the accident trip sequence, the captain flew with a different first officer than the accident first officer. The captain had been on vacation for 7 days prior to the accident and "was not originally scheduled to work on the day of the accident (he was scheduled to continue his vacation through the following days), but he had called crew scheduling on the night of February 17, 2007, to request a trip. He was offered and then accepted a 2-day trip assignment" (p. 9).

The NTSB report goes on to describe the commuting and flight schedule of the captain: "On the day of the accident, the captain traveled as a nonrevenue passenger on a flight from Louisville International Airport-Standiford Field (SDF) Louisville, Kentucky, to ATL [Atlanta International Airport, Atlanta, Georgia] to report for a scheduled 2-day trip. The captain was scheduled to report to SDF at 0525, and the flight to ATL had a scheduled arrival time of 0733. The first flight leg, from ATL to Sarasota-Bradenton International Airport (SRQ), Sarasota, Florida, was delayed because of weather. The flight departed ATL at 0914 and arrived at SRQ at 1042. The second flight leg departed SQR at 1108 and arrived at ATL at 1242. The third flight leg, the accident flight, departed on time (with a different first officer) from ATL at 1305 and had an expected arrival time at CLE of 1451" (p. 1).

In the accident investigation, "the captain reported that he was unable to sleep later that night [February 17], stating that he received 45 minutes to 1 hour of sleep. He went to bed at 2000 but did not fall asleep until 0000 on February 18 and then awoke at 0100. He tossed in bed until about 0200, at which time he decided to get up and prepare for the 0525 report time in SDF [to travel to ATL]" (p. 9).

The report documents additional concerning facts regarding the captain: "At the time of the accident, the captain had been on duty for 9 hours 40 minutes with a total flight time of 5 hours 2 minutes. Also, the captain had been awake for all but about 1 hour of the previous 32 hours; he stated that his lack of sleep affected his ability to concentrate and process information to make decisions" (pp. 9-10). "The captain also reported that he had insomnia, which began 9 months to 1 year before the accident and lasted for several days at a time, and a 10-year chronic cough" (p. 10). "In addition, the captain reported that, for breakfast on the day of the accident, he ate graham crackers and drank orange juice while traveling as a nonrevenue passenger and then drank coffee and ate peanuts and chips later on. The captain stated that he was planning to eat lunch in ATL before the accident flight leg but was unable to do so because of the delays from the earlier flight legs and the change in first officers" (p. 10).

The captain's prior attendance record fear of corrective action may have also contributed to accident: "On January 16, 2007 (about 1 month before the accident), the Shuttle America assistant chief pilot notified the captain, in writing, that his attendance had reached an unacceptable level—nine absence occurrences (seven sick and two unavailable attendance marks) totaling 18 days within the previous 12 months—and that future occurrences would result in corrective action, which could include termination from the company. (According to the company's policy, eight absence occurrences would result in termination.) The captain had not received previous notification from Shuttle America about his attendance. The captain stated that, even though he was tired on the day of the accident, he did not cancel his trip because he thought that could result in his termination" (p. 11).

For this accident, it appears to the committee that fatigue likely resulted from a combination of the captain's inability to sleep the night before the accident flight, the commute from Louisville to Atlanta, and the flight delays that reduced the captain's time between flights and extended his time awake. While the commute appears to have contributed to the fatigue, the committee notes that even without the time spent commuting, the pilot would have still had a period of more than 24 hours in which he only had about an hour's sleep.

The NTSB determined "that the probable cause of this accident was the failure of the flight crew to execute a missed approach when visual cues for the runway were not distinct and identifiable. Contributing to the accident were (1) the crew's decision to descend to the instrument landing system decision height instead of the localizer (glideslope out) minimum descent altitude; (2) the first officer's long landing on a short contaminated runway and the crew's failure to use reverse thrust and braking to their maximum effectiveness; (3) the captain's fatigue, which affected his ability to effectively plan for and monitor the approach and landing; and (4) Shuttle America's failure to administer an attendance policy that permitted flight crew members to call in as fatigued without fear of reprisals" (National Transportation Safety Board, 2008b, p. 67).

Pinnacle Airlines

The NTSB describes the flight history of an April 12, 2007, aircraft accident: "A Bombardier/Canadair Regional Jet (CRJ) CL600-2B19, . . . operated as Pinnacle Airlines flight 4712, ran off the departure end of runway 28 after landing at Cherry Capital Airport (TVC), Traverse City, Michigan. There were no injuries among the 49 passengers (including 3 lap-held infants) and 3 crew members, and the aircraft was substantially damaged" (National Transportation Safety Board, 2008a, p. 1).

The NTSB reports that the accident occurred on the flight crew's first day of a 4-day scheduled trip; the accident flight was the fifth and final flight segment for the day. The captain's home was near Pensacola, Florida, and he commuted to his base at Memphis International Airport (MEM, Memphis, Tennessee). The pilot commuted to Memphis on April 10 and conducted training on a flight to Minneapolis-St. Paul International (Wold-Chamberlain) Airport (MSP). The captain spent the night before the accident at a hotel in Minneapolis-St. Paul, arriving at the hotel at 2200. The captain stated that he had slept soundly the night before the day of the accident flight. Thus, it does not appear to the committee that the commute was a major contributor to the captain's fatigue during the accident flight.

The NTSB determined "that the probable cause of this accident was the pilots' decision to land at Cherry Capital Airport (TVC), Traverse City, Michigan without performing a landing distance assessment, which was required by company policy because of runway contamination initially reported by TVC ground operations personnel and continuing reports of deteriorating weather and runway conditions during the approach. This poor decision making likely reflected the effects of fatigue produced by a long, demanding duty day and, for the captain, the duties associated with check airman functions. Contributing to the accident were (1) the Federal Aviation Administration pilot flight and duty-time regulations that permitted the pilots' long, demanding duty day and (2) the TVC operations supervisor's use of ambiguous and unspecific radio phraseology in providing runway braking information" (National Transportation Safety Board, 2008a, p. 55).

Empire Airlines

The NTSB describes the flight history of an January 27, 2009, aircraft accident: "An Avions de Transport Régional (ATR) Aerospatiale Alenia ATR 42-320 (ATR 42), . . . operating as Empire Airlines flight 8284, was on an instrument approach when it crashed short of the runway at Lubbock Preston Smith International Airport (LBB), Lubbock, Texas. The captain sustained serious injuries, and the first officer sustained minor injuries. The airplane was substantially damaged. The airplane was registered to FedEx Corporation (FedEx) and operated by Empire Airlines, Inc., as a 14 *Code of Federal Regulations* (CFR) Part 121 supplemental cargo flight. The flight departed from Fort Worth Alliance Airport (AFW), Fort Worth, Texas, about 0313" (National Transportation Safety Board, 2011, p. 1).

The captain commuted from his home in Portland, Oregon, to Midland International Airport (MAF), in Midland, Texas, on January 24, 2 days before the start of the trip sequence that culminated in the accident. The first officer commuted from her home in Salt Lake City, Utah, to MAF on January 18, 8 days before the start of the trip sequence that culminated in the accident. The first officer flew a trip sequence ending January 23, and she spent the weekend in Midland, Texas (off duty for over 72 hours prior to beginning the accident flight). Thus, it does not appear to the committee that either pilot's commute from their home to their domicile contributed to their fatigue at the time of the accident.

The NTSB determined "that the probable cause of this accident was the flight crew's failure to monitor and maintain a minimum safe airspeed while executing an instrument approach in icing conditions, which resulted in an aerodynamic stall at low altitude. Contributing to the accident were (1) the flight crew's failure to follow published standard operating procedures in response to a flap anomaly, (2) the captain's decision to continue with the unstabilized approach, (3) the flight crew's poor crew resource management, and (4) fatigue due to the time of day in which the accident occurred and a cumulative sleep debt, which likely impaired the captain's performance" (National Transportation Safety Board, 2011, p. 83).

World Airways

The FAA's ASIAS Brief Report, based on information from the NTSB Aviation Accident/Incident Database, provides the following flight history on a May 6, 2009, abnormal runway contact that resulted in significant damage to the aircraft: "A Boeing DC-10-30, operated by World Airways as flight 8535, experienced a hard landing on runway 10 at Baltimore/Washington-Thurgood Marshall International Airport, Baltimore, [Maryland] (BWI). . . . The captain, flight engineer and 9 flight attendants reported minor injuries" (National Transportation Safety Board, 2009, p. 5).

The report indicates that the captain had been on a multiday trip sequence prior to the accident flight that included flights as captain and as a passenger. On May 3 (3 days prior to the accident), while piloting a flight from the Philippines, the captain reported feeling ill, probably from food poisoning. During the accident flight, the captain reported digestive system discomfort. The report does not contain any information on pilot's commute prior the start of his flight sequence on April 27, but because the captain was at the end of a multiday trip sequence, it does not appear to the committee that commuting prior to the beginning of the trip sequence contributed to the pilot's fatigue.

The NTSB determined that the probable cause of this accident was "the captain's inappropriate control inputs following a firm landing, resulting in two hard nose-gear impacts before executing a go-around. Contributing to the inappropriate control inputs was the captain's fatigue and physical discomfort; and a possible lack of practical consolidation of skills and experience due to a protracted and fragmented training period" (National Transportation Safety Board, 2009, p. 7).

Conclusion

Of the nine accidents examined by the committee during the 1982 through 2010 period and for which NTSB concluded that fatigue was either a probable cause or contributing factor, there was only one in which it appeared that commuting might have contributed to the fatigue on the accident flight. In that accident, the February 18, 2007, Shuttle America runway overrun, it appeared to the committee that fatigue likely resulted from a combination of the captain's inability to sleep the night before the accident flight, followed by the commute as a nonrevenue passenger from Louisville to Atlanta, in turn followed by the flight delays during the duty cycle that extended the captain's time awake.

CURRENT PILOT COMMUTING PATTERNS

The committee was charged to "review the available information related to the prevalence and characteristics of commuting." Unfortunately, the committee was not able to find any systematic or comprehensive data on the frequency of pilot commuting, the lengths of pilot commutes, or the characteristics of their commutes, such as the modes used of commuting by pilots.[10] In the absence of such information, one approach would have been to conduct a survey to acquire systematic reliable data about the prevalence and characteristics of pilots and their commutes. However, developing, testing, implementing, and analyzing a pilot survey to acquire such data would have required time and resources that were not available to the committee.

In the absence of systematic data about actual pilot commutes and in order to gain some insight into likely commuting patterns, the committee requested information about the locations of pilot homes (residences) and domiciles from all Part 121 airlines, using a list of airlines provided by the FAA. Specifically, airlines were asked to provide the zip code of each pilot's home of record (i.e., those designated by the pilots on IRS forms and for the receipt of official notices from the airlines) and the domicile from which that pilot begins his or her duty cycle. The committee received this information for 30,171 pilots. The committee then calculated the straight-line distance from the center of the home zip code to the center of the domicile zip code for each pilot. The straight line distances between zip codes are referred to as "home-to-domicile distances" for convenience, but these calculated home-to-domicile distances have several limitations and are only suggestive of pilot commuting patterns for several reasons. First, the pilots' home zip codes were for their homes of record. Some pilots may have multiple homes, including seasonal residences, and may not always start their commutes from their homes of record. Second, some pilots may arrange for temporary accommodations at or near their domiciles (or at an intermediate location for a multistop commute) and sleep there the night

[10]The only published information appears to be data included in the NTSB report that followed the Colgan Air crash, which reported that 68 percent of the Colgan pilots based at Newark were commuting, with the commutes being various distances (National Transportation Safety Board, 2010, pp. 47-48).

prior to the start of their duty cycles. Third, commutes may be circuitous, particularly those involving multiple connecting flights, so that the actual distances traveled are likely to be longer and may be much longer than the calculated home-to-domicile distances. Fourth, these data are for a single point in time and provide no insight into how commuting patterns might change in response to a pilot's career progression or changes in the patterns of airline operations resulting from mergers, bankruptcies, or changing economic or competitive conditions (see Chapter 2). Finally, the committee does not know the extent to which this sample of pilots is representative of the larger pilot population.

Notwithstanding these limitations and recognizing that the data were not provided by all airlines, the committee believes that the home-to-domicile distance patterns described below provide some insight into pilot commuting patterns found in each of four segments of the industry: Mainline airlines were defined as those that predominately operate scheduled passenger operations in jet aircraft with more than 90 seats (under Part 121 rules). Zip code data were provided by four airlines for 17,519 pilots in this segment. Regional airlines were defined as those that predominately operate scheduled service in aircraft, both jet and turboprop, with 90 or fewer seats (under Part 121 rules). Zip code data were provided by 11 airlines for 7,533 pilots in this segment. Cargo airlines defined as those that conduct scheduled or nonscheduled cargo operations (under Part 121 supplemental rules). Zip code data were provided by four airlines for 4,488 pilots in this segment. Charter airlines were defined as those that conduct nonscheduled passenger operations (under Part 121 supplemental rules). Zip code data were provided by five airlines for 631 pilots in this segment.

To preserve the confidentiality of the pilots, the individual airlines that provided the data were not identified. Not identifying the airlines prevented the committee from examining any relationships between the characteristics and policies of an individual airline and the patterns of home-to-domicile distances for that airline's pilots and thus may limit the lessons that can be drawn from these data. However, the airlines were categorized by the four industry segments—mainline, regional, cargo, and charter.

Table 3-3 summarizes the home-to-domicile patterns by industry segment. When viewing Table 3-3 and the following figure and tables in this section, it's important to keep in mind that a pilot making a short commute may or may not arrive rested and fit for duty depending on what that pilot's activities were prior or during the commute. For example, if the pilot did not sleep well the night prior to reporting for duty or was involved in tiring physical activity earlier in the day, or even was awake since early morning before leaving home to commute to the domicile, the pilot might be fatigued even if the commute was very short. Similarly, a long commute does not necessarily mean that the pilot reported for duty fatigued. The pilot may

TABLE 3-3 Distribution of Home-to-Domicile Distances by Industry Segment (in percentage)

Operation	Less Than 30 Miles	31-90 Miles	91-150 Miles	750-1,500 Miles	1,501-2,250 Miles	Greater Than 2,250 Miles
Mainline	31	14	4	16	4	2
Regional	37	9	4	16	5	1
Cargo	37	4	1	17	7	2
Charter	29	9	4	27	2	1

SOURCE: Data from stakeholders' input to committee.

have made the commute the day prior to reporting for duty and may have had a full night's sleep in a hotel following the commute, prior to reporting for duty. The first column of Table 3-3 shows the percentage of pilots in each of the four industry segments whose home-to-domicile distance is less than 30 miles. This distance is admittedly arbitrary but is intended to represent a relative short commute similar to that experienced by much of the nonpilot workforce. The second column shows the percentage of pilots in each industry segment whose home-to-domicile distance is between 31 and 90 miles while the third column shows the percentage whose home-to-domicile distance is between 91 and 150 miles. These columns represent longer home-to-domicile distances but still ones where a commute is likely to be made by surface transport. By adding the numbers in the first three columns, one can see the percentage of pilots whose home-to-domicile distance is less than or equal to 150 miles. For mainline pilots, this sum is 49 percent; for regional pilots, this sum is 50 percent; for cargo pilots, this sum is 42 percent; and for charter pilots, this sum is also 42 percent.

The fourth, fifth, and sixth columns in Table 3-3 show the percentages of pilots whose home-to-domicile distances are, respectively, between 750 and 1,500 miles, 1,501 and 2,250 miles, and greater than 2,250 miles. These columns represent home-to-domicile distances where one might expect pilots to commute by air transport. To provide some perspective of these distances, the straight-line distance between Dallas and Indianapolis is about 768 miles, the straight-line distance between Salt Lake City and Detroit is 1,487 miles, and the straight-line distance between San Diego and Miami is 2,265 miles. Again, by adding these three columns, one can see that 22 percent of both mainline pilots and regional pilots have home-to-domicile distances of greater than 750 miles while 26 percent of cargo pilots and 30 percent of charter pilots have these longer home-to-domicile distances.

Looking more broadly at the data in Table 3-3, several things stand out. First, the distributions appear to be very similar for mainline and regional pilots even though these two segments of the industry differ in many respects. Second, the distributions for the cargo and charter segments of the industry are different from both each other and from the scheduled passenger segments. Given their differences in operating and basing policies (see Chapter 2), this is not surprising. Finally, looking at the right-most column, it appears that the proportion of pilots who have extremely long home-to-domicile commutes—coast to coast or international—is in about 1-2 percent across these four industry segments.

Figure 3-4 shows the distributions of home-to-domicile distances for mainline and regional pilots. The similarity of these distributions seen in Table 3-3 is even more apparent when the entire distributions are examined. So in spite of differences in average age, pay, average flight length, and industry structure, it appears that the home-to-domicile commuting patterns of mainline and regional pilots are very similar.

Table 3-4 shows the distribution of home-to-domicile distances for mainline pilots by airline. (The total sample line is the same as the line for the mainline airlines in Table 3-3.) The four mainline airlines that provided data included both large, well-established airlines and smaller, more recently established airlines. As can be seen in the table, the top two airlines, both large established carriers, have similar distributions, while the bottom

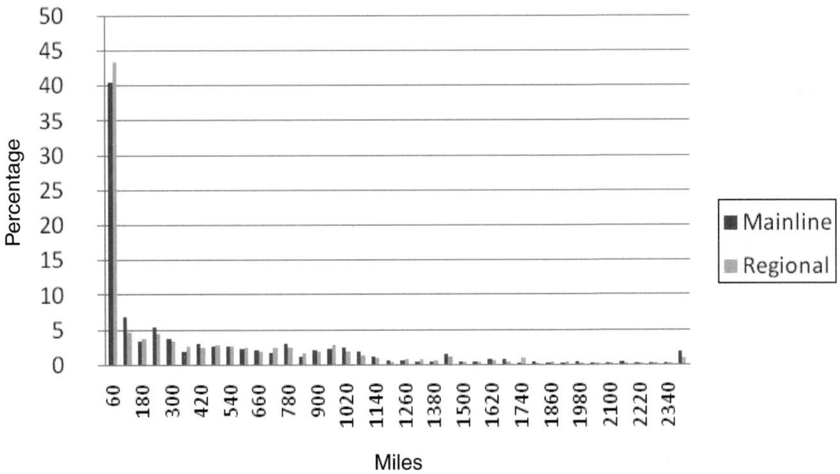

FIGURE 3-4 Distribution of home-to-domicile distances for mainline and regional pilots.
SOURCE: Data from stakeholders' input to committee.

TABLE 3-4 Distribution of Home-to-Domicile Distances for Mainline Pilots by Airline (in percentage)

Mainline Airlines	Less Than 30 Miles	31-90 Miles	91-150 Miles	750-1,500 Miles	1,501-2,250 Miles	Greater Than 2,250 Miles
A	33	12	5	15	3	1
J	34	18	3	18	4	3
N	18	17	4	20	6	3
W	8	6	3	13	23	19
Total Sample 17,519 Pilots	31	14	4	16	4	2

NOTE: For all home-to domicile distance tables the de-identified airlines have coded alphabetically based on the order in which the input was received.
SOURCE: Data from stakeholders' input to committee.

TABLE 3-5 Distribution of Home-to-Domicile Distances for Regional Pilots by Airline (in percentage)

Regional Airlines	Less Than 30 Miles	31-90 Miles	91-150 Miles	750-1,500 Miles	1,501-2,250 Miles	Greater Than 2,250 Miles
C	24	6	4	25	7	2
D	27	4	1	27	3	0
E	47	12	3	6	3	1
F	34	6	13	15	2	2
H	42	12	4	6	3	1
K	22	12	3	18	10	0
O	34	9	4	22	6	1
R	40	6	5	12	4	1
T	100	0	0	0	0	0
U	80	11	0	3	0	2
X	11	16	10	25	5	7
Total Sample 7,533 Pilots	37	9	4	16	5	1

SOURCE: Data from stakeholders' input to committee.

two, both smaller, more recently established airlines, are different both from the two larger airlines and from each other.

Table 3-5 shows the distribution of home-to-domicile distances for regional pilots by airline. The 11 regional airlines that provided data included airlines of varying size and operating in different regions of the country. The data show that there is variation in home-to-domicile patterns across the airlines. One might infer that differences in various characteristics of the airlines are associated with different home-to-domicile patterns.

TABLE 3-6 Distribution of Home-to-Domicile Distances for Cargo Pilots by Airline (in percentage)

Cargo Airlines	Less Than 30 Miles	31-90 Miles	91-150 Miles	750-1,500 Miles	1,501-2,250 Miles	Greater Than 2,250 Miles
B	36	3	1	17	8	3
M	87	13	0	0	0	0
P	81	7	2	3	0	0
S	90	0	3	0	0	3
Total Sample 4,488 Pilots	37	4	1	17	7	2

SOURCE: Data from stakeholders' input to committee.

TABLE 3-7 Distribution of Home-to-Domicile Distances for Charter Pilots by Airline (in percentage)

Charter Airlines	Less Than 30 Miles	31-90 Miles	91-150 Miles	750-1,500 Miles	1,501-2,250 Miles	Greater Than 2,250 Miles
G	59	24	6	6	0	0
I	4	0	4	46	3	2
L	20	8	10	32	0	0
Q	67	25	3	2	0	0
V	57	7	1	8	3	0
Total Sample 631 Pilots	29	9	4	27	2	1

SOURCE: Data from stakeholders' input to committee.

Table 3-6 shows the distribution of home-to-domicile distances for cargo pilots by airline. The four cargo airlines that provided data included airlines of varying size and operating patterns. The data show that there is variation in home-to-domicile patterns across the airlines. One might infer that differences in various characteristics of the airline are to be associated with different home-to-domicile patterns.

Table 3-7 shows the distribution of home-to-domicile distances for charter pilots by airline. The five charter airlines that provided data included airlines of varying size and operating patterns. The data show that there is variation in home-to-domicile patterns across the airlines. One might infer from the table that differences in various characteristics of the airline are to be associated with different home-to-domicile patterns.

Although the data the committee received are neither a complete accounting nor a randomly drawn sample, the committee believes that they provide useful information and some insight into the home-to-domicile patterns of pilots in the Part 121 portion of the industry.

The home-to-domicile patterns of the mainline and regional airlines appear, in aggregate, to be very similar even though these segments of the industry have markedly different operations and industry structure. In all four segments of the industry, however, a breakdown of the home-to-domicile distances by airline suggests that there is considerable variation across individual airlines. Policies directed at addressing concerns about the potential impact of commuting on pilot fatigue should recognize this heterogeneity in the industry.

Time Zone Considerations

The implications of crossing one or more time zones for potential fatigue during duty are complex as such crossings involve the time of day of flight, the direction of travel (whether traveling east to west where time is "gained" or west to east where it is "lost") as well as the standard considerations related to characteristics of the commute. For example, the implications of crossing multiple time zones would be lessened if the pilot was able to plan and implement a commute that enabled him or her to obtain adequate sleep prior to duty (e.g., by arriving the night before). In addition, crossing time zones in and of itself, particularly a single time zone, is not an indicator of potential fatigue as the distance traveled can be quite short or very far. Recognizing these caveats, the committee analyzed the available zip code data to obtain additional descriptive information related to pilot residences and domiciles specific to time zones.

The majority of pilots (73.5 percent) reported a residence in the same time zone as their domicile. A significant additional percentage (18.8 percent) reported a residence one time zone away from their domicile, with much smaller percentages travelling two time zones (5 percent), three time zones (2.3 percent), or four or more time zones (.4 percent) time zones. A similar pattern emerges by type of carrier, particularly when comparing mainline and regional airlines: see Figure 3-5. However, proportionally fewer pilots who work for cargo and charter airlines report residences and domiciles in the same time zone and more report distances that cross one or two time zones.

When looking at time zones in combination with distance, the scenario is more complex. The distance between home and domicile for pilots in the same time zone ranged from less than a mile to 1,288 miles; for pilots who cross a single time zone, the distance ranged from 14 to 2,439 miles. In other words, there are long commutes that stay in a single time zone and short commutes that cross into a different time zone. Similarly, a relatively small percentage of pilots (11.1 percent) who travel across a time zone

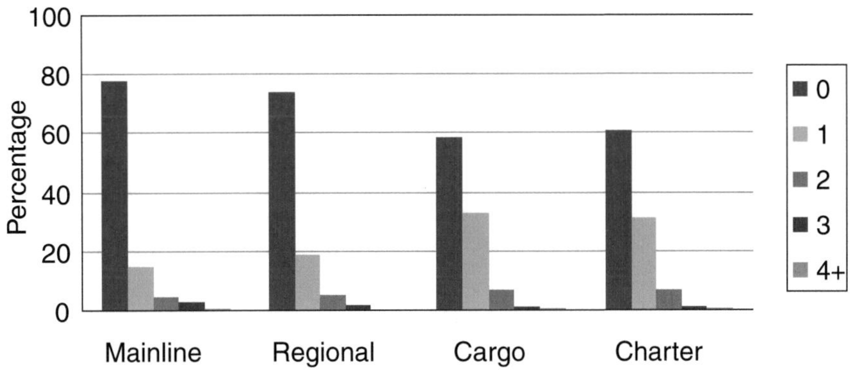

FIGURE 3-5 Share of pilots with home-to-domicile time zone differences.
SOURCE: Data from stakeholders' input to committee.

travel a greater distance than the pilots who have a residence and domicile in the same time zone and some pilots who crossed three time zones reported a shorter distance between domicile and residence than pilots who crossed only one or two time zones. The greatest distances travelled obviously involve travel across multiple time zones. The shortest distance for pilots travelling across two, three, or four or more time zones, respectively, are 1,004, 1,656, and 2,890 miles. Table 3-8 shows detailed data for all pilots as well as by carrier type.

There is little conclusive that can be said about the number of time zones crossed given wide variation in distances travelled and lack of information about how the commute is actually conducted. It is possible that pilots who commute across multiple time zones are fatigued when they arrive for work. It is also possible that these pilots fly to their domicile the night before they are expected to report for duty and obtain adequate sleep prior to duty. Without information about actual commuting practices, these data serve merely a descriptive purpose and should not be used to make any conclusions about the likelihood of fatigue as a result of the corresponding commute.

Additional Considerations

The committee also reviewed data from NASA's Aviation Safety Reporting System (ASRS). ASRS collects, processes, and analyzes voluntarily submitted aviation safety incident reports of unsafe occurrences and hazardous situations from pilots, air traffic controllers, dispatchers, flight

TABLE 3-8 Distance Between Residence and Domicile by Time Zone and Carrier (by percentage within time zone)

	No Time Zones					One Time Zone				
MILES	ALL	ML	Reg'l	Cargo	Chart.	ALL	ML	Reg'l	Cargo	Chart.
0-60	55.8	52.1	58.8	67.8	58.9	0.1		0.1	0.1	
60-120	7.3	8.6	6.1	2.8	9.4	0.7	1.1	0.9		
120-180	3.8	4.0	4.3	1.8	3.1	1.6	1.7	3.2	0.1	
180-240	5.8	6.5	4.9	4.3	4.2	2.1	2.1	4.4	0.1	0.5
240-300	3.4	3.6	3.1	2.1	4.5	4.3	5.9	5.3	0.5	3.0
300-360	2.2	1.8	2.6	3.2	3.4	4.4	2.8	4.1	8.3	
360-420	3.4	3.4	3.1	4.0	0.8	3.0	2.6	0.9	6.0	0.5
420-480	3.0	2.6	3.4	4.7	1.3	2.9	3.8	2.2	2.6	
480-540	2.6	2.6	2.8	2.2	3.1	4.0	4.4	3.2	4.0	3.0
540-600	2.1	2.1	2.0	1.8	4.7	5.4	3.5	5.2	8.4	8.1
600-660	1.8	1.8	1.4	2.1	2.9	5.7	4.3	4.2	9.4	7.6
660-720	0.9	0.7	0.8	1.8	1.0	8.5	8.2	10.0	7.5	8.6
720-780	1.1	1.3	0.8	0.3	0.3	10.4	12.6	10.0	7.2	6.1
780-840	0.6	0.6	0.9	0.3	0.5	5.4	4.5	5.7	6.9	5.1
840-900	0.9	1.1	0.8	0.2	0.3	8.5	7.5	6.8	12.4	4.0
900-960	1.8	2.1	2.0	0.1		5.3	4.2	7.0	4.1	16.7
960-1,020	1.4	1.8	0.8	0.3	0.5	5.7	7.0	6.5	2.0	9.6
1,020-1,080	1.4	1.9	0.9	[a]	0.8	3.3	2.9	3.9	2.4	9.6
1,080-1,140	0.6	0.8	0.4			3.1	3.1	3.0	2.6	6.6
1,140-1,200	0.1	0.2	[a]			2.0	1.6	1.9	2.2	7.1
1,200-1,260	0.1	0.1	[a]		0.3	2.7	1.3	3.4	4.7	1.5

1,260-1,320	[a]	2.0	1.8	2.2	2.2	1.0
1,320-1,380		1.3	2.0	0.9	0.3	1.5
1,380-1,440		4.5	7.4	3.4	1.2	
1,440-1,500		1.0	1.1	0.8	1.4	
1,500-1,560		0.8	1.0	0.2	1.1	
1,560-1,620		0.7	1.0	0.2	0.5	
1,620-1,680		0.1	0.2	0.1	0.1	
1,680-1,740		0.1	0.1			
1,740-1,800			[a]			
1,800-1,860						
1,860-1,920				0.1		
1,920-1,980		0.1	[a]		0.3	
1,980-2,040		0.2			0.7	
2,040-2,100						
2,100-2,160					0.1	
2,160-2,220					0.1	
2,220-2,280						
2,280-2,340		0.1			0.2	
2,340-8,400[b]		0.1	0.1		0.3	

continued

TABLE 3-8 Continued

	Two Time Zones					Three Time Zones				
MILES	ALL	ML	Reg'l	Cargo	Chart.	ALL	ML	Reg'l	Cargo	Chart.
0-60										
60-120										
120-180										
180-240										
240-300										
300-360										
360-420										
420-480										
480-540										
540-600										
600-660										
660-720										
720-780										
780-840										
840-900										
900-960										
960-1,020	0.2	0.3			2.3					
1,020-1,080	0.5				16.3					
1,080-1,140	1.2	1.1	2.2		2.3					
1,140-1,200	3.1	4.6	2.2	0.7						
1,200-1,260	4.7	6.7	3.0	0.3	16.3					
1,260-1,320	3.8	4.1	5.5		11.6					

1,320-1,380	4.6	4.6	7.2	0.3	9.3					
1,380-1,440	7.2	7.5	8.5	4.3	11.6					
1,440-1,500	4.4	5.5	5.0	0.3	9.3					
1,500-1,560	6.4	5.1	6.5	8.3	14.0					
1,560-1,620	12.4	13.1	11.7	12.3	7.0					
1,620-1,680	13.6	15.1	7.7	19.6		0.4	0.4	0.7		
1,680-1,740	6.2	1.2	16.7	6.0		1.0	1.2	0.7		
1,740-1,800	5.6	4.9	5.2	8.6		2.7	3.9			
1,800-1,860	6.9	5.8	6.7	11.0						
1,860-1,920	6.6	2.1	4.5	21.6		6.7	5.9	12.2		
1,920-1,980	2.1	3.5	0.7	0.7		8.6	9.8	7.5		16.7
1,980-2,040	1.5	2.1	1.7			5.3	5.3	6.8		16.7
2,040-2,100	0.7	0.4	2.0			6.0	6.3	7.5		
2,100-2,160	4.3	6.7	3.0	0.7		3.4	3.1	6.1		
2,160-2,220	0.5	0.9				5.1	5.1	7.5		
2,220-2,280	0.3	0.5		0.3		4.9	4.3	8.8		
2,280-2,340	0.3	0.7				3.9	3.5	6.8		
2,340-8,400[b]	2.8	3.5		5.0		52.0	51.3	35.4	100.0	66.7

[a]Less than .05 percent.
[b]The distance between domicile and residence for all pilots who travelled across four time zones were all in this range.

attendants, maintenance technicians, and others.[11] There was limited information available in the reports to determine the degree to which commuting was a factor in the reported incidents. Also, since these reports are voluntarily submitted, in some cases to gain immunity from punishment, it is not clear the extent to which these reports are representative of the experiences of the entire Part 121 pilot population. The committee did not find that these data were useful in the context of the committee's charge, and these data are not discussed in the report.

CONCLUSION

CONCLUSION: There is potential for pilots to become fatigued from commuting. However, there is insufficient evidence to determine the extent to which pilot commuting has been a safety risk in part because little is known about specific pilot commuting practices and in part because the safety checks, balances, and redundancies in the aviation system may mitigate the consequences of pilot fatigue.

[11]For details, see http://asrs.arc.nasa.gov/overview/summary.html [May 2011].

4

Sleep, Wakefulness, Circadian Rhythms, and Fatigue

FATIGUE

Prevention of fatigue as a safety risk in commercial aviation operations has focused on effective management of duty and rest scheduling (Dinges et al., 1996). When considered in the context of work safety, fatigue has been broadly defined as a biological drive for recuperative rest (Williamson et al., 2011). Over the past several decades, the scientific knowledge base about the causes of fatigue and its effects on performance has grown significantly. The *Aviation Fatigue Management Symposium: Partnerships for Solutions*, supported by the Federal Aviation Administration (FAA) (2008), included several presentations summarizing the state of the science relevant to fatigue in aviation (and other transportation modes).[1] Additional work was presented a year later in *International Conference on Fatigue Management in Transportation Operations: A Framework for Progress* (U.S. Department of Transportation, 2009).

It is well established that fatigue has multiple interactive sources. The primary ones that may be relevant to pilots' commutes include duration of time awake prior to work, duration of time slept prior to work, restfulness of sleep (i.e., sleep continuity) prior to work, and the biological time (i.e., circadian phase) at which sleep and/or commuting occur relative to the start of work. The duration of time at work (i.e., time on task) is a regulated factor for fatigue mitigation.

[1]For more information on the Aviation Fatigue Management Symposium: Partnerships for Solutions, see http://www.faa.gov/news/conferences_events/2008_aviation_fatigue/ [June 2011].

In the aviation industry, commutes that involve travel across multiple time zones have the potential to exacerbate the fatigue associated with commuting, as can chronic restriction of sleep for multiple days prior to commuting. It is important to recognize that these fatigue effects can be mitigated to some extent by following good sleep hygiene practices[2] in the period between the end of the commute and the time of reporting for duty. Due to a lack of relevant data, it is unknown to what extent good sleep hygiene practices are followed by commuting pilots to ensure they are alert during their postcommute flight and duty periods.[3]

Extensive scientific evidence exists on the negative effects of fatigue on the performance of many cognitive tasks, including those essential for safely operating a commercial aircraft. The adverse effects of fatigue induced by sleep loss include maintaining wakefulness and alertness; vigilance and selective attention; psychomotor and cognitive speed; accuracy of performing a wide range of cognitive tasks; working and executive memory; and higher cognitive functions, such as decision making, detection of safety threats, and problem solving; and communication and mood (Harrison and Horne, 2000; Thomas et al., 2000; Durmer and Dinges, 2005; Philibert, 2005; Banks and Dinges, 2007, 2011; Goel et al., 2009b; Lim and Dinges, 2010).

The Institute of Medicine (IOM) defines fatigue as "an unsafe condition that can occur relative to the timing and duration of work and sleep opportunities" (Institute of Medicine, 2009, p. 218). It further states:

> In healthy individuals, fatigue is a general term used to describe feelings of tiredness, reduced energy, and the increased effort needed to perform tasks effectively and avoid errors. It occurs as performance demands increase because of work intensity and work duration, but it is also a product of the quantity and quality of sleep and the time of day work occurs.

Pilot commuting practices and individual day-to-day experiences can be quite variable, depending on many factors. The extent to which pilot commuting is contributing to fatigue at work—by reducing sleep time, extending wake time prior to duty, or interrupting a habitual nocturnal sleep period—is not known.

---

[2]Good sleep hygiene practices generally refer to those behaviors that effectively control all behavioral and environmental factors that precede sleep and may interfere with sleep, to ensure the sleep is as restful as possible, in order to promote daytime alertness or help treat or avoid certain sleep disorders (see Thorpy, 2011).

[3]The committee did not consider the use of sleeping medications by pilots during commutes prior to duty because the FAA has restrictions on pilots' use of Federal Drug Administration-approved prescription sleep medications, over-the-counter drugs, and supplements for sleep.

SLEEP AND CIRCADIAN RHYTHMS

A full understanding of the relationship between commuting and pilot fatigue is complicated by the fact that there are inadequate data on the timing, duration, and quality of pilots' sleep before and during commutes. Quality of sleep encompasses factors that can affect the recuperative value of sleep, immediately prior to and during a commute period, such as noise, light, body posture, sleep surface, and ambient temperature.

Time Awake, Sleep Time, and Circadian Time

Scientific understanding of the interaction of circadian biology and homeostatic sleep need is fundamental to identifying how fatigue can occur relative to commuting. Circadian rhythms are daily (24-hour) rhythms, reflected in microbiology, physiology and behavior, that control the timing of the sleep/wake cycle and influence physical and cognitive performance, activity, food consumption, body temperature, cardiovascular rhythms, muscle tone, and aspects of hormone secretion and immune responses, as well as many other physiological functions. When an individual is acutely sleep-deprived by remaining awake into his or her habitual nocturnal sleep period, elevated homeostatic pressure for sleep due to time awake extending beyond 16 hours develops as the internal circadian clock in the brain is withdrawing the drive for wakefulness (Van Dongen and Dinges, 2005; Institute of Medicine, 2009). Performance deficits not apparent up to 16 hours awake can suddenly become evident as a result of these two interactive processes (i.e., increasing sleep pressure and decreasing wake drive). These deficits can be similar to those observed when people are under the influence of alcohol.[4]

The quantifications of fatigue-related performance noted above suggest that pilots should not be awake beyond approximately 16 hours at the time a duty period ends, unless there are unexpected reasons for this to occur or adequate system mitigation (discussed in Chapter 3). To the extent that commute time may lengthen a duty day beyond this threshold, such commutes should be avoided.

The sleep homeostatic drive can produce fatigue during waking per-

---

[4]For example, performance on an unpredictable tracking task after being awake more than 17 hours (after 3:00 a.m.) was equivalent to the effects of a 0.05 percent blood alcohol concentration (Dawson and Reid, 1997). Williamson and Feyer (2000) also reported that after 17-19 hours without sleep (corresponding to 10:30 p.m. and 1:00 a.m.), speed or accuracy on some cognitive tests was equivalent or worse than those found at a 0.05 percent blood alcohol concentration. Depending on the cognitive task measured, 20-25 hours of wakefulness produced performance decrements equivalent to those observed at a blood alcohol concentration of 0.10 percent (Lamond and Dawson, 1999).

formance at work as a result of inadequate sleep duration or poor quality sleep in the day prior to work (e.g., due to environmental disturbances or physical problems within the individual such as illness or a sleep disorder). Whether due to being awake too long prior to work or to sleeping too little prior to work, the elevated pressure for sleep in the human brain results in subjective fatigue and sleepiness, and degradation of attention, working memory, mental speed, and other cognitive performance functions, including higher-order functions involved in decision making (Harrison and Horne, 2000; Killgore et al., 2006; McKenna et al., 2007; Venkatramen et al., 2007). These cognitive changes can result in turn in adverse effects on work performance (Mitler et al., 1988; Dinges, 1995). Fatigue as a risk to individual pilot performance can result from (1) being awake continuously for more than approximately 16 hours, or (2) sleeping too little (especially less than 6 hours on the sleep opportunity prior to work), or (3) when undertaking work at a time when the body is biologically programmed to be asleep (i.e., an individual's habitual nocturnal sleep period), which for most people is between 10:00 p.m. and 7:00 a.m. (Van Dongen and Dinges, 2005; Basner and Dinges, 2009; Institute of Medicine, 2009).[5]

Fatigue-related performance deficits from inadequate sleep can vary markedly across a day and night (without sleep). This variation in performance is due to the fact that sleep and circadian drives in the brain interact nonlinearly in the control of performance and alertness (Dijk et al., 1992; Goel et al., 2011). For example, performance deficits after being awake at night peak between 6:00 and 10:00 a.m. but are less severe by 6:00-10:00 p.m. (12 hours later) (Goel et al., 2011). The detrimental effects of fatigue on performance may be exacerbated by a tendency for individuals to have reduced awareness of their cognitive performance deficits that result, even as these deficits increase in frequency with consecutive days of inadequate sleep (Van Dongen et al., 2003a; Banks et al., 2010).

Although the effects of acute sleep deprivation on performance may be transiently influenced by such factors as social and physical activity (Goel et al., 2011), a recent meta-analysis of 70 articles that covered 147 cognitive tests of several moderators identified time awake as the most significant predictor of behavior during a period of acute sleep deprivation (Lim and Dinges, 2010). This finding could be especially relevant to those instances in which pilots may obtain little to no sleep within the 24 hours before a flight

[5]The period of habitual sleep time at night has also been identified as encompassing the "window of circadian low," defined as the hours between 2:00 a.m. and 6:00 a.m. for individuals adapted to a usual day-wake/night-sleep schedule. This estimate of the window of circadian low is calculated from extensive scientific data on the circadian low in performance, alertness, subjective fatigue, and body temperature (see Dinges et al., 1996).

and then undertake a lengthy duty day. In such an instance, sleep time is reduced and time awake is increased, and both factors contribute to fatigue.

Much is known about the cognitive and functional deficits that result when healthy adult volunteers remain awake for 24-40 hours (Harrison and Horne, 2000; Philibert, 2005; Institute of Medicine, 2006, 2009; Goel et al., 2009b). Scientific understanding of the effects of sleep deprivation on cognitive functions has accumulated for more than a century (for reviews of this extensive literature, see Kleitman, 1963; Dinges and Kribbs, 1991; Harrison and Horne, 2000; Durmer and Dinges, 2005; Institute of Medicine, 2009).

The cognitive effects of sleep deprivation are due to changes in the brain. Recent advances in neuroimaging technologies have provided further insights into physiological changes in the brain and underlying performance functions that manifest themselves when fatigue results from reduced sleep (Portas et al., 1998b; Drummond et al., 1999, 2005; Drummond and Brown, 2000; Thomas et al., 2000; Bell-McGinty et al., 2004; Chee and Chieh, 2004; Habeck et al., 2004; Chee et al., 2006, 2008; Chuah et al., 2006; Wu et al., 2006; Lim et al., 2007, 2010; Venkatramen et al., 2007; Institute of Medicine, 2009).

It is now recognized that although most adults exposed to a night without sleep experience fatigue-related declines in performance, the timing and severity of the declines vary across individuals, including pilots (Doran et al., 2001; Leproult et al., 2003; Van Dongen et al., 2004; Bliese et al., 2006; Institute of Medicine, 2009). These differences in individual cognitive vulnerability to sleep loss may have a basis in biological factors (e.g., normal genetic variation) regulating sleep and circadian rhythms (Goel et al., 2009a, 2010; Institute of Medicine, 2009). People with untreated sleep disorders are also subject to individual vulnerability and may experience negative effects on their performance and safety beyond those experienced by healthy individuals.

Chronic Partial Sleep Deprivation

In addition to acute sleep deprivation, fatigue can be exacerbated by chronic partial sleep loss, also known as cumulative sleep debt, which occurs when the sleep obtained over multiple days is too short in duration to maintain behavioral alertness during the daytime (Van Dongen et al., 2003b). There is scientific evidence that chronic sleep restriction results in cumulative performance deficits across days and that the rate of the performance decline is inversely proportional to the sleep obtained (Dinges et al., 1997; Belenky et al., 2003; Van Dongen et al., 2003a). These conclusions are also supported by data from an experiment in which daily sleep was chronically obtained by supplementing various shortened nocturnal sleep periods with varying-duration daytime naps (Mollicone et al., 2007). In all of these controlled laboratory studies, measures of behavioral alertness decreased and cognitive performance deficits increased cumulatively across consecutive days, at a rate inversely proportional to the amount of sleep provided each day (for reviews, see Banks and Dinges, 2007, 2011).

Performance deficits from chronic sleep restriction can accumulate across days to levels equivalent to those found after even one or two nights without any sleep (Van Dongen et al., 2003a). They are also influenced by the duration of habitual sleep prior to the sleep restriction period (Rupp et al., 2009). Moreover, chronic sleep restriction that is followed by a night of little to no sleep results in severe deficits in cognitive performance (Banks et al., 2010). Recovery of behavioral alertness following chronic sleep loss often requires extended periods of sleep that are 1-3 hours longer than habitual sleep for one or more nights (Belenky et al., 2003; Lamond et al., 2007; Banks et al., 2010).

The threshold at which chronic sleep restriction adversely affects behavioral alertness and cognitive performance in the majority of healthy adults is when time in bed for sleep is 7 hours or less per 24 hours for a number of consecutive days (Belenky et al., 2003; Van Dongen et al., 2003a; Banks and Dinges, 2007, 2011; Mollicone et al., 2007). Since physiological sleep at night in healthy adults aged 25-65 years averages 90 percent (± 5 percent) of time in bed (Ohayon et al., 2004)—this percentage is often less with increasing age and when sleep is taken in the daytime—the duration of actual physiological sleep time during a 7-hour time in bed in a healthy adult can range from 6.0 hours to 6.7 hours of physiological sleep.

What people report as their usual sleep duration is almost always an overestimate. For example, a population-based sample of N = 669 middle-aged adults found that subjective reports of habitual sleep were only moderately correlated (r = 0.47) with an objective measure of sleep time (i.e., wrist actigraphy), and that there was a systematic over-reporting bias—those who actually slept 5 hours overreported their sleep durations by 1.2 hours (i.e., 6.7 hours), and those sleeping 7 hours overreported by their sleep durations by 0.4 hours (Lauderdale et al., 2008).

Although scientific experiments indicate a minimum threshold of 7 hours' time in bed for sleep is appropriate for at least 80 percent of adults (many of whom will require more than 7 hours in bed to achieve the physiological sleep duration necessary to prevent reductions in alertness and cognitive functions), it is unknown whether this threshold should be applied to the estimated 20 percent of adults who report sleeping 6 hours or less per night (Kripke et al., 2002). There is currently no consensus among scientists and public health experts on (1) what proportion of adults are naturally short sleepers (i.e., they require 6 or fewer hours of sleep a night to be alert) and what proportion are simply chronically sleep deprived at this level of daily sleep; and (2) the extent to which caffeine and other stimulant foods and supplements—none of which are chemical substitutes for sleep—can prevent deficits in behavioral alertness and cognitive performance under chronic sleep restriction. Although there are extensive studies on the alertness-promoting effects of caffeine under acute sleep loss conditions, there are few studies on its effects under conditions of chronic sleep restriction, when tolerance can develop within a few days (Bonnet et al., 2005). In addition, many people do not consume caffeine, and the many who do so are not aware of the dose they are ingesting or whether tolerance has developed from chronic use. Therefore it is difficult to estimate whether caffeine is being used effectively to prevent the adverse effects of chronic restriction of sleep (below 7 hours of time in bed) on behavioral alertness and cognitive performance.

Evidence that cognitive performance is adversely affected when sleep per 24 hours is cumulatively less than 7 hours (time in bed) suggests that pilots should seek to obtain sufficient bed time to ensure they are fit for duty. To the extent that time taken for sleep may be reduced by commuting, such commutes should be avoided.

Napping

Naps are most easily defined as periods of sleep less than half the duration of a typical nocturnal sleep period (Dinges, 1989; Dinges and Broughton, 1989). They are also most often identified with sleep obtained in locations other than a bed, and sleep when clothing is not removed. Naps are one of the frequently used fatigue countermeasures (caffeine being the other), and there is substantial scientific evidence that nap sleep can help reduce the severity of fatigue during prolonged duty periods of work (Dinges et al., 1987; Institute of Medicine, 2009). Naps have been found to be beneficial for fatigue mitigation in commercial pilots (Rosekind et al., 1994), although some pilots report that some sleep obtained in sleeping berths on long-haul aircraft—which is most often less than 3.5 hours in duration—often affords less restoration than equivalent-duration sleep in a bed (Rosekind et al., 2000; Roach et al., 2010).

Although nap sleep obtained while sitting has some benefit for reducing fatigue, studies have found that sleeping while sitting upright (with the requirement of at least partial antigravity posture) results in less sleep time and poorer sleep quality than sleeping in a semirecumbent position (Nicholson and Stone, 1987). Sleeping in a semirecumbent position with ambient noise results in more light sleep and less deep sleep than sleeping supine without noise (Dinges et al., 1981). Since pilot commuting can involve sleep opportunities while seated or semirecumbent (e.g., in a car, bus, or plane during a commute), the recovery potential of such sleep may be of less value than an equivalent period of sleep in a bed. These findings make it difficult to estimate the value of naps and longer sleeps obtained by pilots during commutes to work.

Body posture and ambient noise level, as well as physical comfort, are not the only factors that can influence the benefits of nap sleep. Although napping has been shown to be an effective technique for restoring alertness and performance during periods of continued wakefulness, it is the timing and length of a nap, along with the timing of the nap in the 24-hour period (i.e., when it occurs relative to circadian phase), that also moderates the benefits of napping for performance (Dinges et al., 1987; Webb, 1987; Rogers et al., 1989; Bonnet, 1991; Rosa, 1993; Matsumoto and Harada, 1994; Vgontzas et al., 2007; Caldwell et al., 2009). Naps taken following a prolonged period of wakefulness or during the habitual sleep period (and in the window of circadian low) can be associated with more severe and prolonged sleep inertia, which is a period of grogginess and performance deficits immediately after awakening (Jewett et al., 1999b; Tassi and Muzet, 2000). After the sleep inertia dissipates—in 20 minutes to 2 hours, depending on the degree of prenap sleep deprivation and the timing of the nap—the fatigue-reducing benefits of the nap occur, but they will dissipate faster than the benefits of a full nocturnal sleep period.

FATIGUE MANAGEMENT TECHNOLOGIES

Recognition of the complex nature of the multiple interacting factors that influence the buildup and reduction of fatigue as a state that can affect performance has been at the core of the development and application of various fatigue management technologies. The science of fatigue management has developed rapidly over the past decade in civilian transportation sectors, with much of the applied research sponsored originally by the military, where sustained and continuous operations pose acute and chronic fatigue-related challenges. There are now several well-documented candidate technologies for managing fatigue and its negative effects on performance. These fall into two broad categories: fatigue-detection technologies and mathematical models of fatigue risk. Substantial progress has been made in each of these areas.

Development of technologies in the first category—fatigue-detection technologies for management of the fatigue risk—has been of interest to transportation modalities in particular for the past 10-15 years, especially in motor vehicle operations (Balkin et al., 2011). These technologies include development of relatively unobtrusive ways to determine an operator's level of alertness or performance during duty, as well as devices that predict fatigue in advance of a work cycle or trip (Balkin et al., 2004, 2011; Basner and Dinges, 2011). A recent review of fatigue-detection technologies organized them into four categories (Balkin et al., 2011): (1) Fitness-for-duty tests that are designed to assess whether operators have sufficient alertness/performance capacity prior to a work cycle or duty period; (2) online operator monitoring technologies that are designed to provide real-time monitoring of an operator's physiological or behavioral state during work; (3) performance-based monitoring systems that are designed to continuously track operational performance to detect operator conditions/behaviors that can lead to reduced safety; and (4) embedded or secondary-task technologies that are designed to monitor and/or enhance operator performance/alertness by modulating the amount of stimulation provided through a secondary task. Although some of the fatigue-detection technologies have been studied in operational environments and shown promise—especially in combination (e.g., Dinges et al., 2005), there remain important unresolved questions and limitations regarding the validity and reliability of their use relative to actual work performance, and their acceptance by operators and industries (Dinges and Mallis, 1998; Balkin et al., 2011). There is also a need to determine how such technologies could be used most effectively in fatigue management in commercial aviation, especially as it relates to commuting.

The second major category of fatigue management technologies consists of mathematical models of fatigue or the risk fatigue poses to safety. The models make predictions about the likelihood of fatigue as a risk to performances using information on duty time and scheduling, sleep quantity and quality, circadian and time-zone information, and other variables (for reviews see Mallis et al., 2004; Dawson et al., 2011). Over the past decade, a number of federal agencies have supported the continued development and evaluation of mathematical models of fatigue risk (Jewett et al., 1999a; Neri, 2002). A workshop sponsored by the U.S. Department of Defense, the U.S. Department of Transportation, and the National Aeronautics and Space Administration provided an opportunity to conduct an initial evaluation and comparison of seven of these mathematical models from the United States, Europe, and Australia (Mallis et al., 2004). Although predictions of performance were promising, the evaluation showed that further research was needed to demonstrate the models' validity and reliability using real-world data, and that the models could not make reliable predictions of group performance risks from fatigue over multiday schedules (Dinges, 2004; Van Dongen, 2004). In recent years, some of the models have undergone further improvements in the accuracy of their predictions of both the basic dynamics of chronic sleep restriction in relation to fatigue (e.g., McCauley et al., 2009), and in relation to prediction of accidents (e.g., Hursh et al., 2008).

The potential for practical application of the mathematical models in the commercial aviation context—and particularly in relation to pilot commuting—has not yet been determined. A recent review of eight of the

BOX 4-1
Risk Factors for Fatigue-Related Errors and Accidents

Risks of fatigue-related errors and accidents stem from multiple interrelated and interacting aspects of work, rest, and sleep. These include but are not limited to:

1. duration of work periods within a single day and over time,
2. time of day at which work occurs,
3. variation in the timing of work within and between weeks,
4. duration of sleep obtained on work days and on nonwork days,
5. frequency and duration of days off from work,
6. different vulnerabilities of workers to fatigue from these factors, and
7. volume and intensity of work.

SOURCE: Institute of Medicine (2009, pp. 218-219) citing the works of Dinges (1995), Rosa (2001), Drake et al. (2004), Folkard et al. (2005), and Van Dongen (2006).

mathematical models of fatigue in work settings concluded that although the models are intended to provide quantitative information on the likely average level of fatigue risk associated with a given pattern of work and sleep, there is considerable individual variability attributable to personal biology and task variables not included in current models (Dawson et al., 2011; see also Van Dongen et al., 2004). The review also concluded that given the current limitations of the fatigue models, they may be most useful as one element in a fatigue risk management system (Dawson et al., 2011). Considerable research is needed to address how to use these models, and other knowledge in the design and implementation of staffing and work-scheduling programs in order to minimize fatigue (see National Research Council, 2007; Horrey et al., 2011).

The issue of fatigue in safety-sensitive work operations cuts across many industries and has been addressed broadly in the scientific literature. The combination of work demands, sleep restriction, and circadian factors can negatively affect alertness, performance, speed, accuracy, and central nervous system functioning (Cabon et al., 1993; Goel et al., 2009b): see Box 4-1. The next chapter looks more closely at the potential for pilots' commuting patterns to affect their risk of fatigue.

5

Pilot Commuting and Fatigue Risk

In this chapter we relate the scientific evidence presented in Chapter 4 to the manner in which pilot commuting could contribute to these factors and therefore to fatigue as an operational risk.[1] We repeat the caution to readers not to assume that the distance pilots live from the airport reflects their likely commute times. As discussed above, there are very little data to evaluate that assumption.

INADEQUATE SLEEP PRIOR TO FLIGHT DUTY

Consistent with the scientific literature from laboratory experiments (reviewed in Chapter 4), field studies of pilots have found that sleep duration in the 24 hours prior to a flight duty period can contribute to pilot fatigue in flight. In a recent report by Thomas and Ferguson (2010), sleep and performance data from captains and first officers were collected by trained expert observers during 302 normal flight operations of a commercial airline flying short-haul jet operations that primarily occurred between 6:00 a.m. and 10:00 p.m. Crew members provided estimates of their total sleep in the prior 24 hours, their total sleep in the prior 48 hours, and the total time they were awake since their last sleep period at the commence-

[1]We did not consider transportation while crews are laying over during long-haul operations, as these typically involve arranged times, hotels for sleep, and conveyances to and from the airport, and they fall within the flight and duty time regulations. We are also not considering in-flight sleep during long-haul operations with augmented crews, as these also fall within the flight and duty time regulations.

ment of cruise (i.e., early in flight). Observers assessed the crew during normal flight operations using the "threat and error management model" (Helmreich, 2000; International Civil Aviation Organization, 2002; Klinect, 2002). In this model, safety was defined as the active process of crews' effective management of operational threats, which included aspects of normal flight operations that have the potential to negatively affect safety, such as adverse weather or an aircraft system malfunction, and management of the inevitable errors that occur as part of normal human performance. The study found that restricted sleep in both the 24-hour and 48-hour periods prior to each sector was associated with changes in crews' threat and error management performance. Restriction to less than 6 hours of sleep in the prior 24 hours was associated with degraded operational performance and increased error rates (Thomas and Ferguson, 2010). The authors concluded that their findings support prior sleep as a critical fatigue-related variable.

A study of 19 long-haul pilots also found that sleep in the prior 24 hours was a significant predictor of self-rated fatigue and the measured mean response speed of the psychomotor vigilance task after international flight sectors (Petrilli et al., 2006). These investigators concluded that in order to minimize the risk of fatigue, the sleep obtained by pilots should be taken into account in the development of flight and duty time regulations. This provocative suggestion may or may not be considered relative to flight and duty time regulations, but the scientific evidence on how commuting may contribute to fatigue because of inadequate sleep and prolonged wakefulness may suggest that there is a shared responsibility for mitigating fatigue between pilots and carriers.

Sleep is a physiological phenomenon that is defined by measuring brain waves, eye movements, muscle activity, and other physiological processes. As noted in Chapter 4, in order to acquire 6 hours physiological sleep time, an average healthy adult must spend approximately 7 hours in bed, as physiological sleep occurs for 85-95 percent of time in bed for healthy sleepers. Thus, when it is necessary to obtain at least 6 hours of physiological sleep, the time in bed would have to be approximately 7 hours. Moreover, although some people can function at normal levels for a night or two with 6 hours of physiological sleep, repeated days of 6 hours of sleep can result in cumulative fatigue and its attendant cognitive performance deficits in a significant portion of the population (Van Dongen et al., 2003a; Mollicone et al., 2007). Therefore, a requirement of 6 hours of physiological sleep (i.e., 7 hours of time in bed) prior to duty should be considered a bare minimum for alert functioning, and its adequacy for pilot alertness should be periodically evaluated.

EXAMPLES OF "FAVORABLE" AND "UNFAVORABLE" COMMUTES

In order to illustrate how the various dimensions of a pilot's commute may be affected by sources of fatigue, the committee presents illustrations of commute patterns for four different combinations of home-to-domicile distances, timing, and circadian shifts. These commute patterns are drawn from the committee's direct conversations with various stakeholders (including pilots, airlines, unions, and the FAA), in the course of hearings and testimony, during this study. These examples reflect the norms of the industry based on conversations with industry officials, the committee's experience, and the committee's analysis of home-to-domicile distances calculated from zip code data (see Chapter 3). These selections may not reflect the true distribution of commutes but were rather chosen to highlight different patterns. These illustrations are accompanied by examples of "favorable" and "unfavorable" commuting patterns based on the findings from sleep science. Four primary sources of fatigue—time awake, sleep time, sleep quality, and circadian phase—are the dependent variables for determining whether a commute is favorable or unfavorable. These examples begin with place of residence for the pilot and end with the completion of the pilot's first day's duty assignment.[2] The committee had no way to determine how much more risk an unfavorable commute would present as compared to a favorable one.

Example 1: Home, Portland, Oregon; Domicile, San Francisco International Airport (SFO)

Description: Early morning awakening following short sleep
Factors: Time since awakening, with 13 hours duty

Unfavorable: Example 1a

The pilot, on the evening preceding the assignment, goes to bed earlier than usual at 9:00 p.m., but, unaccustomed to the early bedtime, falls asleep at 10:00 p.m. The pilot wakes at 3:00 a.m. at home in Portland after 5 hours of sleep. The pilot departs his home at 3:30 a.m. and arrives at the Portland International Airport (PDX) at 4:00 a.m. The pilot departs PDX at 5:00 a.m. on a 1-hour commuting flight as a passenger to SFO. The pilot reports for duty at 8:00 a.m. for the first assigned flight, which departs at 9:00 a.m. The pilot flies three legs, with the last one landing at

[2]All time references refer to the time associated with the pilot's place of residence (residence time), not time at location of flight legs or aircraft landing.

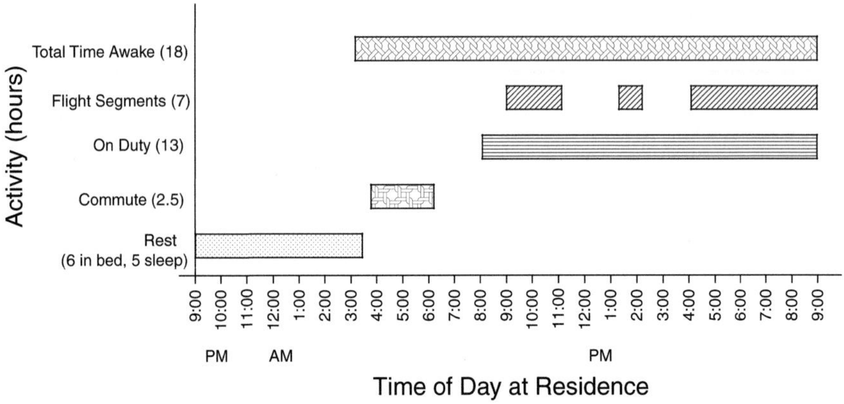

FIGURE 5-1 Example 1a: Unfavorable commuting pattern.
SOURCE: Based on a submission by a pilot to the Aviation System Reporting Systems (ASRS) database. ASRS collects, processes, and analyzes voluntarily submitted aviation safety incident reports of unsafe occurrences and hazardous situations from pilots, air traffic controllers, dispatchers, flight attendants, maintenance technicians, and others. For details, see http://asrs.arc.nasa.gov/overview/summary.html [May 2011].

Bradley International Airport (BDL) in Hartford, Connecticut, at 9:00 p.m. (Oregon time). At this time, the pilot has been awake for 18 hours, including 13 hours of duty, following a short sleep (5 hours). For the graphical representation of this example, see Figure 5-1.

Favorable: Example 1b

The pilot commutes from home to SFO the day before the duty assignment begins. The pilot arrives in San Francisco by 9:30 p.m., sleeps at a hotel near the airport, going to sleep by 11:00 p.m. and awakens at 6:30 a.m. (with 7.5 hours of sleep). Following the same pattern above, ending the duty at BDL, the pilot's time since awakening is 14.5 hours, following a night of 7.5 hours of sleep. For a graphical representation of this example, see Figure 5-2.

Example 2: Home, Alexandria, Virginia; Domicile: John F. Kennedy International Airport (JFK), New York City

Description: Emergent, unplanned circumstance in commute

Factors: Long total awake time without nap, operations during circadian low

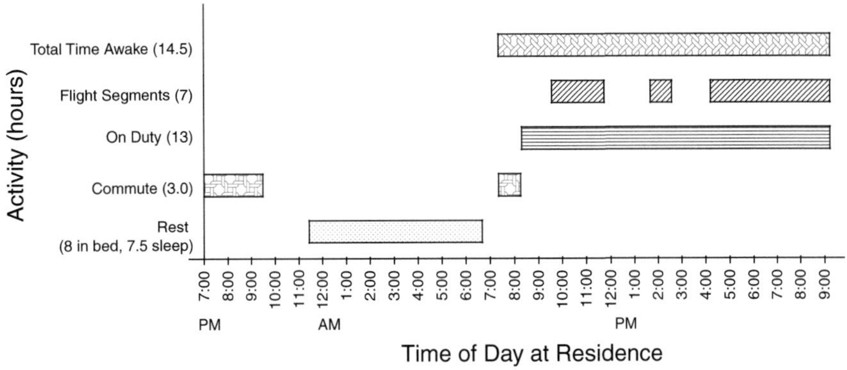

FIGURE 5-2 Example 1b: Favorable commuting pattern.

Unfavorable: Example 2a

The pilot obtains a full night's sleep (7 hours) in the evening prior to duty and awakens at his normal time of 6:00 a.m. After spending the morning and early afternoon at home engaged in normal activities, the pilot leaves at 2:00 p.m., arriving at Ronald Reagan Washington National Airport (DCA) at 2:30 p.m. for a 3:30 p.m. departure to JFK. The flight is late and departs at 4:30 p.m., arriving at JFK at 6:00 p.m. The pilot reports for duty at 7:00 p.m. The pilot begins the single-leg assignment at 8:00 p.m. to Phoenix, Arizona, arriving at 1:00 a.m. (Virginia time). Although the pilot had adequate sleep the night before, the pilot's time awake by the end of the duty day is 19 hours.

Even if the pilot attempted to sleep or nap prior to leaving home for the commute to JFK, the pilot is unlikely to have obtained restful sleep so soon after awakening and during the circadian peak. Moreover, the pilot is waiting for a delayed flight and then taking a short commuting flight during the afternoon circadian low, when a nap attempt may be more successful. Thus, with the commute occupying the best portion of the preduty period for sleep, although several hours are potentially available for sleep prior to duty, it is quite possible that this pilot will be landing the aircraft in Phoenix fatigued, with the length of time since awakening likely to affect individual performance adversely. For the graphical representation of this example, see Figure 5-3.

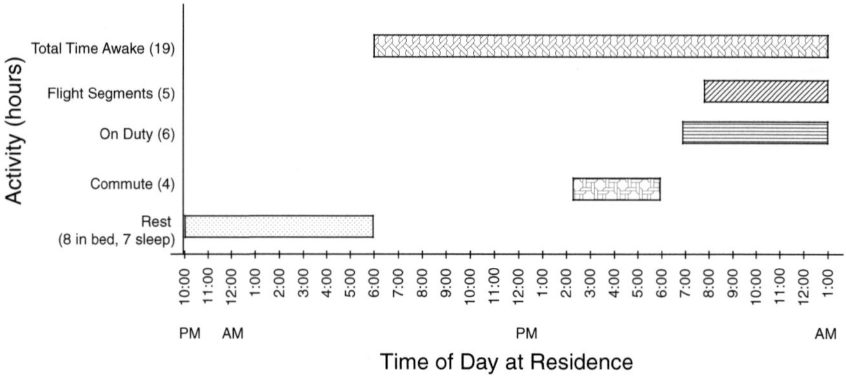

FIGURE 5-3 Example 2a: Unfavorable commuting pattern.
SOURCE: Based on personal testimony from stakeholders at open session meetings.

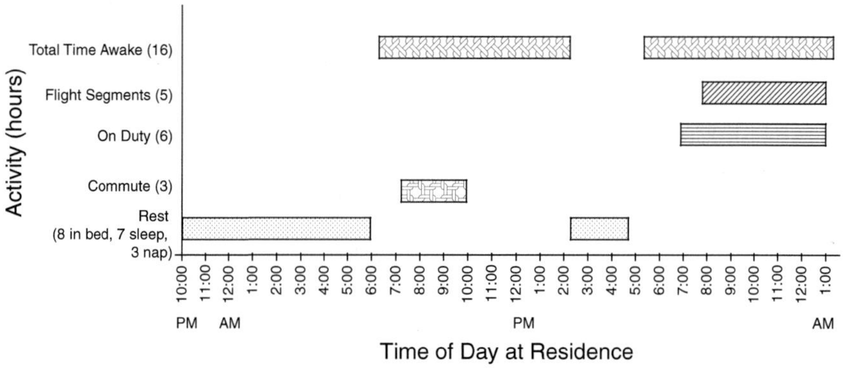

FIGURE 5-4 Example 2b: Favorable commuting pattern.

Favorable: Example 2b

The pilot leaves home earlier, finds a rest facility, and naps in an environment conducive to quality rest during this circadian phase for napping, 2:00 p.m. to 5:00 p.m. For the graphical representation of this example, see Figure 5-4.

Example 3: Home, Concord, California; Domicile, Charlotte/ Douglas International Airport (CLT), Charlotte, North Carolina

Description: Transcontinental commute, cargo airline

Factors: Nocturnal sleep loss and work during circadian low; unrestful sleep environment; early morning awakening; inadequate sleep in 24 hours prior to end of duty; difficulty of sleeping during circadian high; questionable sleep quantity/quality during night-time commuting flight.

Unfavorable: Example 3a

The pilot leaves home in Concord, California, at 9:00 p.m., arriving at SFO at 10:00 p.m. The pilot departs SFO at 11:00 p.m. to commute to CLT, arriving Charlotte at 4:00 a.m. (California time). The pilot checks in for duty at 5:00 a.m. and begins the duty assignment at 6:00 a.m. for a 3-hour flight to Dallas/Fort Worth International Airport (DFW), arriving at 9:00 a.m. (California time).

If the pilot had slept from noon to 8:00 p.m. at home, before departing at 9:00 p.m., the pilot would have obtained adequate sleep. However, by sleeping on the normal pattern, from 11:00 p.m. to 7:00 a.m., and then napping during the afternoon circadian low from 2:00 p.m. to 5:00 p.m. (with actual sleep time 2.5 hours), the amount of time slept within the past 24 hours preceding the projected time of landing in Dallas would be inadequate.

The pilot could then consider the sleep that she might obtain during the 5-hour commuting flight from the West Coast to the East Coast. In favor of obtaining restful sleep during this commute, the all-night timing of the flight spans not only the window of circadian low, but also the pilot's entire habituated sleep period. The duration and quality of sleep actually obtained, though, will depend on factors beyond the immediate control of the pilot, such as whether the available accommodation is in a first-class lie-flat sleeper seat or in an upright coach seat next to a crying baby. On arrival at CLT, the pilot may well be faced with a decision of whether to advise the airline that of being unfit to operate the assigned flight to DFW due to fatigue. For the graphical representation of this example, see Figure 5-5.

Favorable: Example 3b

The pilot commutes in to Charlotte on the day before the assigned flight, and sleeps near the domicile in a hotel or local accommodation, with plenty of time for a complete sleep period before awakening at 3:30 a.m. (in time to report to the domicile, CLT, for duty at 5:00 a.m., including local travel). Although the possibility of obtaining high-quality sleep is likely bet-

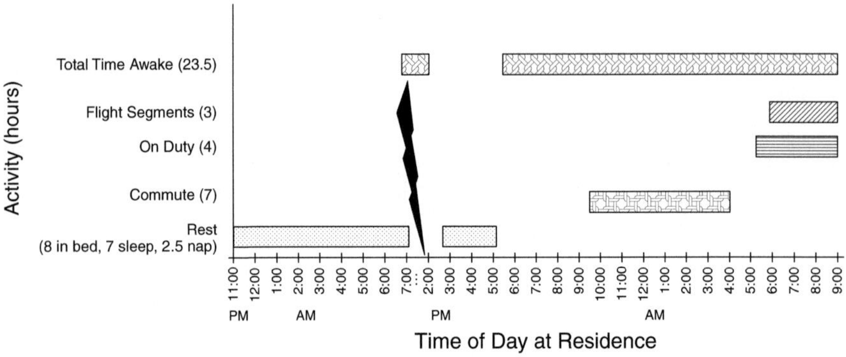

FIGURE 5-5 Example 3a: Unfavorable commuting pattern.
SOURCE: Based on personal testimony from stakeholders at open session meetings.

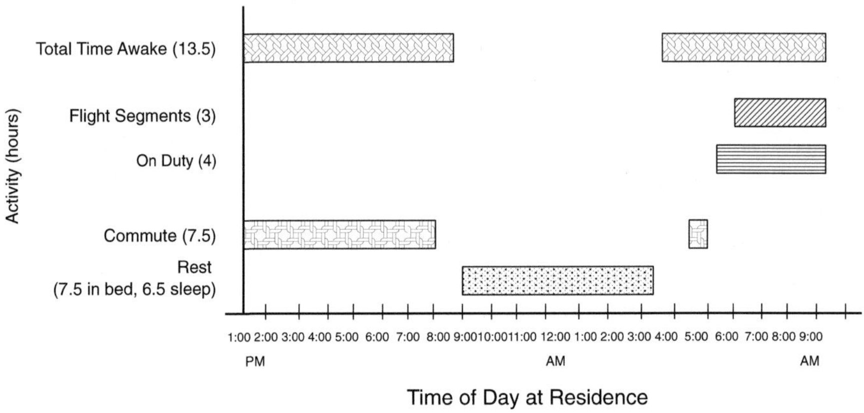

FIGURE 5-6 Example 3b: Favorable commuting pattern.

ter in a bed than on the airplane, it is important to note that the very early wake-up call for the West Coast habituated pilot may make it difficult to obtain a full night's rest due to the interruption of the habitual sleep period. For the graphical representation of this example, see Figure 5-6.

Example 4: Home, Baltimore, Maryland; Domicile: Washington Dulles International Airport (IAD), Chantilly, Virginia

Description: Same 1-day schedule for 3 consecutive days
Factors: Time awake, sleep loss (cumulative), and sleep quality

Unfavorable: Example 4a

A pilot has the same 1-day schedule for 3 consecutive days. On the first night preceding the assignment, the pilot goes to bed at 10:00 p.m. and wakes at 4:00 a.m. for 5 hours of sleep (6 hours in bed). The pilot departs home (her residence in Baltimore) at 5:00 a.m. for the 2-hour commute to her domicile, IAD. The pilot checks in for duty at 7:00 a.m. and begins the first of four flight legs for the day at 8:00 a.m. The pilot concludes the duty day and leaves for the commute home at 8:00 p.m. The pilot repeats this pattern for the next 2 days. However, on the evenings of the first and second days, due to the commute home, the amount of sleep each night decreases by 1 hour to 4 hours (5 hours of time in bed). For the graphical representations of these 1-day and 3-day patterns, see Figures 5-7 and 5-8.

Favorable

Given current scheduling practices, there is no obvious favorable alternative to the commuting pattern for this flight schedule, and it is therefore reflective of shared responsibility between the pilot and the airline. One possible mitigation of fatigue might be for the pilot to take a nap between the hours of 3:00 p.m. and 4:00 p.m. on each afternoon. The value of the nap would be contingent on sleep quality. However, airlines also might be able to effectively limit the negative effects of fatigue on pilots' performance by using both their bidding procedures and their trip pairings (including computerized preference bidding systems) to refrain from assigning mul-

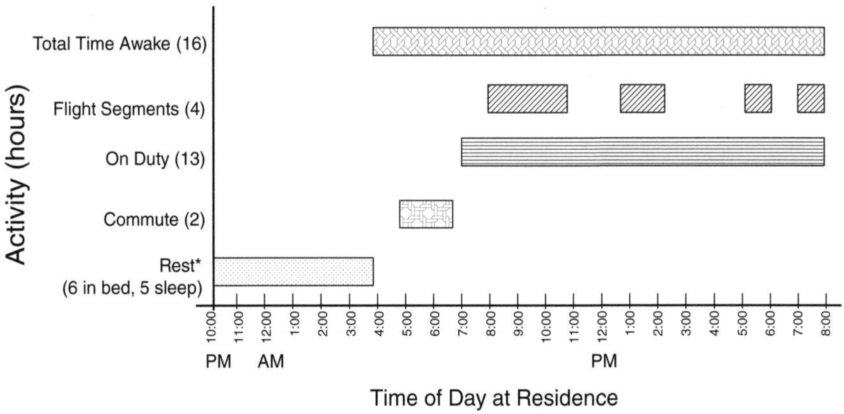

FIGURE 5-7 Example 4a: Unfavorable commuting pattern—day 1 of 3 consecutive days. On second and third days, rest time reduced by 1 hour.
SOURCE: Based on communication with FAA officials.

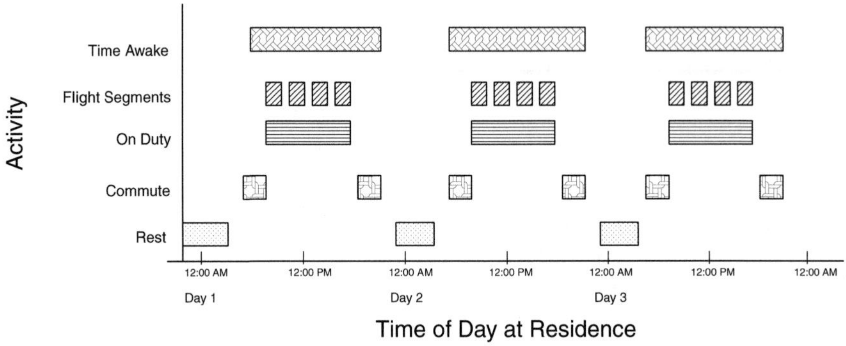

FIGURE 5-8 Example 4a: Unfavorable commuting pattern—overview of 3 consecutive days.
SOURCE: Based on communication with FAA officials.

tiday trip assignments like this one to pilots who are commuting to their domicile, even if the commute is a driving commute of less than 2 hours.

Discussion

Commute time cannot be viewed singularly without considering such factors as the time of the start of the duty day, the length of the duty day, and what the pilot was doing that would add to the overall time awake at the end of the duty day. The end result is a product of the interaction of those factors. Pilots need to consider these several factors when thinking about commuting in a way to minimize fatigue. What is noteworthy about all of these examples is that the favorable commutes all cut into the pilot's time at home; it appears there is often a tradeoff between time at home and beginning the duty cycle adequately rested.

RECOMMENDATION

Extensive scientific evidence exists on the negative effects of fatigue on performance of many cognitive tasks (see Chapter 4), including those essential for safely operating a commercial aircraft. The adverse effects of fatigue induced by sleep loss include maintaining wakefulness and alertness, vigilance and selective attention, psychomotor and cognitive speed, accuracy of performing a wide range of cognitive tasks, working and executive memory, and on higher cognitive functions such as decision making, detection of safety threats, and problem solving, as well as communication and mood. Fatigue is not, however, a binary condition where one is either rested with no negative effects on performance or fatigued with severe negative effects on performance. There are degrees of fatigue and degrees of the negative effects of fatigue on performance. Similarly, the effects of fatigue on performance can vary substantially from one pilot to the next without any untoward effects on the safety of flight.

The scientific literature shows fatigue as a risk to performance can result from three factors: (1) being awake continuously for more than approximately 16 hours, or (2) sleeping too little (especially less than 6 hours on the day prior to work), or (3) when undertaking work at a time when the body is biologically programmed to be asleep (i.e., an individual's habitual nocturnal sleep period), which for most people is between 10:00 p.m. and 7:00 a.m. The evidence that cognitive performance is adversely affected when the amount of sleep in 24 hours is cumulatively less than approximately 6 hours suggests that pilots should seek to obtain sufficient bed time to ensure they are fit for duty. The detrimental effects of fatigue on performance may be exacerbated by a tendency for individuals to have reduced awareness of the cognitive performance deficits that result from fatigue.

Pilots are currently required to report fit for duty. Judging whether a pilot is fit for duty is an individual pilot decision that should take into account the amount of sleep received prior to duty.

> **RECOMMENDATION 1: Pilots should avoid planning commutes or other preduty activities that result in being awake beyond approximately 16 hours before the scheduled end of duty, endeavor to sleep at least 6 hours[3] prior to reporting for duty, and obtain more than 6 hours of sleep per day whenever possible to prevent cumulative fatigue from chronic sleep restriction Pilots should also consider the amount of sleep and time awake in their decision making relative to when to inform their supervisors that they should not fly due to fatigue.**

Although there are currently no agreed-on objective standards in the aviation industry to determine whether a pilot is reporting to duty fatigued, there are provisions in the proposed Notice of Proposed Rulemaking for assessment by others of whether a pilot is fatigued. The validity and reliability of such assessments are unknown, as is the likelihood that they can result in either false positives or false negatives. Consequently it is uncertain whether they can result in effective prevention of fatigue. The proposed regulation is discussed in the next chapter.

---

[3]This refers to at least 6 hours of physiological sleep. Since physiological sleep is typically 85 to 95 percent of total bed time in healthy adults, time in bed for sleep will have to be 6.5 to 7 hours to ensure at least 6 hours of physiological sleep are acquired.

6

Reducing the Risk of Fatigue from Commuting

Current federal flight duty time regulations (14 CFR 91 and 14 CFR 121) do not address pilot commuting. There is only a general requirement (in Part 91.13) that "No person may operate an aircraft in a careless or reckless manner so as to endanger the life or property of another." This provision is interpreted by the Federal Aviation Administration (FAA) and the airline industry as requiring that pilots report fit for duty.

PROPOSED FAA RULE RELEVANT TO FATIGUE

In response to P.L. 111-216 (the Airline Safety and Federal Aviation Administration Extension Act of 2010), the FAA on September 14, 2010, issued a Notice of Proposed Rulemaking (NPRM) (*Federal Register*, Vol. 75, No. 177) related to flight and duty time that attempts to take advantage of the available research on fatigue, sleep, and circadian rhythms and, among other things, to consider the effects of commuting, means of commuting, and the length of the commute on fitness for duty. In referring to the flight duty period (FDP) the NPRM states that "An FDP begins when a crewmember is required to report for duty that includes a flight, series of flights, or positioning flights (including part 91 ferry flights) and ends when the aircraft is parked after the last flight and there is no plan for further aircraft movement by the same crewmember" (p. 55,859). Thus, in the proposed regulations, time spent commuting is not considered duty time. Time spent commuting is also not considered rest by the FAA. As the NPRM states, "The FAA does believe that it is unreasonable to assume that an individual is resting while commuting. Accordingly, time spent commuting, either locally or long-distance, is not considered rest" (p. 55,875).

Background

As part of its efforts to update the regulations, the FAA chartered an Aviation Rulemaking Committee (ARC) in June 2009. The ARC was comprised of representatives from labor, industry, and the FAA, and it was tasked with using fatigue science and a review of international approaches to develop recommendations for revisions of current regulations. The ARC was unable to reach consensus on all issues, however they did reach consensus on the role of commuting in any proposed regulations. With respect to commuting they "unanimously recommended that pilots be reminded of their existing obligations under part 91 to report to work fit for duty, but that the FAA impose no new requirements" (p. 55,874).

Issues Related to the Proposed Rule

The proposed regulations present commuting as fundamentally an issue of fitness for duty, defining a responsible commuter as a pilot who "plans his or her commute to minimize its impact on his or her ability to get meaningful rest shortly before flying, thus fulfilling the proposed requirement that he or she reports for an FDP rested and prepared to perform his or her assigned duty" (p. 55,874). The NPRM places considerable emphasis on education because, as the NPRM states, "The FAA believes a primary reason that pilots may engage in irresponsible commuting practices is a lack of education on what activities are fatiguing and how to mitigate developing fatigue" (p. 55,875). Pilot education is one of the specified objectives of the draft advisory circular on fitness-for-duty mentioned above. The effect of commuting on fatigue is also one element of a recommended training curriculum specified in the NPRM.

In the NPRM (p. 55,875), the FAA further states that "it is inappropriate to simply rely on the existing requirements in Part 91 to report to work fit for duty." FAA proposes a new Part 117 to address fitness for duty. The proposed rule states, "Fit for duty means physiologically and mentally prepared and capable of performing assigned duties in flight with the highest degree of safety" (p. 55,885). The proposed section 117.5 goes on to place specific responsibility on both the flight crew member and the airline: see Box 6-1.

As a complement to issuance of the NPRM, the FAA issued a draft advisory circular (AC 120-FIT) on fitness for duty "to demonstrate acceptable methods of compliance with Title 14 of the Code of Federal Regulations (14 CFR) proposed part 117, § 117.5." The draft circular clearly states

BOX 6-1
FAA Proposed Regulations on Fatigue (Section 117.5)

a. Each flight crew member must report for any flight duty period rested and prepared to perform his or her assigned duties.
b. No certificate holder may assign and no flight crew member may accept assignment to a flight duty period if the flight crew member has reported for a flight duty period too fatigued to safely perform his or her assigned duties or if the certificate holder believes that the flight crew member is too fatigued to safely perform his or her assigned duties.
c. No certificate holder may permit a flight crew member to continue a flight duty period if the flight crew member has reported himself too fatigued to continue the assigned flight duty period.
d. Any person who suspects a flight crew member of being too fatigued to perform his or her duties during flight must immediately report that information to the certificate holder.
e. Once notified of possible flight crew member fatigue, the certificate holder must evaluate the flight crew member for fitness for duty. The evaluation must be conducted by a person trained in accordance with § 117.11 and must be completed before the flight crew member begins or continues an FDP.
f. As part of the dispatch or flight release, as applicable, each flight crew member must affirmatively state he or she is fit for duty prior to commencing flight.
g. Each certificate holder must develop and implement an internal evaluation and audit program approved by the Administrator that will monitor whether flight crew members are reporting for FDPs fit for duty and correct any deficiencies.

that fitness for duty is considered a joint responsibility of the air carrier and the crew member and goes on to say, "Part 117 recognizes the need to hold both air carriers and pilots responsible for making sure crewmembers are working a reasonable number of hours, getting sufficient sleep, and not reporting for flight duty in an unsafe condition. Many of the ways that air carriers and crewmembers negotiate this joint responsibility are handled in the context of labor management relations and agreements."

FATIGUE RISK MANAGEMENT PLANS AND SYSTEMS

There are currently two different regulatory initiatives that are relevant to the discussion of commuting and its effect on fatigue: fatigue risk management plans (FRMPs) and fatigue risk management systems (FRMSs). It is important not to confuse the two.

Fatigue Risk Management Plans

Fatigue risk management plans are an airline's policies and procedures to reduce the risk of flight crew member fatigue and to improve flight crew member alertness (see Federal Aviation Administration, 2010a). P.L. 111-216 required U.S. airlines to submit drafts of their plans to the FAA. On August 19, 2010, the FAA issued an InFO (Information for Operators; see Federal Aviation Administration, 2010a) that provided the necessary information for air carriers regarding the structure and elements involved in the development of a fatigue risk management plan.[1] The FRMP structure should consist of:

- senior-level management commitment to reducing fatigue and improving flight crew member alertness;
- FRMP scope and fatigue management policies and procedures;
- current flight time and duty period limitations;
- rest scheme consistent with limitations;
- fatigue reporting policy;
- education and awareness training program;
- fatigue incident reporting process;
- system for monitoring flight crew fatigue; and
- an FRMP evaluation program (Federal Aviation Administration, 2010a).

The guidance instructs that FRMPs should be updated every 24 calendar-months. In support of the development of FRMPs, the FAA issued another InFO that provides an FRMP checklist for operators to ensure that all of the relevant elements of an FRMP were included in their submission (Federal Aviation Administration, 2010b).

According to the FAA (Federal Aviation Administration, 2010a, p. 1):

> A FRMP is an air carrier's management plan outlining policies and procedures for reducing the risks of flightcrew member fatigue and improving flightcrew member alertness. The FRMP policies and procedures should focus on the air carrier's specific kind of operations (e.g., domestic, flag, and supplemental) and the type operations (e.g., continuous duty overnights, night vs. day operations, cargo vs. passenger operations, short-haul vs. long-haul, etc.).

---

[1]The checklist can be found at http://www.faa.gov/other_visit/aviation_industry/airline_operators/airline_safety/info/all_infos/media/2010/InFO10017.pdf [June 2011], and the supplemental document can be found at http://www.faa.gov/other_visit/aviation_industry/airline_operators/airline_safety/info/all_infos/media/2010/info10017SUP.pdf [June 2011], respectively.

The FAA issued guidance as to the structure of the plan as well as the submittal, review, and acceptance processes. Of relevance to commuting, the FAA checklist identifies "The effects of fatigue as a result of commuting" as one of 15 elements and tasks for the fatigue education and awareness training program to be referenced in the FMRP (see Federal Aviation Administration, 2010b).

The following question regarding FRMPs was posed to airlines from whom the committee requested input for this study, "Does your Fatigue Risk Management Plan include any reference or consideration of commuting? If so, please provide a copy of the plan."

Out of the 33 airlines that provided input to the committee, 17 responded with comments relevant to the FRMP. Eleven provided a statement on the status of their FRMP, if indeed they had one. For the most part, these responses included statements that the plan was submitted and pending approval. In one instance, the airline mentioned that commuting was not referenced as commuting is not allowed. Another airline pointed out that commuting was not relevant because the airline practiced home basing. In yet another case, a very small airline wrote that it was not relevant because of the few fatigue calls they had had in the past 5 years, none was related to commuting.

Among the six airlines that provided copies of plans, five included the wording, noted above, from the FAA guidance document regarding commuting as a factor to be addressed in a fatigue education and awareness training program. Two of these five included an additional statement that commuting information was to be collected when fatigue was reported by a pilot. One of these five airlines had a statement in its FRMP that fatigue was a factor under review for event evaluation.

In one other case an airline includes the following statement in its FRMP (personal communication):

> Crewmembers commuting greater than two hours from the company facility are required to overnight in their domicile, if their bid assignment includes an early morning departure between the hours of 0000-0600, thus elevating the potential of fatigue. The STBY crew understands the time zone they are on STBY for and are expected to be rested and prepared to report to duty as needed.

Fatigue Risk Management Systems

New developments both in the science of fatigue and performance and in management and regulatory philosophies have led to the other regulatory approach in the transportation domain, usually termed fatigue risk management systems (FRMSs).[2] These systems are focused on integrating scientific knowledge about fatigue and its management with the realities of airline operations. In essence, these systems recognize that responsibility for managing fatigue-related safety risks is a shared responsibility of regulatory authorities, operators, and individual pilots.

In an effort to collect additional data, the committee approached many international regulatory and safety oversight organizations, operators, and pilot associations—including the International Civil Aviation Organization (ICAO), the International Air Transport Association, the Flight Safety Foundation, and the International Federation of Airline Pilots' Association—to obtain information regarding existing regulations, policies, and best practices regarding commuting outside the United States. It is interesting to note that little information was received as to relevant aspects to commuting and fatigue with the exception of FRMSs.

The ICAO established a FRMS task force to review scientific and operational knowledge and to develop detailed regulatory standards and guidance for member countries on implementation of such systems (see International Civil Aviation Organization, 2009). The proposed Standard and Recommended Practice (SARP) was approved for adoption by the ICAO Council on June 13, 2011. It will become effective for member states on October 15 and applicable on December 15, 2011.

FRMS, according to the new ICAO standard, promotes addressing flight crew fatigue in a comprehensive and proactive manner by gathering objective data regarding sleep, fatigue, and operational parameters to manage the risk which fatigue can pose to flight safety (International Civil Aviation Organization, 2011a, 2011b). This approach is in stark contrast to managing the risk through prescriptive limits of flight time or duty periods based on the assumption that a pilot is safe to fly as long as he or she is operating within prescribed hourly limits. It is important to note that hours spent commuting are not included in such limits.

When an airline chooses to implement FRMS within an approved regulatory framework it commits to specifying both predictive and proactive processes that it will use to identify potential fatigue hazards and the resulting safety risks. The predictive processes are applied when developing monthly crew rostering schedules and can include the use of scientifically derived biomathematical computer models as well as operational experience to take into account factors known to affect sleep and fatigue and their effects on performance (International Civil Aviation Organization, 2011a, 2011b).

[2]An FRMS is a data-driven and scientifically based process to continuously manage and monitor fatigue-related risks to ensure that personnel are performing at adequate levels of alertness in flight operations.

After the rostering schedules are implemented then the proactive processes are used to identify hazards during current operations on an ongoing basis. These processes can include crew self-reports of fatigue as well as more objective measures of sleep, using actigraphs (a wristwatch-like device that is worn continuously), and crew performance, using simple tests developed in the laboratory, such as the widely accepted Flight Data Monitoring (also known as Flight Operations Quality Assurance or FOQA) to identify deviations from planned flight parameters in airplane handling performance during approach and landing. The operator must also ensure that remedial actions, necessary to effectively mitigate the risks associated with the hazards, are implemented promptly, and it must specify the methods it will use to actively monitor the effectiveness of those actions taken to mitigate fatigue risks (International Civil Aviation Organization, 2011a, 2011b).

According to the FAA, "An FRMS can be part of an organization's SMS [safety management system] or a stand-alone system" (U.S. Department of Transportation, 2010a, p. 4). If an airline has a safety management system, then the data collection and analysis would preferably be carried out in a manner consistent with that SMS.[3] Sample crews are selected with no regard to whether or not they have commuted long distances by car, bus, train, or air before starting duty. Given the prevalence of commuting, described elsewhere in this report, it can be assumed that a substantial number of the sampled crews will include commuters who travel long distances by all forms of transportation.

Thus, FRMSs provide a rigorous method to assure that crews are operating at a suitable level of alertness without regard to the characteristics of their commutes. FRMSs can offer both the operator and regulators a valid "snapshot" of crew alertness during normal operations and thereby provide at least a partial assessment that the contribution of commuting to fatigue is or is not within an acceptable level. Such limited assurance offers a significant benefit beyond simply requiring the crew and the operator to adhere to prescriptive limits when no data are routinely gathered to assess the specific risk that fatigue may pose to a particular set of flights. Furthermore, if an operator wishes to assess whether some types of commuting produce more fatigue for a specific trip pairing, an FRMS provides a ready method to do so. FRMSs are currently under development by several foreign carriers. Industry and professional groups, as well as U.S. state regulatory agencies, are also involved in development and implementation efforts.

An FRMP includes some elements of an FRMS (e.g., management policy, event reporting and evaluation, and fatigue education and awareness training), but it is still based on flight time and duty period limita-

[3]For explanation of an SMS, see http://www.icao.int/anb/safetymanagement/DOC_9859_FULL_EN.pdf [June 2011].

tions and a focus on reported events. It does not include the key proactive FRMS element of routinely assessing fatigue risk on specific trip pairings. Consequently, its ability to address commuting is limited to education and training and reactive analyses of reported unsafe events.

When FRMS becomes applicable as an ICAO worldwide standard in December 2011, member states will each have to decide how to implement the new standard within their aviation regulations. The proposed SARPs combine all standards for fatigue management under a general heading of "Fatigue Management" rather than being dispersed as they are now throughout Annex 6, Part I. This consolidation will enable states to allow operators the option of utilizing FRMS as the basis for some or all of their operations in place of prescriptive regulations. In anticipation, ICAO has worked with industry (International Air Transport Association, IATA) and labor (International Federation of Airline Pilots' Association, IFALPA) to draft complementary FRMS Manuals for Operators and Regulators, which are scheduled to be released in July 2011.

Although an FRMS is not mandatory for U.S. carriers, the FAA did issue an Advisory Circular (AC 120-103) on FRMSs on August 3, 2010 (U.S. Department of Transportation, 2010a). The circular identifies the basic components of an FRMS and how it may be implemented in aviation operations as a means of improving safety and performance. In the circular, an FRMS is described as "a data-driven and scientifically based process that allows for continuous monitoring and management of safety risks associated with fatigue-related error. It is part of a repeating performance improvement process. This process leads to continuous safety enhancements by identifying and addressing fatigue factors across time and changing physiological and operational circumstances." The circular notes that it may be implemented as part of the organization's safety management system or as a stand-alone system.

The components for an FRMS include (a) a fatigue risk management policy, (b) an education and awareness training program, (c) a fatigue analysis and reporting system, (d) monitoring fatigue in flight and cabin crew, (e) an incident reporting process, and (f) performance evaluation. Roles and responsibilities in the FRMS process include the operator, the employees/crew, and the regulator. The regulator's responsibility is to audit the process and ensure that the FRMS is responsive to feedback and provides a level of safety that is equivalent to those established by existing regulations. The data-driven approach of an FRMS is derived from the guidance developed by the Flight Safety Foundation for regulatory authorities to use for approving flights greater than 16 hours (Flight Safety Foundation Editorial Staff, 2005). The process was used first for Singapore Airlines, and it has since been by several other airlines, including the current effort by the FAA to assess fatigue on ultra-long-range flights by Delta, American, and Continental Airlines. In the NPRM, related to fatigue, the FAA has proposed that carriers use a similar FRMS approach for flights not covered by the new regulations. In order to be consistent with other states, the FAA will need to adjust the circular to be consistent with the ICAO FRMS SARPs recently approved by the ICAO Council.

The FAA approach is compatible with ICAO's initiative on fatigue risk management systems and the trend over the past two decades of many U.S. federal regulatory agencies to shift more responsibility to the organizations they regulate and to encourage cooperative rather than adversarial relationships. Generally, these initiatives rely on management systems that use continuous monitoring to identify and mitigate potential risks before they have safety consequences.[4]

Pilot Decision Making

Decision making is central to pilots' efforts to avoid flying their aircraft while they are fatigued. Once a pilot has made a strategic decision of where to live in relation to his or her domicile, there are three major circumstances in which such tactical decision making has special significance: (1) when the pilot is developing plans for commuting to the domicile; (2) when the pilot must make adjustments in plans necessitated by arising contingencies (e.g., bad weather); and (3) when the pilot has to decide whether and how to cancel a duty assignment because of (anticipated) fatigue. The decisions in all such situations arc highly challenging. For instance, they typically involve multiple, often conflicting considerations, numerous stakeholders with competing interests (e.g., family members, colleagues, and supervisors), and the need to be informed by nonobvious and sometimes counterintuitive facts about the biology of fatigue and rest.

Regulatory Considerations: General Issues

A major concern in establishing any regulation is designing it so that it achieves its intended effect. Negative unintended consequences often emerge when a seemingly simple regulation is implemented in a complex system. Regulators may not have enough knowledge about the detailed operation of the systems and so may adopt seemingly simple regulations that fail to anticipate how the system will respond to those regulations. An early analysis of the general problem of unintended consequences found that one of its sources is "imperious immediacy of interest," which is where

[4]Such voluntary FAA programs include the Aviation Safety Action Program and the Flight Operational Quality Assurance Program.

the intended consequence of an action is desired so strongly that potential unintended effects are purposely ignored (Merton, 1936).

The committee is concerned that a rush to establish regulation regarding pilot commuting and fatigue without an adequate understanding of how pilot commuting and fatigue interact with the aviation system might trigger unanticipated and unintended consequences that have not yet been carefully anticipated.

Such unanticipated and unintended consequences can reduce the effectiveness of the regulation in achieving its goal, and in some cases may even result in a regulation having the opposite effect of what had been intended. A noteworthy example occurred with the 55 mph speed limit, established in March 1974 in response to the 1973 oil embargo (see National Research Council, 1984). Following this adoption, highway fatalities dropped. Although multiple factors contributed to the decline in fatalities, the general consensus was that the reduced speed limits had resulted in fewer highway fatalities. As the fuel shortage eased, the speed limit was retained largely on the grounds of the increased safety it apparently provided. However, in response to other pressures and interests, in 1987, 40 states raised the speed limit to 65: many anticipated that highway fatalities would again increase due to the higher speeds. Although highway fatalities did increase, so did vehicle miles traveled. A study that examined statewide fatality rates, considering not only the roads on which the speed limits were changed but also the non-interstate roads on which they were not, found that the higher 65 mph speed limit reduced the statewide fatality rates by 3.4-5.1 percent in comparison with other states (Lave and Elias, 1994). It appears that this unexpected and initially counterintuitive result was because enforcement and highways are integrated systems. The federal government had threatened to impose financial penalties if the 55 mph speed limit was not enforced, so states devoted considerable patrol resources to rural interstates and reduced both enforcement on other highways and other safety activities. In addition, it appears that the higher level of enforcement on rural interstates may have caused some drivers to switch to parallel noninterstate highways, which are more dangerous in terms of fatalities but which had the same speed limit and less speed enforcement. Where the 55 mph speed limit was raised and the threat of federal financial sanctions removed, highway patrols reallocated their activities to a better balance from a safety perspective and with the higher interstate speed limits, some drivers switched from parallel rural roads to the safer interstate highways.

This experience offers two cautionary lessons for safety regulation. One is that complex systems may react to regulation in ways that were unanticipated and, in this case, counter to the goal of improved highway safety. The second is that patterns of enforcement can have important and often unanticipated effects on how a system reacts to regulation.

In aviation safety regulation, another possible unintended consequence of regulation can come from modal shift effects. A regulation that increases costs to the airline industry will likely result in some portion of those costs being passed on to travelers in the form of higher airline ticket prices. Higher airline ticket prices would cause some travelers to switch their mode of travel from airplanes to automobiles. Since travel by private automobile is more dangerous than travel by commercial airline, the result of such a shift would be an increase in highway fatalities. Thus, however many airline passenger and crew lives are saved by the airline safety regulation, the net savings of life from the regulation would be less because of the increase in highway fatalities. In some cases, the net effect may actually be a net loss of lives from a regulation intended to save lives.

This potential for an outcome other than that intended was forecast for a proposed regulation to mandate the use of child safety seats on commercial airlines. One study of the proposed regulation (Windle and Dresner, 1991) concluded that more lives would be lost from the switch to highway travel from the higher travel costs for families with children than would be saved from the added safety benefit of child safety seats.

Regulatory Considerations: Pilot Commuting

Developing a regulation to address pilot commuting would face several challenges. The first would be to determine how many lives the elimination of commuting-related fatigue would be expected to save. Although there is no doubt that, in principle, commuting can contribute to pilot fatigue, that pilot fatigue can contribute to reduced pilot performance and that reduced pilot performance can contribute to aviation accidents that can result in fatalities, the magnitudes of any of these effects are not well understood. In particular, there is very little knowledge about the extent to which pilot commuting contributes to pilot fatigue in practice, in part because there are almost no systematic data on current pilot commuting patterns.

Determining the extent to which fatigue may have contributed to an accident is difficult in an accident investigation, the committee's examination of 863 accidents found only 9 in which fatigue was judged to be a probable cause or contributing factor (see Chapter 3). In none of the accidents was commuting-related fatigue judged by the National Transportation Safety Board to be a probable cause or contributing factor, and, of the nine fatigue-related accidents, there was only one in which a commute may have been one of the contributors to that fatigue. Although the limitations of the accident investigation process means that the role of fatigue may be difficult to detect so that these figures may well understate the role of fatigue, it is still difficult to conclude that commuting-related fatigue is a major source of aviation accidents.

The second challenge would be to determine what proportion of commuting-related fatigue accidents a proposed regulation would prevent. Commuting occurs during a pilot's off-duty time and, collectively, from a diverse array of home locations to a large number of domiciles using a wide variety of transportation options. Enforcement of a regulation designed to alter pilots' behavior during their off-duty hours would be difficult. In such situations, as suggested by the enforcement of the 55 mph speed limit, different patterns of enforcement could have different impacts on the actual effect of the regulation. Enforcement might well prevent some fatigue-inducing commutes, depending on how a regulation was implemented, but the form of enforcement could also induce some counterproductive behavior.

The third challenge would be to determine what the regulation would cost to both pilots and airlines and the subsequent effects of those added costs would be on airline ticket prices. Higher ticket prices would cause some travelers to switch from airline travel to auto travel, with the result of some increase in highway deaths. At first glance, it might appear that only the direct costs to the airlines would influence ticket prices, but costs the regulation might impose on pilots might also have an effect. If the regulation imposed costs on pilots, it could make being an airline pilot a less attractive career than it had been prior to the regulation. If that caused some pilots to choose a different profession, then the airlines might have to pay higher wages to attract a sufficient number of pilots to the industry. Those higher wages, should they be necessary, would result in higher costs to the airlines and eventually higher ticket prices. With these considerations in mind, it is important to note that assessing the impact of cost on airline ticket prices and, in turn, on increased highway fatalities is beyond the scope of the current requirements for cost-benefit analysis of proposed regulations. There are other possible adverse consequences from regulations: see Viscusi (1994) and Viscusi and Zeckhauser (1994).

Given that there is some potential for commuting to contribute to fatigue and clear evidence that fatigue can decrease performance, the committee believes it is important to reduce the likelihood that commuting could contribute to pilot fatigue during duty. At the same time, the safety risk posed by commuting-induced fatigue is unknown. There is a need to understand the extent to which the risk posed by fatigue resulting from some commutes may be mitigated by individual, airplane (e.g., flight deck systems), or aviation system (e.g., crew resource management) characteristics.

There is also tremendous variability across individual pilot commuting practices and day-to-day experiences. Attempting to determine a one-size-fits-all delineation on what constitutes a fatiguing commute on the basis of either time or distance is difficult because the length of the commute, measured either by distance or time spent commuting, does not necessarily determine whether or not the pilot reports fit for duty and well rested. And as discussed above, regulations specific to commuting could inadvertently lead to increased safety problems and additional loss of lives due to unintended and unanticipated consequences. Consequently, although action is warranted to reduce the likelihood that commuting will present a safety risk, there is a lack of evidence to support the basis for issuance of regulations pertaining to commuting.

CONCLUSIONS AND RECOMMENDATIONS

CONCLUSION: With regard to the proposed provisions in Section 117.5, there are no valid and reliable tools and techniques feasible to achieve the goals of detecting fatigue and fitness for duty in pilots in an operational setting. To achieve these goals, further research would be needed to scientifically validate the tools and techniques, demonstrate that they are technically feasible in an operational environment, and evaluate their relationship to operational safety and the extent to which they can be integrated into an operational context.

CONCLUSION: There are inadequate data to specify or determine the effectiveness of regulations regarding pilot commuting. Additional information is needed to determine if a regulatory approach would be appropriate.

Potential fatigue is an inherent component of a system that functions 24 hours a day, 7 days a week. Recognizing this, the aviation industry has been developing an approach through FRMSs to better understand when fatigue is a concern and how to best mitigate that risk. Airlines develop FRMSs specific to their operational environment. To date, commuting has not been a major consideration in these systems. Incorporating data on commuting in relation to pilots' duty hours and sleep prior to duty would help inform these systems and allow airlines to consider mitigation strategies specific to their operations.

RECOMMENDATION 2: The potential of commuting on pilot fatigue should be addressed as part of an airline's strategies to manage fatigue risk. If airlines develop fatigue risk management systems (FRMSs), they should gather information about preduty sleep and wake time relative to commuting practices and duty cycle. FRMSs should provide a mechanism for identifying problematic patterns and addressing them. FRMSs can offer both the airline and the Federal Aviation Administration an improved assessment of crew alertness

during normal operations and thereby provide some information on the contribution of commuting to fatigue and whether fatigue is or is not within an acceptable level of risk.

FRMPs are the airline carriers' management plans outlining policies and procedures reducing the risk of flight crew member fatigue and improving flight crew member alertness. P.L. 111-216 requires each U.S. carrier operating under Part 121 to submit to the FAA their draft FRMP for review and acceptance. Provided in the FAA's guidance on the development of an FRMP is a requirement for a fatigue education and awareness training program element, one of the subtasks of this element is the effects of commuting on fatigue.

This requirement reflects the perspective that managing the effects of commuting on fatigue is a joint responsibility of airlines and pilots, a position with which the committee agrees. Although the FRMP approach is not as rigorous as the FRMS process, it is required of all Part 121 airlines and therefore presents an opportunity to reach a wider audience than FRMS.

RECOMMENDATION 3: The committee supports fatigue education and awareness training as part of an airline's fatigue risk management plan. Training relative to commuting should include guidelines regarding the effects of inadequate or disturbed sleep or prolonged wakefulness on fatigue and performance. Fatigue education and awareness training should be annually updated with particular attention to incorporating relevant new developments in sleep science.

As part of its data collection, the committee requested that airlines submit information on their policies on pilot commuting, sick leave, and fatigue, if available. Although only a relatively small proportion of airlines responded (39 percent), it is clear from the information submitted and from comments provided in public comments that there is considerable diversity in these policies. In addition, not all airlines have commuting or fatigue policies, with pilots relying instead on sick leave availability to address potential fatigue. Airlines should consider policies that would help pilots plan predictable commutes that do not promote fatigue on duty and policies that minimize negative consequences when unanticipated events alter their commuting plans and lead to fatigue. The effects of these policies on pilot behavior are currently not well understood.

RECOMMENDATION 4: The Federal Aviation Administration should convene a joint industry, labor, and government working group, under the auspices of an independent organization (such as the Flight Safety Foundation), to assess industry policies on pilot commuting, sick

leave, attendance/reliability, and fatigue and to develop industry best practices. The output of this joint working group should inform the development and updating of airlines' fatigue risk management plans and should be validated periodically.

Pilots make decisions about commuting in the context of other factors in their lives, the specifics of their flights, the policies in place at their airlines, including sick leave and commuting policies, and other environmental factors. It is unclear to what extent pilots are aware of the findings from current decision science or consider this information in their decision making. Decision-making strategies informed by this science could be incorporated into FRMP training and considered in the development of industry best practices.

RECOMMENDATION 5: The Federal Aviation Administration should commission efforts to develop protocols and materials for training pilots to make decisions regarding commuting easily and effectively and to ensure that they are informed by current decision science.

As described above, little is known about pilots' commuting patterns and the extent to which their commuting patterns may affect the amount or quality of sleep or the amount of time awake prior to duty. A better understanding of the relationship of commuting to primary risk factors for fatigue would represent a first step in increasing understanding of the relationship between commuting and fatigue. This information, combined with information that is recommended for inclusion in the required FRMPs or in FRMSs, when such systems are required, will provide input needed to inform further research and industry policies.

RECOMMENDATION 6: To inform the development of industry best practices and policies relative to commuting, the Federal Aviation Administration should fund a study to determine the relationships between distance from domicile and five primary fatigue risk factors: (1) sleep quantity 48 hours prior to the end of duty on each day of the trip; (2) sleep quality 48 hours prior to the end of duty on each day of the trip; (3) time awake in the 48 hours prior to the end of duty on each day of the trip; (4) cumulative sleep time in the 72 hours prior to the end of a duty period; and (5) circadian phase at which sleep is obtained and at which duty is undertaken. In order to be maximally useful, the study should include a large random sample of pilots from multiple companies representing the major industry segments. The study should provide objective data on fatigue risk antecedents by using a well-

validated technology that provides reliable information on sleep and wake periods, such as wrist actigraphy, as well as sleep-wake diaries.

Collecting data on a 48- to 72-hour period is needed to fully understand pilots' commuting experiences within the context of multiple factors. The results of the study can help identify situations that may warrant specific attention or additional research.

Bibliography and References

Air Transport Association of America, Inc. (2011). *Annual Results: U.S. Airlines*. Available: http://www.airlines.org/Economics/DataAnalysis/Pages/AnnualResultsUSAirlines.aspx [May 2011].

Air Transport Association of America, Inc. (n.d.). *Safety Record of U.S. Air Carriers*. Available: http://www.airlines.org/Economics/DataAnalysis/Pages/SafetyRecordofUSAirCarriers.aspx [May 2011].

Balkin, T.J., Bliese, P.D., Belenky, G., Sing, H., Thorne, D.R., Thomas, M., Redmond, D.P., Russo, M., and Wesensten, N.J. (2004). Comparative utility of instruments for monitoring sleepiness-related performance decrements in the operational environment. *Journal of Sleep Research 13*(3):219-227.

Balkin, T.J., Horrey, W.J., Graeber, R.C., Czeisler, C.A., and Dinges, D.F. (2011). The challenges and opportunities of technological approaches to fatigue management. *Accident Analysis & Prevention 43*(2):565-572.

Banks, S., and Dinges, D.F. (2007). Behavioral and physiological consequences of sleep restriction. *Journal of Clinical Sleep Medicine 3*(5):519-528.

Banks, S., and Dinges, D.F. (2011). Chronic sleep deprivation. In M.H. Kryger, T. Roth, and W.C. Dement (Eds.), *Principles and Practice of Sleep Medicine* (5th edition, pp. 67-75). Philadelphia, PA: Elsevier.

Banks, S., Van Dongen, H.P.A., Maislin, G., and Dinges, D.F. (2010). Neurobehavioral dynamics following chronic sleep restriction: Dose-response effects of one night for recovery. *Sleep 33*(8):1,013-1,026.

Basner, M., and Dinges, D.F. (2009). Dubious bargain: Trading sleep for Leno and Letterman. *Sleep 32*(6):747-752.

Basner, M., and Dinges, D.F. (2011). Maximizing sensitivity of the Psychomotor Vigilance Test (PVT) to sleep loss. *Sleep 34*(5):581-591.

Belenky, G., Wesensten, N.J., Thorne, D.R., Thomas, M.L., Sing, H.C., Redmond, D.P., Russo, M.B., and Balkin, T.J. (2003). Patterns of performance degradation and restoration during sleep restriction and subsequent recovery: A sleep dose-response study. *Journal of Sleep Research 12*(1):1-12.

Bell-McGinty, S., Habeck, C., Hilton, H.J., Rakitin, B., Scarmeas, N., Zarahn, E., Flynn, J., DeLaPaz, R., Basner, R., and Stern, Y. (2004). Identification and differential vulnerability of a neural network in sleep deprivation. *Cerebral Cortex 14*(5):496-502.

Bliese, P.D., Wesensten, N.J., and Balkin, T.J. (2006). Age and individual variability in performance during sleep restriction. *Journal of Sleep Research 15*(4):376-385.

Boeing Commercial Airplanes. (2011). *Statistical Summary of Commercial Jet Airplane Accidents, Worldwide Operations, 1959-2009*. Available: http://www.boeing.com/news/techissues/pdf/statsum.pdf [April 2011].

Bonnet, M.H. (1991). The effect of varying prophylactic naps on performance, alertness and mood throughout a 52-hour continuous operation. *Sleep 14*(4):307-315.

Bonnet, M.H., Balkin, T.J., Dinges, D.F., Roehrs, T., Rogers, N.L., and Wesensten, N.J. (2005). The use of stimulants to modify performance during sleep loss: A review by the Sleep Deprivation and Stimulant Task Force of the American Academy of Sleep Medicine. *Sleep 28*(9):1,163-161,187.

Boorman, D. (2001). Today's electronic checklists reduce likelihood of crew errors and mishaps. *ICAO Journal 56*(1):17-20.

Bureau of Transportation Statistics. (n.d.-a). *Air Carrier Summary: T3: U.S. Air Carrier Airport Activity Statistics*. Research and Innovation Transportation Administration. Available: http://www.transtats.bts.gov/Fields.asp?Table_ID=273 [May 2011].

Bureau of Transportation Statistics. (n.d.-b). *Load Factor (Passenger-Miles as a Proportion of Available Seat-Miles in percent (%). All Carrier—All Airports*. Research and Innovation Transportation Administration. Available: http://www.transtats.bts.gov/Data_Elements.aspx?Data=5 [May 2011].

Bull, M. (2004). Automobility and the power of sound. *Theory, Culture & Society 21*(4/5):243-249.

Cabon, P., Coblentz, A., Mollard, R., and Fouillot, J.P. (1993). Human vigilance in railway and long-haul flight operation. *Ergonomics 36*(9):1,019-1,033.

Caldwell, J.A., Mallis, M.M., Caldwell, J.L., Paul, M.A., Miller, J.C., and Neri, D.F. (2009). Fatigue countermeasures in aviation. *Aviation Space and Environmental Medicine 80*(1):29-59.

Chee, M.W.L., and Wei Chieh, C. (2004). Functional imaging of working memory after 24 hours of total sleep deprivation. *Journal of Neuroscience 24*(19):4,558-4,567.

Chee, M.W.L., Chuah, L.Y.M., Venkatraman, V., Chan, W.Y., Philip, P., and Dinges, D.F. (2006). Functional imaging of working memory following normal sleep and after 24 and 35 hours of sleep deprivation: Correlations of fronto-parietal activation with performance. *NeuroImage 31*(1):419-428.

Chee, M.W.L., Jiat Chow, T., Hui, Z., Parimal, S., Weissman, D.H., Zagorodnov, V., and Dinges, D.F. (2008). Lapsing during sleep deprivation is associated with distributed changes in brain activation. *Journal of Neuroscience 28*(21):5,519-5,528.

Chuah, Y.M.L., Venkatraman, V., Dinges, D.F., and Chee, M.W.L. (2006). The neural basis of interindividual variability in inhibitory efficiency after sleep deprivation. *Journal of Neuroscience 26*(27):7,156.

Code of Federal Regulations. (2009). *Title 49: Transportation, Section 830.2*. Available: http://ecfr.gpoaccess.gov/cgi/t/text/text-idx?c=ecfr&sid=2b80b170524ad90add524d1a42b8a618&rgn=div8&view=text&node=49:7.1.4.1.12.1.1.2&idno=49 [May 2011].

Crosby, R., DiClemente, R., and Salazar, L. (2006). *Research Methods in Health Promotion*. Hoboken, NJ: John Wiley and Sons.

Dargay, J.M., and Hanly, M. (2003). *Travel to Work: An investigation Based on the British Household Panel Survey*. Paper presented at the NECTAR Conference No. 7, Umeå, Sweden. Available: http://www2.cege.ucl.ac.uk/cts/tsu/papers/BHPSNectar03.pdf [May 2011].

Dawson, D., and Reid, K. (1997). Fatigue, alcohol and performance impairment. *Nature 388*(6,639):235-235.

Dawson, D., Ian Noy, Y., Härmä, M., Åkerstedt, T., and Belenky, G. (2011). Modeling fatigue and the use of fatigue models in work settings. *Accident Analysis & Prevention 43*(2):549-564.

Dijk, D.J., Duffy, J.F., and Czeisler, C.A. (1992). Circadian and sleep/wake dependent aspects of subjective alertness and cognitive performance. *Journal of Sleep Research 1*(2):112-117.

Dinges, D.F. (1989). Nap patterns and effects in human adults. In D.F. Dinges and R.J. Broughton (Eds.), *Sleep and Alertness: Chronobiological, Behavioral and Medical Aspects of Napping* (pp. 171-204). New York: Raven Press.

Dinges, D.F. (1995). An overview of sleepiness and accidents. *Journal of Sleep Research 4*:4-14.

Dinges, D.F. (2004). Critical research issues in development of biomathematical models of fatigue and performance. *Aviation Space and Environmental Medicine 75*(3):A181-A191.

Dinges, D.F., and Broughton, R.J. (1989). The significance of napping: A synthesis. In D.F. Dinges and R.J. Broughton (Eds.), *Sleep and Alertness: Chronobiological, Behavioral and Medical Aspects of Napping* (pp. 299-308). New York: Raven Press.

Dinges, D.F., and Kribbs, N.B. (1991). Performing while sleepy: Effects of experimentally induced sleepiness. In T. Monk (Ed.), *Sleep, Sleepiness and Performance* (pp. 97-128). Chichester, UK: John Wiley and Sons.

Dinges, D.F., and Mallis, M.M. (1998). Managing fatigue by drowsiness detection: Can technological promises be realized? In L.R. Hartley (Ed.), *Managing Fatigue in Transportation: Proceedings of the Third International Conference on Fatigue and Transportation.* Oxford, UK: Pergamon Press.

Dinges, D.F., Orne, E.C., Evans, F.J., and Orne, M.T. (1981). Performance afternaps in sleep conducive and alerting environments. In L.C. Johnson, D.I. Tepas, W.P. Colquhoun and M.J. Colligan (Eds.), *Biological Rhythms, Sleep and Shift Work. Advances in Sleep Research* (Vol. 7, pp. 539-552). New York: Spectrum.

Dinges, D.F., Orne, M.T., Whitehouse, W.G., and Orne, E.C. (1987). Temporal placement of a nap for alertness: Contributions of circadian phase and prior wakefulness. *Sleep 10*(4): 313-329.

Dinges, D.F., Graeber, R.C., Rosekind, M.R., and Samel, A. (1996). *Principles and Guidelines for Duty and Rest Scheduling in Commercial Aviation.* NASA Technical Memorandum 110404. Ames Research Center, National Aeronautics and Space Administration. Available: http://www.icao.int/fsix/_Library%5CDuty%20times%20fatigue.pdf [May 2011].

Dinges, D.F., Pack, F., Williams, K., Gillen, K.A., Powell, J.W., Ott, G.E., Aptowicz, C., and Pack, A.I. (1997). Cumulative sleepiness, mood disturbance, and psychomotor vigilance performance decrements during a week of sleep restricted to 4-5 hours per night. *Sleep 20*(4):267-277.

Dinges, D.F., Maislin, G., Brewster, R.M., Krueger, G.P., and Carroll, R.J. (2005). Pilot test of fatigue management technologies. *Journal of the Transportation Research Board* (1922):175-182. Available: http://www.med.upenn.edu/uep/user_documents/Dingesetal.--TRBProceedingspaper05-1234.pdf [July 2011].

Doran, S.M., Van Dongen, H.P.A., and Dinges, D.F. (2001). Sustained attention performance during sleep deprivation: Evidence of state instability. *Archives Italiennes De Biologie 139*(3):253-267.

Drake, C.L., Roehrs, T., Richardson, G., Walsh, J.K., and Roth, T. (2004). Shift-work sleep disorder: Prevalence and consequences beyond that of symptomatic day workers. *Sleep 27*(8):1,453-1,462.

Drummond, S.P.A., and Brown, G.G. (2000). Altered brain response to verbal learning following sleep deprivation. *Nature 403*(6,770):655.

Drummond, S.P.A., Brown, G.G., Stricker, J.L., Buxton, R.B., Wong, E.C., and Gillin, J.C. (1999). Sleep deprivation-induced reduction in cortical functional response to serial subtraction. *Neuroreport 10*(18):3,745-3,748.

Drummond, S.P.A., Bischoff-Grethe, A., Dinges, D.F., Ayalon, L., Mednick, S.C., and Meloy, M.J. (2005). The neural basis of the psychomotor vigilance task. *Sleep 28*(9):1,059-1,068.

Durmer, J.S., and Dinges, D.F. (2005). Neurocognitive consequences of sleep deprivation. *Seminars in Neurology 25*(1):117-129.

Evans, G.W., Wener, R.E., and Phillips, D. (2002). The morning rush hour. *Environment & Behavior 34*(4):521.

Federal Aviation Administration. (2008). *Aviation Fatigue Management Symposium: Partnerships for Solutions.* Washington, DC: Author.

Federal Aviation Administration. (2010a). *Fatigue Risk Management Plan (FMRP) Checklist.* InFO 10017SUP. Available: http://www.faa.gov/other_visit/aviation_industry/airline_operators/airline_safety/info/all_infos/media/2010/InFO10017SUP.pdf [May 2011].

Federal Aviation Administration. (2010b). *Fatigue Risk Management Plans (FRMP) for Part 121 Air Carriers—Part Two.* InFO 10017. Available: http://www.faa.gov/other_visit/aviation_industry/airline_operators/airline_safety/info/all_infos/media/2010/InFO10017.pdf [May 2011].

Federal Aviation Administration. (2010c). Notice of proposed rule making: Flight crewmember duty and rest requirements. *Federal Register 75*(177): 55,855. Available: http://www.gpo.gov/fdsys/pkg/FR-2010-09-14/pdf/2010-22626.pdf [May 2011].

Federal Aviation Administration. (n.d.). *Aviation Safety Information Analysis and Sharing System* (ASIAS). Available: http://www.asias.faa.gov/portal/page/portal/asias_pages/asias_home/datainfo:databases:k-o) [May 2011].

Fetterman, D.M. (2010). *Ethnography: Step by Step–Third Edition.* Applied Social Research Methods Series (Vol. 17). Thousand Oaks, CA: Sage.

Flight Safety Foundation Editorial Staff. (2005). Fourth workshop yields insights into early ultra-long-range flight experience. *Flight Safety Digest 24*(8):1-15.

Folkard, S., Lombardi, D.A., and Tucker, P.T. (2005). Shift work: Safety, sleepiness, and sleep. *Industrial Health 43*(1):20-23.

Foushee, H.C., Lauber, J.K., Baetge, M.M., and Acomb, D.B. (1986). *Crew Factors in Flight Operations: III. The operational significance of exposure to short-haul air transport operations.* NASA Technical Memorandum 88322. Moffett Field, California: NASA Ames Research Center. Available: http://human-factors.arc.nasa.gov/zteam/PDF_pubs/Flight_Ops/Short_Haul_III/Flight_Ops_III.pdf [June 2011].

Gallup, Inc. (2007). *Workers Average Commute Round-Trip Is 46 Minutes in a Typical Day.* Gallup News Service. Available: http://www.gallup.com/poll/28504/workers-average-commute-roundtrip-minutes-typical-day.aspx [May 2011].

Goel, N., Banks, S., Mignot, E., and Dinges, D.F. (2009a). PER3 polymorphism predicts cumulative sleep homeostatic but not neurobehavioral changes to chronic partial sleep deprivation. *PLoS ONE 4*(6):e5874.

Goel, N., Rao, H., Durmer, J.S., and Dinges, D.F. (2009b). Neurocognitive consequences of sleep deprivation. *Seminars in Neurology 29*(4):320-339.

Goel, N., Banks, S., Mignot, E., and Dinges, D.F. (2010). DQB1*0602 predicts inter-individual differences in physiologic sleep, sleepiness, and fatigue. *Neurology 75*(17):1,509-1,519.

Goel, N., Van Dongen, H.P.A., and Dinges, D.F. (2011). Circadian rhythm in sleepiness, alertness and performance. In M.H. Kryger, T. Roth, and W.C. Dement (Eds.), *Principles and Practice of Sleep Medicine* (5th edition, pp. 4,445-4,455). Philadelphia, PA: Elsevier.

Habeck, C., Rakitin, B.C., Moeller, J., Scarmeas, N., Zarahn, E., Brown, T., and Stern, Y. (2004). An event-related fMRI study of the neurobehavioral impact of sleep deprivation on performance of a delayed-match-to-sample task. *Cognitive Brain Research 18*(3):306.

Harrison, Y., and Horne, J.A. (2000). The impact of sleep deprivation on decision making: A review. *Journal of Experimental Psychology: Applied* 6(3):236-249.

Helmreich R.L. (2000). On error management: Lessons from aviation. *British Medical Journal* 320:781-785.

Helmreich, R.L., and Foushee, H.C. (2010). Why CRM? Empirical and theoretical bases of human factors training. In B. Kanki, R. Helmreich, and J. Anca (Eds.), *Crew Resource Management* (2nd ed., pp. 3-58). San Diego, CA: Academic Press.

Helmreich, R.L., Merritt, A.C., and Wilhelm, J.A. (1999). The evolution of crew resource management training in commercial aviation. *International Journal of Aviation Psychology* 9(1):19.

Hennessy, D.A., and Wiesenthal, D.L. (1999). Traffic congestion, driver stress, and driver aggression. *Aggressive Behavior* 25(6):409-423.

Horrey, W.J., Noy, Y.I., Folkard, S., Popkin, S.M., Howarth, H.D., and Courtney, T.K. (2011). Research needs and opportunities for reducing the adverse safety consequences of fatigue. *Accident Analysis & Prevention* 43(2):591-594.

Hursh, S.R., Raslear, T.G., Kaye, A.S., and Fanzone, J.F. (2008). *Validation and Calibration of a Fatigue Assessment Tool for Railroad Work Schedules, Final Report.* Washington, DC: U.S. Department of Transportation. Available: http://www.fra.dot.gov/downloads/research/ord0804.pdf [June 2011].

Institute of Medicine. (2006). *Sleep Disorders and Sleep Deprivation: An Unmet Public Health Problem.* Committee on Sleep Medicine and Research, H.R. Colten and B.M. Altevogt, Eds. Board on Health Sciences Policy. Washington, DC: The National Academies Press.

Institute of Medicine. (2009). *Resident Duty Hours: Enhancing Sleep, Supervision, and Safety.* Committee on Optimizing Graduate Medical Trainee (Resident) Hours and Work Schedule to Improve Patient Safety, C. Ulmer, D.M. Wolman, and M.M.E. Johns, Eds. Washington, DC: The National Academies Press.

International Civil Aviation Organization. (2002). *Line Operations Safety Audit (LOSA).* Montreal, Canada: International Civil Aviation Organization.

International Civil Aviation Organization. (2009). *The ICAO Fatigue Risk Management Systems Task Force.* Presentation by M.A. Fox, Chief, Flight Safety Section, ICAO. Available: http://www.icao.int/nacc/meetings/2009/RASGPA02/Pres/Day3/3-3/rasg-pa_2%20fatigue.pdf [August 2010].

International Civil Aviation Organization. (2011a). *FRMS Manual for Regulators.* Available: http://www2.icao.int/en/FatigueManagement/FRMS%20Tools/Doc%209966%20-%20FRMS%20Manual%20for%20Regulators.pdf [July 2011].

International Civil Aviation Organization. (2011b). *Proposed Amendment to International Standards and Recommended Practices Operation of Aircraft.* Annex 6, Part 1, Chapter 4.10 Fatigue Management and Appendix 8. Fatigue Risk Management System Requirements. Available: http://frmsc.com/services-2/frmsc-implementation/icao-sarp/ [July 2011].

Jain, J., and Lyons, G. (2008). The gift of travel time. *Journal of Transport Geography* 16(2):81-89.

Jewett, M.E., Borbely, A.A., and Czeisler, C.A. (Eds.). (1999a). Proceedings of the workshop on biomathematical models of circadian rhythmicity, sleep regulation, and neurobehavioral function in humans. *Journal of Biological Rhythms* 14(6).

Jewett, M.E., Wyatt, J.K., Ritz-De Cecco, A., Khalsa, S.B., Dijk, D.-J., and Czeisler, C.A. (1999b). Time course of sleep inertia dissipation in human performance and alertness. *Journal of Sleep Research* 8(1):1-8.

Killgore, W.D.S., Balkin, T.J., and Wesensten, N.J. (2006). Impaired decision making following 49 hours of sleep deprivation. *Journal of Sleep Research* 15(1):7-13.

Kleitman, N. (1963). *Sleep and Wakefulness* (revised and enlarged edition). Chicago, IL: University of Chicago Press.

Klinect, J. (2002). LOSA searches for operational weaknesses while highlighting systemic strengths. *ICAO Journal 57*(4):8-9.

Kluger, A.V. (1998). Commute variability and strain. *Journal of Organizational Behaviour 19*:147–165.

Kripke, D.F., Garfinkel, L., Wingard, D.L., Klauber, M.R., and Marler, M.R. (2002). Mortality associated with sleep duration and insomnia. *Archives of General Psychiatry 59*(2):131-136.

Kuchar, J.K., and Drumm, A.C. (2007). The traffic alert and collision avoidance system. *MIT Lincoln Laboratory Journal 16*(2):277-295.

Lamond, N., and Dawson, D. (1999). The dynamics of neurobehavioural recovery following sleep loss. *Journal of Sleep Research* 16:33-41.

Lamond, N., Jay, S.M., Dorrian, J., Ferguson, S.A., Jones, C., and Dawson, D. (2007). The dynamics of neurobehavioural recovery following sleep loss. *Journal of Sleep Research 16*(1):33-41.

Lauderdale, D.S., Knutson, K.L., Yan, L.L., Liu, K., and Rathouz, P.J. (2008). Self-reported and measured sleep duration: How similar are they? *Epidemiology 19*(6):838-845.

Lave, C., and Elias, P. (1994). Did the 65 mph speed limit save lives? *Accident Analysis and Prevention 26*(1):49-62.

Leproult, R., Colecchia, E.F., Berardi, A.M., Stickgold, R., Kosslyn, S.M., and Van Cauter, E. (2003). Individual differences in subjective and objective alertness during sleep deprivation are stable and unrelated. *American Journal of Physiology: Regulatory, Integrative & Comparative Physiology 53*(2):R280.

Lim, J., and Dinges, D.F. (2010). A meta-analysis of the impact of short-term sleep deprivation on cognitive variables. *Psychological Bulletin 136*(3):375-389.

Lim, J., Choo, W., and Chee, M. (2007). Reproducibility of changes in behavior and FMRI activation associated with sleep deprivation in a working memory task. *Sleep 30*:363.

Lim, J., Tan, J.C., Parimal, S., Dinges, D.F., and Chee, M.W.L. (2010). Sleep deprivation impairs object-selective attention: A view from the ventral visual cortex. *PLoS ONE 5*(2):e9087.

Lyons, G., and Chatterjee, K. (2008). A human perspective on the daily commute: Costs, benefits and trade-offs. *Transport Reviews 28*(2):181-198.

Lyons, G., Jain, J., and Holley, D. (2007). The use of travel time by rail passengers in Great Britain. *Transportation Research Part A—Policy and Practice 41*(1):107-120.

Mallis, M.M., Mejdal, S., Nguyen, T.T., and Dinges, D.F. (2004). Summary of features of seven biomathematical models of human fatigue and performance. *Aviation Space and Environmental Medicine 75*(3):A4-A14.

Matsumoto, K., and Harada, M. (1994). The effect of night-time naps on recovery from fatigue following night work. *Ergonomics 37*(5):899-907.

McCauley, P., Kalachev, L.V., Smith, A.D., Belenky, G., Dinges, D.F., and Van Dongen, H.P.A. (2009). A new mathematical model for the homeostatic effects of sleep loss on neurobehavioral performance. *Journal of Theoretical Biology 256*(2):227-239.

McKenna, B.S., Dicjinson, D.L., Orff, H.J., and Drummond, S.P.A. (2007). The effects of one night of sleep deprivation on known-risk and ambiguous-risk decisions. *Journal of Sleep Research 16*(3):245-252.

Merton, R.K. (1936). The unanticipated consequences of purposive social action. *American Sociological Review 1*(6):894-904.

Mitler, M.M., Carskadon, M.A., Czeisler, C.A., Dement, W.C., Dinges, D.F., and Graeber, R.C. (1988). Catastrophes, sleep and public policy-consensus report. *Sleep 11*(1):100-109.

Mokhtarian, P.L., and Salomon, I. (2001). How derived is the demand for travel? Some conceptual and measurement considerations. *Transportation Research Part A—Policy and Practice 35*(8):695-719.

Mollicone, D.J., Van Dongen, H.P.A., and Dinges, D.F. (2007). Optimizing sleep/wake schedules in space: Sleep during chronic nocturnal sleep restriction with and without diurnal naps. *Acta Astronautica 60*(4-7):354-361.

Morse, J., and Richards, L. (2002). *Read Me First: A User's Guide to Qualitative Methods.* Thousand Oaks, CA: Sage.

National Aeronautics and Space Administration. (n.d.). *Aviation Safety Reporting System (ASRS).* Available: http://asrs.arc.nasa.gov/search/database.html [May 2011].

National Research Council. (1984). *A Decade of Experience, Special Report 204.* Transportation Research Board. Washington, DC: National Academy Press.

National Research Council. (2007). *Human-System Integration in the System Development Process: A New Look.* Committee on Human-System Design Support for Changing Technology. R.W. Pew and A.S. Mavor, Eds. Washington, DC: The National Academies Press.

National Research Council. (2010). *Achieving Traffic Safety in the United States: Lessons from Other Nations.* Transportation Research Board, TRB Special Report 300. Washington, DC: The National Academies Press.

National Research Council. (2011). *The Effects of Commuting on Pilot Fatigue.* Committee on the Effects of Commuting on Pilot Fatigue, Board on Human-Systems Integration, Division of Behavioral and Social Sciences and Education. Washington, DC: The National Academies Press. Available: http://www.nap.edu/catalog.php?record_id=13097 [May 2011].

National Transportation Safety Board. (1994a). *American International Airways: Uncontrolled Collision with Terrain.* Washington, DC. Available: http://libraryonline.erau.edu/online-full-text/ntsb/aircraft-accident-reports/AAR94-04.pdf [May 2011].

National Transportation Safety Board. (1994b). *A Review of Flightcrew-Involved Major Accidents of U.S. Air Carriers, 1978 Through 1990.* Washington, DC: National Transportation Safety Board.

National Transportation Safety Board. (1999). *Accident Report in Brief, American Eagle: Overrun.* Available: http://www.asias.faa.gov/portal/pls/portal/STAGE.NTSB_BRIEF_REPORT?EV_ID=20001212X18850&AC_VAR=FALSE&ENG_VAR=FALSE&INJ_VAR=FALSE&FT_VAR=FALSE&OCC_VAR=FALSE&WTHR_VAR=FALSE&PNARR_VAR=FALSE&FNARR_VAR=FALSE&CNARR_VAR=FALSE&NARR_VAR=american%20eagle%0D%0A [May 2011].

National Transportation Safety Board. (2001). *Runway Overrun During Landing, American Airlines Flight 1420, McDonnell Douglas MD-82, N215AA, Little Rock, Arkansas, June 1, 1999. Aircraft Accident Report NTSB/AAR-01/02.* Washington, DC. Available: http://www.ntsb.gov/publictn/2001/AAR0102.pdf [May 2011].

National Transportation Safety Board. (2004). *Collision with Trees on Final Approach, Federal Express Flight 1478, Boeing 727-232, N497FE, Tallahassee, Florida, July 26, 2002. Aircraft Accident Report NTSB/AAR-04/02.* Washington, DC. Available: http://www.ntsb.gov/publictn/2004/AAR0402.pdf [May 2011].

National Transportation Safety Board. (2006). *Collision with Trees and Crash Short of Runway, Corporate Airlines Flight 5966, British Aerospace BAE-J3201, N875JX, Kirksville, Missouri, October 19, 2004. Aircraft Accident Report NTSB/AAR-06/01.* Washington, DC. Available: http://www.ntsb.gov/doclib/reports/2006/AAR0601.pdf [May 2011].

National Transportation Safety Board. (2008a). *Runway Overrun During Landing, Pinnacle Airlines, Inc., Flight 4712, Bombardier/Canadair Regional Jet CL600-2B19, N8905F, Traverse City, Michigan, April 12, 2007. Aircraft Accident Report NTSB/AAR-08/02.* Washington, DC. Available: http://www.ntsb.gov/doclib/reports/2008/AAR0802.pdf [May 2011].

National Transportation Safety Board. (2008b). *Runway Overrun During Landing, Shuttle America, Inc., Doing Business as Delta Connection Flight 6448, Embraer ERJ-170, N862RW, Cleveland, Ohio, February 18, 2007. Aircraft Accident Report NTSB/AAR 08/01*. Washington, DC. Available: http://www.ntsb.gov/doclib/reports/2008/AAR0801.pdf [May 2011].

National Transportation Safety Board. (2009). *Accident Report in Brief, World Airways: Landing-Flare/Touchdown—Abnormal Runway Contact* Available: http://www.asias.faa.gov/portal/pls/portal/STAGE.NTSB_BRIEF_REPORT?EV_ID=20090507X00926&AC_VAR=FALSE&ENG_VAR=FALSE&INJ_VAR=FALSE&FT_VAR=FALSE&OCC_VAR=FALSE&WTHR_VAR=FALSE&PNARR_VAR=FALSE&FNARR_VAR=FALSE&CNARR_VAR=FALSE&NARR_VAR=world%20airways [May 2011].

National Transportation Safety Board. (2010a). *Aviation: Statistical Review NTSB/ARC 10-01*. Available: http://www.ntsb.gov/publictn/2010/ARC1001.pdf [May 2011].

National Transportation Safety Board. (2010b). *Loss of Control on Approach, Colgan Air, Inc., Operating as Continental Connection Flight 3407, Bombardier DHC-8-400, N200WQ, Clarence Center, New York, February 12, 2009. NTSB/AAR-10/01*. Washington, DC. Available: http://www.ntsb.gov/publictn/2010/AAR1001.pdf [May 2011].

National Transportation Safety Board. (2011). *Crash During Approach to Landing, Empire Airlines Flight 8284, Avions de Transport Régional Aerospatiale Alenia ATR 42-320, N902FX, Lubbock, Texas, January 27, 2009. Aircraft Accident Report NTSB/AAR-11/02*. Washington, DC. Available: http://www.ntsb.gov/doclib/reports/2011/AAR1102.pdf [May 2011].

National Transportation Safety Board. (n.d.). *Aviation Accident Statistics*. Available: http://www.ntsb.gov/aviation/Stats.htm [May 2011].

Neri, D.F. (2004). Preface: Fatigue and performance modeling workshop, June 13-14, 2002. *Aviation Space & Environmental Medicine 75*:A1-A3.

Nicholson, A.N., and Stone, B.M. (1987). Influence of back angle on the quality of sleep in seats. *Ergonomics 30*(7):1,033-1,041.

Ohayon, M.M., Carskadon, M.A., Guilleminault, C., and Vitiello, M.V. (2004). Meta-analysis of quantitative sleep parameters from childhood to old age in healthy individuals: Developing normative sleep values across the human lifespan. *Sleep 27*(7):1,255-1,273.

Oster, C.V., and Strong, J.S. (2006). Evolution of U.S. domestic airline route networks since 1990. *Transportation Research Record: Journal of the Transportation Research Board* (1951):52-59.

Oster, C.V., Strong, J.S., and Zorn, K.C. (1992). *Why Airplanes Crash: Aviation Safety in a Changing World*. New York: Oxford University Press.

Petrilli, R.M., Roach, G.D., Dawson, D., and Lamond, N. (2006). The sleep, subjective fatigue, and sustained attention of commercial airline pilots during an international pattern. *Chronobiology International: The Journal of Biological & Medical Rhythm Research 23*(6):1,347-1,362.

Petrilli, R.M., Thomas, M.J.W., Lamond, N., Dawson, D., and Roach, G.D. (2007). Effects of flight duty and sleep on the decision making of commercial airline pilots. In J.M. Anca (Ed.), *Multimodal Safety Management and Human Factors* (pp. 259-270). Aldershot, UK: Ashgate.

Philibert, I. (2005). Sleep loss and performance in residents and nonphysicians: A meta-analytic examination. *Sleep 28*(11):1,392-1,402.

Portas, C.M., Bjorvatn, B., Fagerland, S., Gronli, J., Mundal, V., Sorensen, E., and Ursin, R. (1998a). On-line detection of extracellular levels of serotonin in dorsal raphe nucleus and frontal cortex over the sleep/wake cycle in the freely moving rat. *Neuroscience 83*(3):807-814.

Portas, C.M., Rees, G., Howseman, A.M., Josephs, O., Turner, R., and Frith, C.D. (1998b). A specific role for the thalamus in mediating the interaction of attention and arousal in humans. *Journal of Neuroscience 18*(21):8,979-8,989.

Pronovost, P., Needham, D., Berenholtz, S., Sinopoli, D., Chu, H., Cosgrove, S., Sexton, B., Hyzy, R., Welsh, R., Roth, G., Bander, J., Kepros, J., and Goeschel, C. (2006). An intervention to decrease catheter-related bloodstream infections in the ICU. *New England Journal of Medicine 355*(26):2,725-2,732.

Roach, G.D., Darwent, D., and Dawson, D. (2010). How well do pilots sleep during long-haul flights? *Ergonomics 53*(9):1,072-1,075.

Rogers, A.S., Spencer, M.B., Stone, B.M., and Nicholson, A.N. (1989). The influence of a 1-H nap on performance overnight. *Ergonomics 32*(10):1,193-1,205.

Rosa, R.R. (1993). Napping at home and alertness on the job in rotating shift workers. *Sleep 16*(8):727-735.

Rosa, R.R. (2001). Examining work schedules for fatigue: It's not just hours of work. In P.A. Hancock and P.A. Desmond (Eds.), *Stress, Workload, and Fatigue* (pp. 513-528). Mahwah, NJ: Lawrence Erlbaum Associates.

Rosekind, M.R., Graeber, R.C., Dinges, D.F., Connell, L.J., Rountree, M.S., Spinweber, C.L., and Gillen, K.A. (1994). *Crew Factors in Flight Operations IX: Effects of Planned Cockpit Rest on Crew Performance and Alertness in Long-Haul Operations.* NASA Technical Memorandum 108839. Moffett Field, CA: NASA Ames Research Center. Available: http://human-factors.arc.nasa.gov/zteam/PDF_pubs/Flight_Ops/Cockpit_Rest_IX/NASA_TM_94_108839.pdf [May 2011].

Rosekind, M.R., Miller, D.L., Gregory, K.B., and Dinges, D.F. (2000). *Crew Factors in Flight Operations XII: A Survey of Sleep Quantity and Quality in On-Board Crew Rest Facilities.* NASA Technical Memorandum 2000-209611. Moffett Field, CA: NASA Ames Research Center. Available: http://human-factors.arc.nasa.gov/zteam/PDF_pubs/Flight_Ops/Flight_Ops_XII_CrewRestSurv.pdf [May 2011].

Rupp, T.L., Wesensten, N.J., Bliese, P.D., and Balkin, T.J. (2009). Banking sleep: Realization of benefits during subsequent sleep restriction and recovery. *Sleep 32*(3):311-321.

Tassi, P., and Muzet, A. (2000). Sleep inertia. *Sleep Medicine Reviews 4*(4):341-353.

Thomas, M.J.W., and Ferguson, S.A. (2010). Prior sleep, prior sake, and crew performance during normal flight operations. *Aviation Space and Environmental Medicine 81*(7):665-670.

Thomas, M., Sing, H., Belenky, G., Holcomb, H., Mayberg, H., Dannals, R., Wagner, H., Thorne, D., Popp, K., Rowland, L., Welsh, A., Balwinski, S., and Redmond, D. (2000). Neural basis of alertness and cognitive performance impairments during sleepiness. Effects of 24 hours of sleep deprivation on waking human regional brain activity. *Journal of Sleep Research 9*(4):335-352.

Thomas, M.J.W., Petrilli, R.M., Lamond, N., Dawson, D., and Roach, G.D. (2006). Australian long-haul fatigue study. *Proceedings of the 59th Annual International Aviation Safety Seminar.* Paris, France: Flight Safety Foundation.

Thorpy, M.J. (2011). Circadian rhythm in sleepiness, alertness and performance. In M.H. Kryger, T. Roth, and W.C. Dement (Eds.), *Principles and Practice of Sleep Medicine* (5th ed., pp. 680-693). Philadelphia, PA: Elsevier.

Ulin, P., Robinson, E., and Tolley, E. (2004). *Qualitative Methods in Public Health: A Field Guide for Applied Research.* San Francisco, CA: Jossey-Bass.

U.S. Department of Transportation. (2009). *2009 International Conference on Fatigue Management in Transportation Operations: A Framework for Progress.* Boston, MA. Available: http://depts.washington.edu/uwconf/fmto/ [May 2011].

U.S. Department of Transportation. (2010a). *Federal Aviation Administration Advisory Circular, Subject: Fatigue Risk Management Systems for Aviation Safety.* AC No: AC 120-103. Available: http://www.airweb.faa.gov/Regulatory_and_Guidance_Library/rgAdvisory Circular.nsf/0/0fce45047cad59278625777d006ae5ca/$FILE/AC%20120-103.pdf [May 2011].

U.S. Department of Transportation. (2010b). *Federal Aviation Administration Advisory Circular, Subject: Fitness for Duty.* AC No: AC 120-FIT. Available: http://www.regulations.gov/#!documentDetail;D=FAA-2009-1093-0022 [May 2011].

Van Dongen, H.P.A. (2004). Comparison of mathematical model predictions to experimental data of fatigue and performance. *Aviation Space and Environmental Medicine 75*(3):A15-A36.

Van Dongen, H.P.A. (2006). Shift work and inter-individual differences in sleep and sleepiness. *Chronobiology International: The Journal of Biological & Medical Rhythm Research 23*(6):1,139-1,147.

Van Dongen, H.P.A., and Dinges, D.F. (2005). Circadian rhythms in sleepiness, alertness, and performance. In M.H. Kryger, T. Roth, and W.C. Dement (Eds.), *Principles and Practice of Sleep Medicine* (pp. 435-443). Philadelphia, PA: Elsevier.

Van Dongen, H.P.A., Maislin, G., Mullington, J.M., and Dinges, D.F. (2003a). The cumulative cost of additional wakefulness: Dose-response effects on neurobehavioral functions and sleep physiology from chronic sleep restriction and total sleep deprivation. *Sleep 26*(2):117-126.

Van Dongen, H.P.A., Rogers, N. L., and Dinges, D.F. (2003b). Sleep debt: Theoretical and empirical issues. *Sleep and Biological Rhythms 1*(1):5-13.

Van Dongen, H.P.A., Baynard, M.D., Maislin, G., and Dinges, D.F. (2004). Systematic interindividual differences in neurobehavioral impairment from sleep loss: Evidence of trait-like differential vulnerability. *Sleep 27*(3):423-433.

Venkatraman, V., Chuah, Y.M.L., Huettel, S.A., and Chee, M.W.L. (2007). Sleep deprivation elevates expectation of gains and attenuates response to losses following risky decisions. *Sleep 30*(5):603-609.

Vgontzas, A.N., Pejovic, S., Zoumakis, E., Lin, H.M., Bixler, E.O., Basta, M., Fang, J., Sarrigiannidis, A., and Chrousos, G.P. (2007). Daytime napping after a night of sleep loss decreases sleepiness, improves performance, and causes beneficial changes in cortisol and interleukin-6 secretion. *American Journal of Physiology: Endocrinology & Metabolism 55*(1):E253-E261.

Viscusi, W.K. (1994). Risk-risk analysis. *Journal of Risk and Uncertainty 8*(1):5-17.

Viscusi, W.K., and Zeckhauser, R.J. (1994). The fatality and injury costs of expenditures. *Journal of Risk and Uncertainty 8*(1):19-41.

Walsleben, J.A., Norman, R.G., Novak, R.D., O'Malley, E.B., Rapoport, D.M., and Strohl, K.P. (1999). Sleep habits of Long Island rail road commuters. *Sleep 22*(6):728-734.

Webb, W.B. (1987). The proximal effects of two and four hour naps within extended performance without sleep. *Psychophysiology 24*(4):426-429.

Werfelman, L., Rash, C.E., and Manning, S.D. (2009). Rest in place. *AeroSafety World 4*(12):38-42.

Wiener, E.L., and Nagel, D.C. (1988). *Human Factors in Aviation.* San Diego, CA: Academic Press.

Williamson, A.M., and Feyer, A.M. (2000). Moderate sleep deprivation produces impairments in cognitive and motor performance equivalent to legally prescribed levels of alcohol intoxication. *Occupational and Environmental Medicine 57*(10):649-655.

Williamson, A., Lombardi, D.A., Folkard, S., Stutts, J., Courtney, T.K., and Connor, J.L. (2011). The link between fatigue and safety. *Accident Analysis & Prevention 43*(2):498-515.

Windle, R.J., and Dresner, M.E. (1991). Mandatory child safety seats in air transport: Do they save lives? *Journal of the Transportation Research Forum 31*(2):309-316.

Wolcott, H. (1994). *Transforming Qualitative Data: Description, Analysis and Interpretation.* Thousand Oaks, CA: Sage.

Wu, J.C., Gillin, J.C., Buchsbaum, M.S., Chen, P., Keator, D.B., Khosla Wu, N., Darnall, L.A., Fallon, J.H., and Bunney, W.E. (2006). Frontal lobe metabolic decreases with sleep deprivation not totally reversed by recovery sleep. *Neuropsychopharmacology 31*(12):2,783-2,792.

Acronyms

ARC	Aviation Rulemaking Committee
ASIAS	Aviation Safety Information Analysis and Sharing
ASRS	Aviation Safety Reporting System
BOHSI	Board on Human-System Integration
BTS	Bureau of Transportation Statistics
CASS	Cockpit Access Security System
CFR	Code of Federal Regulations
CRM	Crew Resource Management
DBASSE	Division of Behavioral and Social Sciences and Education
FAA	Federal Aviation Administration
FAR	Federal Aviation Regulation
FDP	flight duty period
FRMP	fatigue risk management plan
FRMS	fatigue risk management system
GPWS	Ground Proximity Warning System
ICAO	International Civil Aviation Organization
IOM	Institute of Medicine
NAS	National Academy of Sciences

NASA	National Aeronautics and Space Administration
NPRM	Notice of Proposed Rulemaking
NTSB	National Transportation Safety Board
SARP	Standards and Recommended Practice
TCAS	Traffic Collision Avoidance Systems

Glossary

14 CFR Part 121: federal flight duty time regulations.

AC-120 FIT: As a complement to issuance of the NPRM, the FAA issued a draft advisory circular (AC 120-FIT) on fitness for duty.

Air carriers: a commercial carrier utilizing aircraft as its means of transport; an airline, as for passengers or freight.

Airport/standby reserve: a defined duty period during which a crew member is required by a certificate holder to be at, or in close proximity to, an airport for a possible assignment.[1]

Cargo airlines: air carriers with flights for the purpose of delivering goods to locations.

Charter airlines: air carriers that provide nonscheduled passenger flights.

Circadian rhythms: daily (24-hour) rhythms instantiated in microbiology, physiology and behavior that control the timing of the sleep-wake cycle and influence physical and cognitive performance, activity, food consumption, body temperature, cardiovascular rhythms, muscle tone, and aspects

[1]*Federal Register,* "Notice of Proposed Rule Making: Flight Crew Member Duty and Rest," September 14, 2010, Volume 75, Number 177.

of hormone secretion and immune responses, as well as many other physiological functions.

Commuting: the period of time and the activity required of pilots from leaving home to arriving at the domicile (airport—in the crew room, dispatch room, or designated location at the airport) and from leaving the domicile back to home.

Crash pads: temporary living arrangements shared among groups of pilots.

Crew pairing: a flight duty period or series of flight duty periods assigned to a flight crew member which originate or terminate at the flight crew member's home base.[2]

Crew Resource Management (CRM): the application of procedure and training through a team management system designed to address the challenge of optimizing the human/machine and human/human interfaces. Includes all groups routinely working with the flight crew who are involved in decisions required to operate a flight safely.

Deadhead transportation: transportation of a crew member as a passenger, by air or surface transportation, as required by a certificate holder, excluding transportation to or from a suitable accommodation.[3]

Deadheading: term used when travel is provided to members of a flight crew in order to position them appropriately for duty. According to FAA regulations, deadheading is considered to be part of their work, or duty time.

Domicile: the airport where a pilot begins and ends a duty period.

Duty: any task, other than long-call reserve, that a crew member performs on behalf of the certificate holder, including but not limited to airport/standby reserve, short-call reserve, flight duty, preflight and postflight duties, administrative work, training, deadhead transportation, aircraft positioning on the ground, aircraft loading, and aircraft servicing.[4]

Duty period: a period that begins when a certificate holder requires a crew

[2]Ibid.
[3]Ibid.
[4]Ibid.

member to report for duty and ends when that crew member is free from all duties.[5]

Fatigue: a physiological state of reduced mental or physical performance capability resulting from lack of sleep or increased physical activity that can reduce a crew member's alertness and ability to safely operate an aircraft or perform safety-related duties.[6]

Fatigue risk management plans (FRMPs): the airline carriers' management plans outlining policies and procedures reducing the risk of flight crew member fatigue and improving flight crew member alertness.

Fatigue risk management systems (FRMSs): a data-driven and scientifically based process that allows for continuous monitoring and management of safety risks associated with fatigue-related error. It is part of a repeating performance improvement process. This process leads to continuous safety enhancements by identifying and addressing fatigue factors across time and changing physiological and operational circumstances.[7]

First officer: the member of a flight crew who is second in command to the captain.

Fit for duty: physiologically and mentally prepared and capable of performing assigned duties in flight with the highest degree of safety.[8]

Flight crew: the people involved in operating an aircraft in flight, includes pilots, flight engineers, flight navigators, and cabin attendants assigned to duty in an aircraft during flight time.

Flight duty period (FDP): a period that begins when a flight crew member is required to report for duty with the intention of conducting a flight, a series of flights, or positioning or ferrying flights, and ends when the aircraft is parked after the last flight and there is no intention for further aircraft movement by the same flight crew member. A flight duty period includes deadhead transportation before a flight segment without an intervening required rest period, training conducted in an aircraft, flight simulator or flight training device, and airport/standby reserve.[9]

---

[5]Ibid.
[6]Ibid.
[7]Ibid.
[8]Ibid.
[9]Ibid.

Gateway basing: the airline arranges a flight (when necessary) from a specified gateway city to the departure city of the pilot's first flight, and the pilot is responsible for the commute from home to the gateway city.

Home: the pilot's residence.

Home basing: the airline arranges a reserved seat on a flight from the pilot's home location to the city from which the pilot's flight departs.

Hub: a focal airport for the routing of aircraft and passengers.

Hub-and-spoke: a system where many flights converge on one airport (the hub) at about the same time so that passengers and cargo can connect conveniently to a flight that is going to the ultimate destination (a spoke).

Jumpseat: an additional observer seat on the flight deck available to other pilots by courtesy of the captain.

Long-call reserve: a reserve period in which a crew member receives a required rest period following notification by the certificate holder to report for duty.[10]

Long-haul: flights are that involve long distances, typically beyond 6 hours in length, and often are nonstop flights.

Mainline airlines: air carriers that predominately operate scheduled service in jet aircraft with more than 90 seats and often provide intercontinental service.

Nonrevenue travel: free or reduced-rate (nonrevenue) travel.

Overnighting: assignment by an airline for a flight crew member to spend a required rest period at a location that is not the pilot's domicile, normally including prearranged accommodations and local transportation; see also layover.

Part 91 ferry: a flight with no paid passengers or cargo aboard, performed to position an aircraft to a desired location such as to perform its next

[10]Ibid.

revenue flight; alternatively, a flight of an aircraft that is not airworthy, performed under provisions of a "ferry permit."[11]

Part 121: This phrase refers to most passenger and cargo airlines that fly transport-category aircraft with 10 or more seats.

Regional airlines: air carriers that predominately operate scheduled service in aircraft, both jet and turboprop, with 90 or fewer seats.

[11]Federal Aviation Administration. (n.d.). *Special Flight Permits*. Available: http://www.faa.gov/about/office_org/field_offices/fsdo/phl/local_more/media/ferry_permit.pdf [June 2011].

Appendix A

Airlines, Associations, and Groups That Provided Written Input

The committee received a wide range of written input from airlines, associations, and groups. This input was comprised of either one or more of the following: general responses to the questions posed by written requests (see Box 1-3, in Chapter 1), home-to-domicile zip code information for airline pilots (for 24 airlines); and information specific to relevant airline policies and fatigue risk management plans.

AIRLINES

ADI
Air Wisconsin Airlines Corporation
Aloha Air Cargo
Ameristar Air Cargo, Inc.
Atlantic Southeast Airlines, Inc.
Atlas Air Worldwide (Atlas and Polar Air Cargo)
Capital Cargo
Colgan
CommutAir Champlain Enterprises
Compass Airlines
Delta Air Lines
Empire
Era Aviation
Everts Air Cargo
Federal Express
Florida West International Airways, Inc.

GoJet_Trans States Holdings
JetBlue
Miami Air International, Inc.
North American Airlines
Omni Air International, Inc.
Pinnacle
PSA Airlines, Inc
Seaborne Airlines
Trans States Airlines
United Continental
UPS
US Airways
USA Jet Airlines
USA 3000 Brendan Airways
Virgin America
World Airways
Unidentified Airline*

ASSOCIATIONS AND GROUPS

Cargo Airline Association
Coalition of Airline Pilots Associations
National Air Carriers Association
U.S. Airline Pilots Association

*This airline requested not to be identified.

Appendix B

Public Meeting Agendas

Meeting 1: Monday, November 22, 2010

9:45 am Public Welcome and Study
- *Connie Citro*, interim deputy director, Division of Behavioral and Social Sciences and Education (DBASSE)
- *Clint Oster*, chair, Committee on the Effects of Commuting on Pilot Fatigue

Committee Member and Staff Introductions
Participant Introductions

10:00 am Sponsor Perspective
Charge and Expectations of the Study
- *Dale E. Roberts*, aviation safety inspector, Air Transportation Division, Federal Aviation Administration (FAA)

Questions and Discussion

11:00 am NTSB Comments
- *Mark Rosekind*, member, National Transportation Safety Board

Questions and Discussion

12:00 pm Working Lunch
Topics: Informal Discussion with Presenters

12:45 pm Relevant Research
Flight Attendant Fatigue Study
- *Thomas Nesthus*, Civil Aerospace Medical Institute, FAA

Human Factors Monitoring Program: Fatigue Risk Management Scientific Study
- *Jessica Nowinski*, National Aeronautics and Space Administration Ames Research Center (with Irving Statler participating by phone)

Questions and Discussion

2:15 pm Stakeholder Comments
- *Charlotte O'Connell*, pilot
- *Jeff Skiles*, U.S. Airline Pilots Association

Questions and Discussion

3:00 pm Adjourn Open Session

Meeting 2: Monday, December 20, 2010

10:00 am Welcome and Introductions
- *Robert M. Hauser*, interim executive director, DBASSE
- *Clint Oster*, committee chair

10:15 am Stakeholder and Public Comments: Part I
- *Captain (retired) Bill Mims*, A Pilot's Perspective
- *Steven Sargent*, Compass Airlines

11:15 am An Ongoing Study on Commuting and Pilot Fatigue
- *Lori Brown*, faculty specialist, Western Michigan University College of Aviation (via teleconference)

12:15 pm Working Lunch
Lunch will be served in the meeting room.
Topics: Discussion with Presenters

1:00 pm Stakeholder and Public Comments: Part II
- Airline Pilots Association, Intl., *Captain Bill Soer,* flight and duty time committee member
- National Air Carriers Association, *George Paul*, director, Technical Services
- Coalition of Airline Pilots Associations, *Captain Bob Coffman*

2:30 pm General Discussion with Guests

3:00 pm Break

3:15 pm Learning Lessons for the Railroad Industry
- *Jeff Moller*, assistant vp, Operations Systems and Practices, Association of American Railroads, Washington, DC

4:15 pm Final Questions and Discussion

4:30 pm Adjourn Open Session

Meeting 3: Monday, February 21, 2011

10:00 am Welcome and Introductions
- *Clint Oster*, committee chair

10:15 am Stakeholder and Public Comments Presentations and Discussion
- *Captain William McDonald*, managing director, Flight Operations Contract Administration, FedEx

Meeting 3: Tuesday, February 22, 2011

9:45 am Welcome and Introductions
- *Clint Oster*, committee chair

10:00 am FAA Presentation on NPRM
- *Dale E. Roberts*, aviation safety inspector, Air Transportation Division, FAA
- *Greg Kirkland*, assistant division manager, Flight Standards Service Air Transportation Division, FAA

Appendix C

Summary of Stakeholder Response to Committee Request for Input

To help inform the committee's deliberations, requests for data were sent to a variety of different stakeholders in the airline industry, including 84 individual airlines, 8 airline associations, and 7 commercial pilot associations. Because of the extremely short turnaround (a few weeks) between our sending these requests and the meetings of the committee, the response rates from the stakeholders considered here were relatively modest, a total of 29. The committee conducted a qualitative review of written input received by March 23, 2011, which included responses from 25 individual airlines (4 mainline passenger carriers, 8 regional passenger carriers, 9 cargo carriers, and 4 nonscheduled charter carriers), 2 of the airline associations, and 2 of the pilot associations. (Some airlines responded with written input after this date but their input could not be included in this review.)

The committee received written statements from three individual commercial pilots who volunteered their thoughts on issues being addressed by the committee which was considered in the review of stakeholder response. During the committee's meetings, several of these individuals as well as some officials from particular airlines and professional associations met with the committee to present their views orally. Overall, the obtained data bear on the set of issues and questions outlined in Box 1-3 (in Chapter 1), as well as other related policies and practices of the particular air carriers and the Federal Aviation Administration (FAA).

This appendix summarizes what the committee learned from that input on the specific issues of interest to its work regarding commuting[1]: definition, prevalence, reasons, effects, and suggestions for improvement.

DEFINITIONS OF COMMUTING

In response to requests for definitions of what "commuting" means to pilots and crew members of commercial air carriers, the committee received a heterogeneous mix of replies from 17 of the queried stakeholders (1 airline association, 2 pilot associations, 3 individual pilots, and 11 individual airlines). Two of the respondents did not offer definitions, stating that "any definition of 'commuting' would be purely subjective" and "commuting cannot be defined." Four respondents emphasized that a "one-size-fits-all" definition of commuting would be inappropriate because pilot and crewmember commutes may involve multiple different modes of travel, as well as widely variable travel distances and times, with a variety of en route activities.

For 11 respondents, however, there was some consistency of views about the airlines industry's interpretations of "commuting." In particular, they explicitly defined "commuting" as referring specifically to travel arranged by pilots and other crew members acting as independent agents for going to and from home and work. Seven respondents specifically constrained the commuting activity to involve travel by air. For example, one senior pilot for a major passenger carrier said: "I would say a 'commuting' pilot is one who takes a flight instead of driving. 'Commuting' should be defined as a flight. This is a starting point of how to define the corporate responsibility in numbers of commuting pilots." Consistent with this view, three other respondents even said that "commuting" refers specifically to traveling by air from home to base using available jumpseats. However, seven other respondents at least implicitly said that "commuting" might entail not only air travel but also other modes (e.g., driving) if that travel takes 2 hours or more.

PREVALENCE OF COMMUTING

Several factors make it challenging to precisely characterize the prevalence of commuting by pilots and other crew members across the airline industry. Some stakeholders who responded explicitly on this issue were reluctant to offer numerical estimates due to the ambiguity of defining "commuting." For example, an official of a pilot association said: "prevalence can't be quantified, because 'commuting' can't be defined."

[1]There may be some subjective biases in the coding and quantification of the data, due to a need for treating similar statements by various stakeholders as paraphrases of each other.

Even if one accepts a nominal definition of "pilot commuting" as air travel from home to domicile, there would still be challenging aspects to quantifying the prevalence of commuting because of its variability. At one extreme, for some airlines (e.g., some unscheduled charter passenger carriers) none of the pilots travel to work by air, because they all live within a 90-minute drive time of their domicile. At the opposite extreme, for other airlines nearly 90 percent of their pilots and other crew members travel to work by air, with 10-20 percent of them taking more than 2 hours for doing so, and 10 percent or more of them traveling at least 1,000 miles. For example, one major cargo carrier reported that for one of its principal domiciles, 73 percent of the pilots commute at least 6 hours by air. Commuting to a domicile may change because of airlines restructuring. For example, according to a pilot from one mainline carrier, commuting to one specific domicile increased by a factor of 2—from 30 to 60 percent—when flights operated from another domicile of that carrier were substantially reduced.

Summarizing the responses from two airline associations, two pilot associations, two individual pilots, and nine individual airlines, the percentages of pilots who commute by air range from less than 5 percent to nearly 90 percent depending on a wide range of factors, including type of airline, particular domicile, and phase of airline restructuring. Some examples from respondents include a major cargo carrier that reported 47 percent of its pilots commute by air, and another major cargo carrier that reported commuting by air varies from 37 percent for one domicile to 88 percent for another domicile. In terms of distance, the number of long-distance air commutes (more than 1,000 miles) will likely continue to change over time given the economic dynamism of the industry.

REASONS FOR COMMUTING

The 10 stakeholders (2 airline associations, 2 pilot associations, 3 individual pilots, and 3 individual airlines) who explicitly addressed this issue noted several interrelated factors that explain why considerable numbers of pilots choose to commute from home locations that are several hours and hundreds to thousands of miles from their domiciles. Those factors included the high cost of living at the domiciles (mentioned by six respondents); frequent domicile closings and future unpredictability of the airline industry (mentioned by five respondents); the desire to maintain family stability (mentioned by five respondents); low pay, especially for regional carriers (mentioned by four respondents); lifestyle preferences, e.g., for good weather and outdoor living (mentioned by three respondents); and absence of adequate coverage for costly moving expenses (mentioned by one respondent).

EFFECTS OF COMMUTING ON PILOT FATIGUE

Especially relevant to the committee's central concerns were replies received from 12 stakeholders (2 airline associations, 2 pilot associations, 2 individual pilots, and 6 airlines) who explicitly commented on the effects of commuting on pilot fatigue. Although some degree of subjectivity and economic or personal self-interest undoubtedly colors these views, they nevertheless provide some useful perspectives. For example, six respondents acknowledged that commuting is a potentially fatiguing activity. Extending this line of commentary, five responded and explicitly noted or strongly hinted that fatigue can have negative effects on pilots' performance of flight deck duties and ought to be addressed.

At the same time, however, four respondents emphasized how challenging it is to measure the effects of commuting on pilot readiness and fitness for duty, given the difficulties with defining "commuting," quantifying its prevalence, and accounting for the heterogeneous ways in which pilots commute. In particular, six respondents noted that the fatiguing effects of various types of commutes may be quite different. For example, a 90-minute commute through chaotic rush-hour traffic to reach a domicile airport might elevate stress and fatigue levels substantially more than would a relaxed 3-hour commute by air. One respondent also pointed out that there are individual differences among pilots in terms of how their commutes may affect them.

With these sorts of caveats in mind, five respondents stated that commuting done responsibly by flight crew members would not necessarily increase their fatigue levels significantly. Also, six respondents said that commuting pilots—especially those who travel relatively long distances—should plan their commutes for proper rest at their domiciles before reporting for operational duty. In this vein, six respondents said that commuting directly into a work period from a remote location without proper rest along the way is a bad practice. Four respondents mentioned the unpredictability and stress-inducing aspects of direct, long, no-break commutes before duty assignments as exacerbating factors. Indeed, three respondents who discussed the fatigue issue in detail emphasized how stress itself is a primary contributor to the effects of commuting on pilot fatigue.

Several stakeholders provided concrete examples in which pilot fatigue could result from problematic commuting. The following scenario from one respondent, redacted to provide confidentiality, is illustrative of input to the committee:

> A crewmember lives [on the East Coast], is based in [the Mid-West], and has an 11-day trip commencing [from the domicile] with a flight to [central Europe]. The initial flight is scheduled to depart in the morning at 0630 local time and arrive approximately 8 hours later. To arrive at domicile, the crewmember must leave home at 1900 local time in the evening [be-

> fore duty begins] and drive 2 hours to a major [East Coast] metropolitan airport. The crewmember then commutes via cockpit jump seat on a flight [to the domicile] that arrives there at 0015 local time [early in the next morning]. The crewmember now has almost five hours until report time for the first scheduled segment to [Europe]. Because of this imprudent, unregulated commuting practice, this crewmember [might] be awake, and for all practical purposes on duty, for over 21 hours upon landing [later that day] in Europe.

Different points of view were provided to the committee by 12 respondents (2 airline associations, 2 pilot associations, 3 individual pilots, and 5 individual airlines) regarding the prevalence of problematic commuting. At one extreme, three respondents claimed that commuting almost never significantly increases pilot fatigue or affects pilots' fitness for duty. Typifying these comments is the response from one pilot association, such as: "For commuting pilots, the impact of commuting on pilot fatigue is minimal. . . . Pilots, as professionals, carefully restrict their own activity and commute responsibly, because they are in the same airplane at the end of the day as their passengers." The respondent added, "Pilots are professionals and as a group we ensure we show for work 'fit to fly'." One explanation offered for this optimistic view was that "the present method of pilots self-policing their own physiological needs has been, and still remains, an effective deterrent of fatigue. . . . Pilots have ably borne this responsibility since man first took to the skies. . . . A pilot who has a difficult or lengthy commute to work recognizes the effect this will have on him . . . and will commute the day before to give himself time for adequate rest [before reporting for operational duty]."

At the opposite extreme, three other respondents claimed that pilots' commutes can sometimes be problematic. Illustrating this opposing viewpoint are the following quotes from input to the committee: "[T]he impact of commuting on pilot fatigue is not minimal." "[T]he reality is that . . . pilots [sometimes] commute directly into a trip, allowing for more time at home and saving a few dollars. But this practice sacrifices rest and compromises professionalism." The official of one major cargo carrier wrote: "Many crew members commute directly into their [very early morning] duty assignments, which increases the level of fatigue and, in some cases, would increase their effective duty days beyond proposed FAR [Federal Aviation Regulation] maximums." Such strong negative opinions were expressed not only by some air carriers but also by individual pilots.

Three respondents also noted that having to pay for hotel rooms and "crash pads" is a disincentive for responsible commuting. One respondent also mentioned that inadequate base facilities contribute to the effects of commuting on pilot fatigue and that the adverse effects of commuting are especially problematic for crew members of regional air carriers. One individual pilot stated that, "the effects of commuting for the regional pilot are symptoms of a greater system failure."

SUGGESTIONS FOR HOW TO IMPROVE THE SYSTEM

Not surprisingly, 12 stakeholders (2 airline associations, 2 pilot associations, 3 individual pilots, and 5 individual airlines) offered a range of suggestions for how to improve the commercial airlines system with respect to commuting.

The viewpoint of the airline carriers is embodied in a set of related replies from three respondents. They stated explicitly that current airline commuting policies and practices—to the extent any exist—are already adequate, that no major new changes need be made, and that the burden of ensuring that flight crew members are fit for duty should not be shifted to the air carriers. Rather, in their opinion, fatigue management in the context of commuting should remain solely the responsibility of flight crew members. Their comments also suggested that the FAA should more tightly regulate the commuting practices of pilots, but not by imposing additional burdens on air carriers to monitor pilot behavior. For example, two urged that commuting overnight on "red-eye" flights directly prior to subsequent duty periods should be strongly discouraged or banned outright.

Contrasting with these views were the responses from individual airline pilots and their professional associations. Specifically, three such respondents said that no new rules and regulations should be imposed on pilots who commute by air to work nor should their commuting practices be scrutinized by their employers. Instead, they suggested that the FAA should more tightly regulate the policies of air carriers that influence the ease or difficulty of commuting. They urged that a new regulation be put in place whereby all commercial air carriers would institute standardized nonpunitive sick leave, fatigue, and commuting policies, unlike the wide variety of punitive, nonpunitive, and nonexistent policies that currently prevail. Furthermore, one respondent suggested that airlines' commuting policies should be coordinated with the scheduling of back-up commuter flights through CASS (the Cockpit Access Security System).

Three respondents also suggested that specific rules regarding regional air carriers need to be strengthened. Along these same lines, three responses expressed considerable enthusiasm for requiring airlines to improve their support of pilots whose domiciles are changed, including additional provision of paid moves, cost-of-living adjustments (COLAs), and positive-space tickets rather than merely jumpseats for flights used for commuting. Supplementing these suggestions, one respondent noted as well that rest facilities at airlines' bases (domiciles, hubs, and spokes) should be upgraded with more comfortable and quiet sleeping quarters.

Appendix D

Qualitative Analysis of Selected Public Comments to Proposed FAA Rules

The Department of Transportation and Federal Aviation Administration (FAA) issued a Notice of Proposed Rulemaking (NPRM), "Flight Crew Member Duty and Rest," on September 14, 2010. The FAA's proposed rules were developed in response to requests made by President Obama and Congress to issue final regulations by August 1, 2011. The NPRM specifies "limitations on the hours of flight and duty time allowed for pilots to address problems relating to pilot fatigue" (*Federal Register*, September 14, 2010), aspects of which relate to the commuting practices of pilots.

The FAA invited the public to submit questions and comments about "any matters they consider relevant" and indicated that "we may incorporate any such recommendation in a Final Rule" (*Federal Register*, September 14, 2010). The NPRM suggested that individuals provide comments and suggestions on specified topics:

- same or better protection against the problems of fatigue at a lower cost;
- factors to consider in calculating the maximum of flight duty periods (FDPs);
- when to permit flight crew members or carriers to operate beyond a scheduled FDP;
- reliability of proposed reporting requirements;
- parameters of proposed reporting requirements;
- intervals between reporting requirements; and
- length of time for air carriers to report a problematic crew pairing.

Some of the public comments and suggestions addressed the issue of commuting and possible consequences of the proposed duty and rest rules on commuter pilots. It is those comments that we considered in our qualitative investigation.

ANALYTIC METHOD

Qualitative methods are used to investigate the *why* and *how* of decision making, rather than the *what*, *where*, *when*. For the purposes of this investigation, the public comments expressed the viewpoints of a group of volunteer respondents, both individuals and representatives of a variety of organizations, who submitted their thoughts and ideas about the NPRM to the FAA.

The qualitative data set was comprised of a purposeful sample of the public comments selected as relevant to the following topic areas:

- definitions of commuting;
- prevalence of commuting;
- perceptions of commuting as being problematic (e.g., when the unplanned occurs, such as weather disturbances or mechanical difficulties that delay flights);
- characteristics and examples of responsible commuting;
- perceptions of commuting as less of a choice and more related to external factors (e.g., frequent domicile changes, low salaries, and other industry-related factors); and
- suggestions and rationale for modifying the NPRM.

Sample

The FAA electronic database containing 2419 submitted comments was searched. Comments were sorted using three key words: "commut"; "commute"; and "commuting" (N = 176). A total of 85 comments were selected for inclusion: see Table D-1. In many cases, an individual comment contained multiple opinions of relevance (e.g., on both the definition of commuting and he prevalence of commuting practices, as well as some suggestions for the NPRM). As a result, over 400 statements relevant to the study were considered.

Data Analysis

The analysis of qualitative data is an iterative process of examining and reexamining the narrative data set throughout all phases of analytic inquiry (Wolcott, 1994; Morse and Richards 2002; Ulin et al., 2004; Crosby et al.,

TABLE D-1 Number of Comments Reviewed and Selected for Inclusion in Analysis, by Key Words

Key Words Used	Number of Comments Reviewed	Number of Comments Selected
"commut" "commute"	53	27
"commuting"	123	58
Total	176	85

2006; Fetterman, 2010). The continuous process of visiting and revisiting the narrative data, with an eye toward identifying similarities and differences in meaning and content, results in an interpretive description of the range of meanings associated with each of the topics under investigation.

Several procedures were systematically followed to analyze the data set and are presented below as Phases 1-4.

Phase 1 After an analyst completed four readings of the data set, each response was tagged by a one-sentence description. Especially vivid and "to-the-point" responses were highlighted for later consideration as illustrative quotes. The responses were then sorted by relevance to each of the topic areas under investigation (see above). Below is an example of a one-sentence description (in italics) and of a quote for consideration.

> *As long as a pilot is fit for duty, the air carrier should not have the right to know whether or not a pilot commuted by air.*
>
> "I also disagree with the FAA's views that discourage commuting. Pilots should have a right to live where they want to, and can afford it, rather than trying to exist in an expensive city, with poor family life situations. Pilots should not be open to discipline of any type as long as they show up fit for duty. As long as a pilot shows up fit for duty, the airline should not have any right to be concerned with whether a pilot commuted in or not."

Phase 2 Preliminary codes were developed to experiment with sorting the content of the responses in each of the topic areas. "Coding" is the process of assigning descriptive labels, or codes, to "chunks" of the narrative data set (see Wolcott, 1994; Morse and Richards, 2002; Ulin et al., 2004; Crosby et al., 2006). For example, the following chunks of the narrative data (one-sentence descriptions [in italics] and quotes) have been assigned to the code "most pilots commute responsibly:"

> *It is rare for pilots to commute irresponsibly.*
>
> "I highly disagree with the FAA's proposal. The FAA is attempting to control a vast minority of pilots that commute irresponsibly. The majority of pilots that I know, work with and offer jumpseats to, are commuting responsibly. I rarely have a pilot that cuts commuting down to the wire with no back-ups or rest prior to report time."
>
> *The majority of pilots commute responsibly by using hotels or crash pads to rest.*
>
> "The high majority of pilots that I know, work with and have had in the jumpseat from other carriers demonstrate responsibility with reporting to duty fit. Most commute the evening before a trip the next day, others commute in the morning for an evening sign in and head to a hotel or crash pad to rest."
>
> *Let the record speak for itself—thousands of pilots commute every day without incident.*
>
> "Any language that includes restrictions on where a pilot shall live compared to his base is not going to increase safety one bit. Let these professionals decide what is best for themselves about how to get adequate rest while still commuting. Their record speaks for itself and thousands of pilots commute every day without incident."

Phase 3 After six rounds of sorting with a variety of codes, final codes were selected to sort the content and meaning of the responses in each topic area. For example, the final code "frequent moving of domicile bases to new locations" was used to sort the following data:

> *During the last decade, industry-related factors have forced airlines to move the location of their domicile bases on a frequent basis. In response, a majority of pilots no longer live close to their domicile bases and most feel they are forced to commute to keep the location of family residences stable and affordable. Estimates of one-half or more pilots commute to work by air. Long commutes are never desirable and the "commuter adaptation" to the industry-wide change is viewed by many pilots as being "part of the job"* (N = 42). All of these respondents perceived the frequent changes in the location of domicile bases as the major reason for the increased numbers of commuters by air. One of the 42 respondents wrote: "[R]egional carriers open and close bases more frequently due to contracts with legacy carriers and their pilots are less likely to be able to afford re-location."

One respondent provided a brief overview of commuting and domicile relocation practices during the 20th century and the early 21st century:

> "In decades past, commuting was not permitted, and crews lived within driving distance of base. In that era, flight crews were paid about fifty to four hundred percent more in current dollars, allowing them to afford high cost of living areas. During this period, it was also less common for air carrier to change bases. When it did occur, it was rare and the economic impact wasn't as great given the wages afforded to the crews. In the last decade, it has been more common for air carriers to open and close crew bases due to economic conditions and outsourcing agreements. Crews that had moved into bases were now required to commute, with relocation being both financially and emotionally difficult, if not impossible. A large portion of flight crews commute via airlines to their crew base over hundreds of miles, and even over several times zones. Regional carriers are especially prone to opening and closing bases due to contracts with legacy carriers, and their pilots are less likely to be able to afford relocation. The regional carrier I worked for had numerous crew bases on the east coast to the mid-continent. Some of these crew bases had opened and closed several times. Also, Junior First Officers earning \$20,000 to \$30,000 annually were more prone to being assigned and reassigned to these bases."

Phase 4 The last step of the qualitative analysis was the writing. During the writing process, the interpretive analysis is fine-tuned and streamlined to provide readers with an increasingly crisp presentation of the results.

RESULTS

This section presents the results of the analysis described above. See Table D-2 for a summary of results by number of respondents.

Definitions of Commuting

Thirty-nine respondents perceived the topic of commuting to be "an area of extreme ambiguity." One of the respondents described a definitional ambiguity related to defining lengthy commutes by air or car:

> Trying to mandate rest "in area" prior to duty is noble but burdensome. With the sprawl of today's large metroplex population centers many local pilots have at least a 1-2 hr commute, when including the drive to the airport, parking, movement from parking area to crew sign-in areas, etc.

TABLE D-2 Summary of Results by Number of Respondents

Topic	Number*
Definitions of Commuting	
Commuting is an area of extreme ambiguity, involving short- and long-distance commuters who travel by car and/or airplanes to arrive at their domicile bases.	39
Prevalence of Commuting	
The majority of pilots commute to work via air.	7
*Between 50-60 percent of pilots commute to work via air.	6
The majority of part 135 pilots often choose to work at cargo carriers because they can avoid commuting long distances to their domicile bases.	4
A minority of pilots commute to work over long distances.	2
Perceptions of Commuting as Problematic	
The majority of pilots have adapted to the energy demands of commuting and successfully manage their need for rest; their safety record speaks for itself. Commuting is now perceived as "part of the job."	22
Commuting does not impact pilots' fatigue level.	2
Characteristics and Examples of Responsible Commuting	
Commuters who report to duty too fatigued to safely fly are not responsibly commuting.	34
Commuters who can afford to schedule opportunities for resting in a bed, as needed, are responsible commuters.	24
Pilots who commute overnight on "red-eye" flights, and do not have opportunities to rest, most appropriately in a bed, are not properly rested for late afternoon or evening flights.	14
Pilots who are up early in the morning to commute to their domicile bases, and do not have opportunities to rest as needed, are often not fit for flight duty for a late afternoon or evening and are not adequately rested.	11
The majority of pilots commute responsibly.	6
Very few pilots commute irresponsibly and those that do are employed by small regional carriers.	6
Perceptions of Commuting as Less of a Choice and More Related to External Factors	
Frequent changes in the location of domicile bases are perceived as the major reason for the increased numbers of pilots commuting by air.	42
One of the consequences of dramatically lower pilot salaries over the past 25 years is that some low-paid commuters cannot afford the cost of resting in a hotel or shared apartment as needed.	24
Pilots who reflect on their years of experience residing close to their domicile bases and commuting short and/or long distances contend that postcommute rest in a bed, in a quiet, dark, and secluded area is necessary to combat the fatiguing effects of commuting, and as stated above, some low-paid commuters cannot afford to rest appropriately.	14

TABLE D-2 Continued

Topic	Number*
The FAA should develop regulations mandating that air carriers subsidize the cost of rest accommodations to lower-paid pilots who want to rest following their commutes.	6
As a result of the above, if the proposed rules are authorized, pilots without difficult commutes will regularly fly with pilots who have been awake for 24 hours.	2
Regional carriers open and close bases more frequently due to contracts with legacy carriers and their pilots are less likely to be able to afford relocation.	1
Suggestions to the FAA by Respondents	
1. The FAA should continue to mandate that pilots are held accountable for reporting to work fit for duty and not give airlines the authority to measure pilots' fitness for duty, e.g., fatigue level, or to ask employees to report on the preflight activities of peers.	52
2. In addition to the proposed mandate for airlines to develop fatigue management plans and strategies, the FAA should also require airlines to implement no-fault fatigue policies.	27
3. Postpone regulations related to commuting until evidence-based, fatigue-mitigating practices are identified. Not enough is known about the current number of pilots commuting by air, their commute flight patterns (distances covered and the time it takes), and their rest patterns prior to reporting for duty. There is also little research evidence about the relationships between commuting practices and job performances.	15
4. The FAA should mandate that airline companies provide positive space to pilots commuting by air, if requested, because 'space-available' travel can be highly stressful.	11
5. To best ensure public safety, the FAA should mandate that air carriers are responsible for calculating the start of flight duty periods differently for pilots who commute by air.	8

*The total number of respondents was 85. In many cases, individually submitted comments contained multiple opinions of relevance. As a result, over 400 statements relevant to the study were considered.

> For instance, I'm relatively "close" to the airport in DFW, but usually give myself 1 hr for the drive in and bus ride from the employee lot. Those in slightly more distant suburbs or exurbs might be unrealistically burdened by a 1.5 hr commuting limit.

Prevalence of Commuting

Perceptions about the prevalence of commuting were discussed primarily in the context of respondents' opinions about the proposed on-base rest requirement for commuters. There were 16 respondents on this topic: 6 said that between 50-60 percent of pilots commute by air to work; 7 said that "a majority" commute by air; 1 wrote that the vast majority of pilots commute by air; and 2 said that a "minority of pilots commute to work over long distances." One of the respondents in the last group made a distinction between short- and long-distance commuters, estimating that "many pilots commute 1½ to 3 hrs via airplane, while only a small percentage of pilots commute long distances to their home domicile."

A pilot with more than 30 years of industry experience provided a historical perspective on the recent increase in the number of crew members who commute by air to their domiciles:

> In the last decade, it has been more common for air carriers to open and close crew bases due to economic conditions and outsourcing agreements. Crews that had moved into bases were now required to commute, with relocation being both financially and emotionally difficult, if not impossible. A large portion of flight crews commute via airlines to their crew base over hundreds of miles, and even over several times zones.

One respondent, representing the views of an organization, provided an overview of issues related to commuting in the context of the airline industry:

> Commuting is common in the airline industry, in part because of life-style choices available to pilots by virtue of their being able to fly at no cost to their duty station, but also because of economic reasons associated with protecting seniority on particular aircraft, frequent changes in the flight crew member's home base, and low pay and regular furloughs by some carriers that may require a pilot to live someplace with a relatively low cost of living.

Three respondents agreed with an experienced cargo pilot who shared his rationale for having chosen to work for a long time for a cargo company: "[T]he overwhelming majority of part 135 pilots live in close proximity to their assigned bases or points of departure. Most commonly, this is specifically why pilots choose to fly part 135, as it allows them to spend their off duty hours at their own residences."

Respondents made several distinctions in the types of commuting: long-distance commuting by air; shorter distance commuting by air (1.5-3 hours); and varying number of hours/car commute (2-4 hours), which are not covered by the proposed regulation.

Perceptions of Commuting as Problematic

Twenty-two respondents did not perceive commuting to be problematic and did not see the need for additional regulations about mandated opportunities for rest. Their responses included statements that commuters had "adapted to the fatigue challenges of commuting," that "commuting is part of the job," and that "commuting is a way of life and many of us have no other way to get to work. We can continue to manage our rest as we have learned to do for decades." Eighteen of the respondents argued that, as one respondent wrote, "the safety record of commuters speaks for itself."

Two respondents did not consider same-day commuting to be a problem, with one contending that this type of commuting "does not impact crew members' fatigue levels." However, another respondent wrote that "a crew member who is up all day before an evening departure is not properly rested." One representative of an airline carrier wrote that commuting is a "significant issue in fatigue and its mitigation" and also that "as carriers develop training programs for FRMP and for this regulation, commuting must be addressed. This will place significant pressure on labor-management relations. However, we see no regulatory solution at this time."

Characteristics and Examples of Responsible Commuting

Six respondents agreed that the majority of pilots commute responsibly. Twenty-four respondents agreed that those who commute long distances and can afford to pay hotels or portions of the rent for apartments ("crash pads") and do rest are responsible commuters.

Thirty-four respondents wrote comments that agreed with one, that "commuters who report to duty too fatigued to safely fly are not responsible commuters." Fourteen respondents wrote comments that agreed with one, who said that pilots who commute overnight on "red eye" flights and do not have opportunities to rest are "not properly rested for late afternoon or evening flights." Eleven respondents wrote that pilots who are up early in the morning to commute to their domicile bases without opportunities to rest are often not fit for duty for flights later in the day. Six respondents commented in the vein of one who wrote that, "very few pilots commute irresponsibly, and those that do, are employed by small regional carriers."

One respondent suggested that the desire to maximize the number of days off can lead some commuters to report to duty not fully fit, noting that:

> there are a very small percentage of pilots (mostly employed at small regional carriers) who choose to commute at irresponsible times, largely due to income restraints (unable to afford to pay for lodging) and not wanting to have fewer days off within the month (lowering personal quality of life).

Commuting Related to External Factors

Many respondents to the NPRM said that commuting decisions are related less to pilots' choices than to two external factors: frequent moving of domicile bases to new locations and a significant decrease in salary levels, for both veteran and new pilots, in recent decades. The rest of this section presents our summary of the issues, in italics, and quotes on the subject from respondents.

Frequent Moving of Domicile Bases to New Locations

> *During the last decade, industry-related factors have forced airlines to move the location of their domicile bases on a frequent basis. In response, a majority of pilots no longer live close to their domicile bases and most feel they are forced to commute longer distances to keep the location of family residences stable and affordable. Estimates of one-half or more pilots commute to work by air. Long commutes are never desirable and the "commuter adaptation" to the industry-wide change is viewed by many pilots as being "part of the job."* (N = 42)

All of the respondents on this issue perceived the frequent changes in the location of domicile bases as the major reason for the increased numbers of long-distance commuters. One of the respondents stated that "regional carriers open and close bases more frequently due to contracts with legacy carriers and their pilots are less likely to be able to afford re-location."

One respondent provided a brief overview of commuting and domicile relocation practices during the 20th century and the early 21st century:

> In decades past, commuting was not permitted, and crews lived within driving distance of base. In that era, flight crews were paid about fifty to four hundred percent more in current dollars, allowing them to afford high cost of living areas. During this period, it was also less common for air carrier to change bases. When it did occur, it was rare and the economic impact wasn't as great given the wages afforded to the crews.
>
> In the last decade, it has been more common for air carriers to open and close crew bases due to economic conditions and outsourcing agreements. Crews that had moved into bases were now required to commute, with relocation being both financially and emotionally difficult, if not impossible. A large portion of flight crews commute via airlines to their crew base over hundreds of miles, and even over several times zones. Regional carriers are especially prone to opening and closing bases due to contracts with legacy carriers, and their pilots are less likely to be able to afford relocation. The regional carrier I worked for had numerous crew bases on the east coast to the mid-continent. Some of these crew bases had opened and closed

several times. Also, Junior First Officers earning $20,000 to $30,000 annually were more prone to being assigned and reassigned to these bases.

Deceases in Salary Levels

Pilot salaries have significantly decreased over the past decades. As a result, some low-paid pilots are not able to afford the cost of resting in a hotel or a shared apartment ("crash pad") prior to starting work on a same-day flight. (N = 24)

Fourteen respondents agreed that proper rest for pilots meant sleeping or resting in a bed in a quiet location. One respondent—with "over 30 years of continuous experience as a line pilot . . . the first 15 of those years spent residing in domicile and the more recent 15 years living on the West Coast and commuting" to several domicile locations on the East Coast and the Midwest—represented the viewpoints of the respondents on this issue:

> [E]xperience has shown me that *the* most important antidote to combating fatigue is the opportunity for sleep when needed. It does not take an expensive study to tell us what is already intuitively known—that adequate rest requires an adequate bed—in a quiet, dark, and secluded area that is isolated in such a manner as to not be subject to disturbance.

One respondent argued that there would be an important consequence of instituting the proposed NPRM due to the low pay of some pilots who cannot afford to pay for a place to rest: "[I]f the new rules go through as written, those of us who don't have a more difficult commute will be flying with pilots who will regularly be up for 24 hours." A solution to the problem was proposed by six respondents who suggested that the FAA should require airlines to subsidize accommodations at low or no cost to the individual commuters. As stated by one of the six: "[T]here just needs to be a provision for commuter pilots to have adequate accommodations to rest. I suggest that air carriers pay for hotels for the low paid pilots who are forced to commute." One respondent contended: "[I]f the air carrier was responsible for the rest of commuters by providing them with lodging for a period prior to the start of duty, the rule [to rest] would be easily enforceable."

Nine respondents referred to their perceptions of the role of low-paid, fatigued pilots in the Colgan crash. One of them said that, "the event that caused this [proposed] rule change was the Colgan accident . . . its cause was inexperienced pilots and a crew that could not afford to sleep in a bed. Their commute to work was not the problem, low pay was."

Suggestions to the FAA

Pilots' Responsibility to Report Fit for Duty

To date, the FAA and airline companies have held pilots responsible for assessing their own fitness for duty status. If unfit for any reason, regulations require a pilot to step aside and report for duty as a sick person, temporarily unfit for duty. The FAA should continue to mandate that pilots are held accountable for reporting to work fit for duty and not give airlines the authority to measure pilots' fitness for duty, e.g., fatigue level, or to ask employees to report on the pre-flight activities of peers. (N = 52)

The strong support for this idea appears to be related to three major factors: (1) pilots' professional pride in being responsible for assessing their own level of fitness for duty (N = 45); (2) the view that individuals alone are responsible for their life circumstances and have the right to privacy in all possible matters (N = 30); (3) the contrary view (to 2) that airlines are responsible for ensuring safe working conditions of their employees (N = 11). One of the respondents noted that, "pilots are the experts in how fit for duty they are or are not—regulations that dictate where a pilot must live or be before duty would be erroneous at best, would not enhance safety, and would place an unreasonable burden on pilots." Another respondent described how reporting fit for duty is a source of professional pride and adult status for pilots and then made the case that regulations to involve airlines in this assessment are an "onerous intrusion into lives of pilots." This respondent wrote:

> Pilots are scrutinized more than probably any other profession, including and especially doctors. We are trusted with the lives of hundreds of people at a time, yet I fear the FAA is about to enact a set of regulations that would treat us like children by not allowing us the responsibility of determining for our own self whether or not we are fit for duty. Any such regulations would be a one-size-fits-all, onerous intrusion into the lives of pilots that would do nothing to increase fitness for duty. We are already held accountable for our actions while on duty; I think we can handle the responsibility of knowing how to show up in a condition of fitness for that duty.

Another respondent wrote:

> The new regulation, as written, may put pilots in a position of changing their life in a way that will NOT enhance safety, and may actually decrease it. Commuting to work in a coach seat where rest is possible, is no more dangerous than a pilot that works in his yard for 5 hours before he reports for duty. Yet, the first pilot is under scrutiny because he commuted and the second pilot is not under scrutiny. Pilots are the experts in how fit for

> duty they are or are not. Please ensure that all liability for pilots ensuring fitness for duty is removed from this NPRM. Further, please remove all regulation that might dictate where a pilot must live or be before duty. These regulations would be erroneous at best, would not enhance safety, and would place an unreasonable burden on pilots.

Another respondent expressed a special concern for rights to privacy, stating that, "as long as a pilot shows up fit for duty, the airline should not have any right to be concerned with whether a pilot commuted in or not." Yet a somewhat different comment came from a respondent who wrote that "it is best to ensure crewmembers are not exposed to fatiguing conditions rather than assess them after fatigue occurs."

One respondent discussed the separate domains of responsibility between labor and management:

> The concept of the air carrier's ability to manage an individual employee's fitness to fly is erroneous. Airlines have direct control over the time of day of the operations, the number of takeoffs and landings scheduled, and controlling the effects of crossing multiple time zones. The flight crew member is the only one who can control the effects of commuting.

Forty-nine individual respondents and five respondents who represented the views of their organizations emphasized the importance of not tracking pilots' arrival and departure times at their domiciles because it is an unwarranted invasion of privacy. As one organizational respondent wrote:

> We support the concept that a flight crewmember must be fit for duty prior to operating an aircraft. The fitness for duty is and must be a joint responsibility of the certificate holder and the flight crew member. While it is important that both the flight crew member and the certificate holder be involved in fit for duty determinations, we cannot create an environment that requires tracking and reporting the activities of an individual flight crew member prior to their reporting for flight duty. Such tracking would be difficult and costly for the certificate holder and constitute an unwarranted invasion of the personal privacy of the flight crew member.

Two of the individual respondents pointed out that tracking is not the only option for ensuring responsible commuting; one wrote:

> While it is important for all stakeholders to be involved in the fitness-for-duty equation, we simply cannot operate in an environment that places a priority on the tracking and reporting of commuting over educating and encouraging responsible, jointly managed commuting policies.

Another respondent further questioned the FAA on the issue of individual rights and responsibilities:

> [T]o start with, whatever happened to personnel responsibility? Existing rules and regulations require a crew member to show up fully rested and ready for work. That is a crew member responsibility, not a company responsibility. Commuting needs to be a crew members' responsibility.

Six respondents discussed the role of personal choice and responsibility in commuting and other off-the-clock behaviors. One wrote:

> [C]ommuting should not be touched. Pilots are required to show up for work rested and fit to fly. That is the law. If they choose to commute all night or stay up and watch television all night at home before work, then they should call in sick. That is already the mandate. Making more rules does not help anything.

Fatigue Policies

> *In addition to the proposed mandate for airlines to develop fatigue management plans and strategies, the FAA should also require airlines to implement no-fault fatigue policies.* (N = 27)

Several respondents expressed the view that many pilots fear negative consequences if they report unfit to fly, due to fatigue, on the day of flight. One respondent described the advantages of instituting a "no-questions-asked" fatigue policy:

> Getting hired at Southwest Airlines (SWA) represents reaching my goal destination. One of the most amazing and effective policies for combating fatigue that the pilots at SWA have is a no-questions-asked fatigue policy. What this means is that if a pilot calls in fatigued, s/he is done. Scheduling will pull the pilot from the trip and the pilot's job is not in jeopardy!!! The pilot is not going to be disciplined or penalized for calling in fatigued.
>
> Pilots have a great deal of responsibility, and what an outstanding policy like this does is to allow the pilot to focus on the most important priority, that of public safety, while recognizing and accommodating to his/her personal limitations. In my five years at SWA, I have not once called in fatigued. I have called in sick a few times, and I have only praise for the courteous, professional treatment I have received in those circumstances. No pressure to get back to work until ready to do so. Based on those experiences, I have full confidence that the no-questions-asked fatigue policy

> works as promoted. A pilot who thinks his/her job is in jeopardy is not going to call in fatigued!

Another respondent expressed disappointment that the proposed NPRM did not address a basic need of pilots:

> I am disappointed with the FAA's view on pilot commuting. I've read that 60% of pilots commute by air to work. If the FAA believes that fatigue mitigation is a joint responsibility between crewmembers and the airline, then the airlines need to be required to have some type of a non-punitive fatigue policy.

A third respondent advocated for crew members' right to "cry Uncle" when fatigued:

> The creation of a no-fault fatigue program where a crewmember may, without fear of discipline or any financial considerations, declare himself unfit to fly (due to fatigue) and be provided a rest period accordingly, would mitigate day-of-flight fatigue issues. Consider the long day with bad weather, deicing, holding, diverting, etc. Giving crew the opportunity to cry, "Uncle" would be invaluable.
>
> It is a crewmember's responsibility to arrive rested and ready prior to flight and properly modifying the Rest and Duty Time regulations will give them more tools to proactively manage their fatigue. However, if a crew becomes fatigued they should not feel pressured to complete a flight segment nor penalized for any reason. It is a crewmember's responsibility to arrive rested and ready prior to flight and properly modifying the Rest and Duty Time regulations will give them more tools to proactively manage their fatigue.

Inadequate Data on Commuting

> *Postpone regulations related to commuting until evidence-based fatigue-mitigating practices are identified. Not enough is known about the current number of pilots commuting by air, their commute flight patterns (distances covered and the time it takes), and their rest patterns prior to reporting for duty. There is also little research evidence about the relationships between commuting practices and job performances.* (N = 15)

The lack of information about commuting practices and their relationships with job performance was the reason behind the advise to delay any regulations. Two of the 15 respondents identified another topic missing from the knowledge base, which one characterized as "the lack of reliable estimates of how fatigued pilot commuters become as their flight duty periods progress, especially for long distance commuters." Five of the 15 respondents, representing the views of organizations, commented on lack of supporting data in the Advisory Circular, AC 120-FIT; one wrote:

> The practice of personal commuting must remain each flight crew member's responsibility to be fit for duty for every flight duty period to which they are assigned. The FAA's accompanying Advisory Circular, AC 120-FIT, should clearly be withdrawn. It is premature, wholly lacks any scientific study or supporting data, and raises the same issues with regard to incorrectly involving certificate holders in the commuting practices of their flight crew members.

One of the 15 respondents provided an explanation as to why individual variation in experiencing fatigue is a key factor in understanding predictors of fatigue among pilots: "[F]atigue is definitely a threat in our environment, but it is so individual and so unique. I have had 20 hour layovers with a good 8 hour sleep and find myself fatigued sometimes." Given the knowledge gaps, another respondent discussed an alternative to regulatory mandates. "[A]n advisory approach may be more effective than a regulatory approach at this time."

Required Space for Commuting

> *The FAA should mandate that airline companies provide positive space to pilots commuting by air, if requested, because 'space available' travel can be highly stressful.* (N = 11)

One of the 11 respondents noted that "a number of cargo airlines already provide positive space for all pilots to whatever domicile that the airline requires them to be based at." Three respondents said that the FAA should provide pilots with positive space; as one wrote, "so they can plan their commutes with more accuracy thus giving them the chance to get the required rest before their flight." Another respondent elaborated this point of view, concluding:

> For pilots who choose to commute, give them the option to add deadhead legs both before and after their scheduled trips. These deadhead trips would get the pilots from their homes to their domicile bases with much less stress and without the uncertainty of space available travel. This increase in quality of life would take away much of the risk in irresponsible commuting. The decreased stress would also decrease one of the factors leading to fatigue.

Duty Period Calculations

> *To best ensure public safety, the FAA should mandate that air carriers are responsible for calculating the start of flight duty periods differently for pilots who commute by air.* (N = 8)

Two respondents expressed the need for FAA action; one wrote that "airline management will not voluntarily safely schedule crews unless they are under threat from the FAA." Two pilots commented on the fact that some pilots commute over one or two time zones to their domiciles. One of them wrote that the public "should be protected from pilots commuting to work from distant locations" and that it was "unacceptable to have a pilot reside in Florida and report for duty in Los Angeles after a long commuting flight."

All eight respondents said that public safety would increase if the flight schedules factored in pilots' time zone acclimation. One of them reported that "the legacy carrier I worked for took the issue of fatigue very seriously—schedules and assignments were made with consideration of circadian rhythms, time zone changes, and prior schedules."

Five respondents argued in favor of commuter-specific rules about the start of duty periods. One wrote that rules "should be implemented when commuting exceeds a defined number of miles and/or hours spent commuting." One suggested that "the only clear solution is a regulation requiring pilots to commute 'on-duty' in terms of calculating rest prior to flight." Also in this vein, one of them thought that the duty period "should begin one hour prior to their intended commuting flight and should not go over 12 hours, including commuting and working segments, and up to 14 hours with crew consent." Another of the five respondents concluded that "it is then only fair, in order to protect the public, to enforce the regulation by subjecting a commuter pilot to random checks."

Appendix E

Mainline Airlines Departures by City

This appendix presents the committee's analysis of changes in the number of aircraft departures discussed in Chapter 2 for mainline airlines. Figures E-1 through E-24, ordered alphabetically by airline, show total departures by airport code (refer to Table E-1 for corresponding cities) and by airline, in the cities most frequently served by that airline and thus in the cities most likely to serve as domiciles for pilots. The data used for this analysis were scheduled aircraft departures taken from Air Carrier Summary: T3: U.S. Air Carrier Airport Activity Statistics provided by the Bureau of Transportation Statistics (n.d.-a) of the U.S. Department of Transportation. The data were from the third quarter of 2000, 2005, and 2010. All carriers that reported more than 20,000 aircraft departures in the third quarter of 2010 were examined. This group consisted of 12 mainline airlines. Two of the airlines were all-cargo airlines, FedEx and UPS, and the rest were passenger airlines.

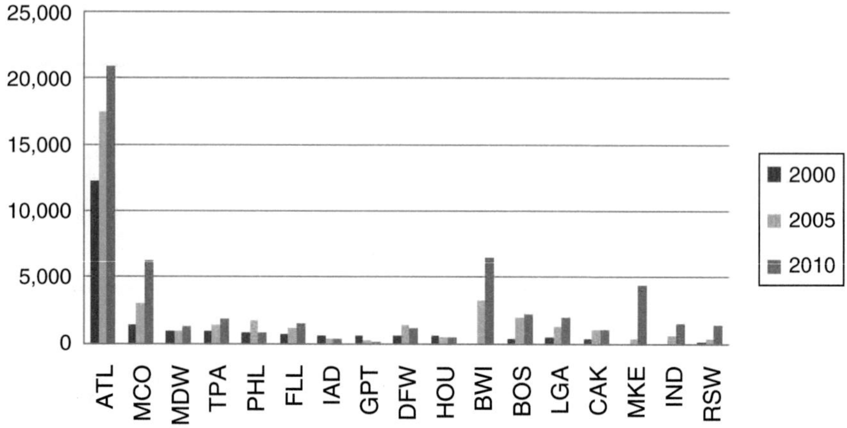

FIGURE E-1 Air Tran departures by city.
SOURCE: Data from Bureau of Transportation Statistics (n.d.-a).

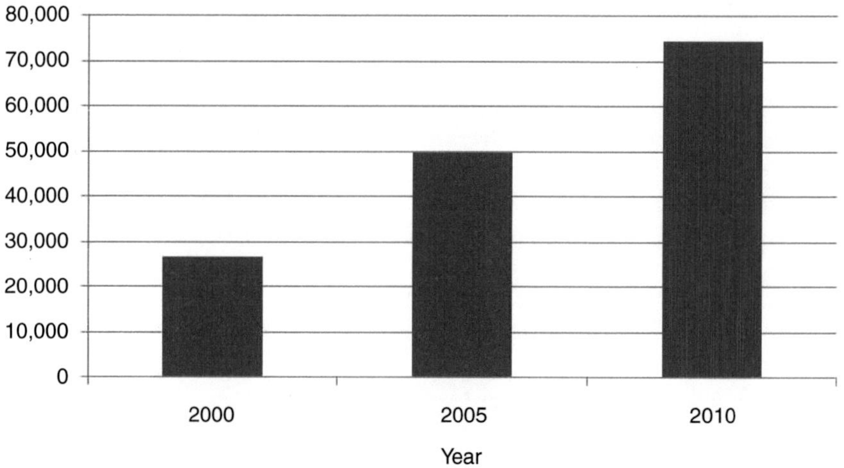

FIGURE E-2 Air Tran total departures.
SOURCE: Data from Bureau of Transportation Statistics (n.d.-a).

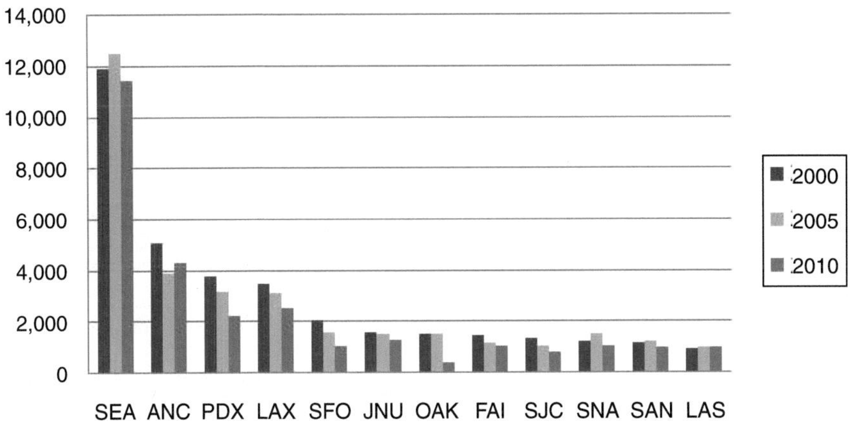

FIGURE E-3 Alaska departures by city.
SOURCE: Data from Bureau of Transportation Statistics (n.d.-a).

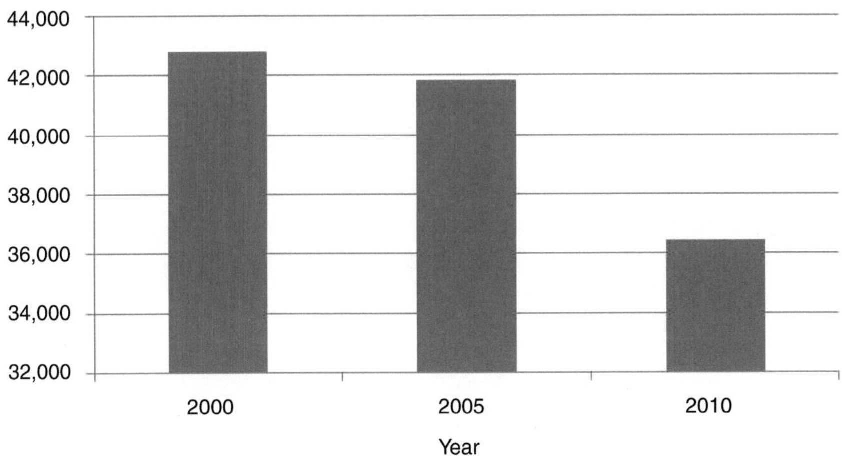

FIGURE E-4 Alaska total departures.
SOURCE: Data from Bureau of Transportation Statistics (n.d.-a).

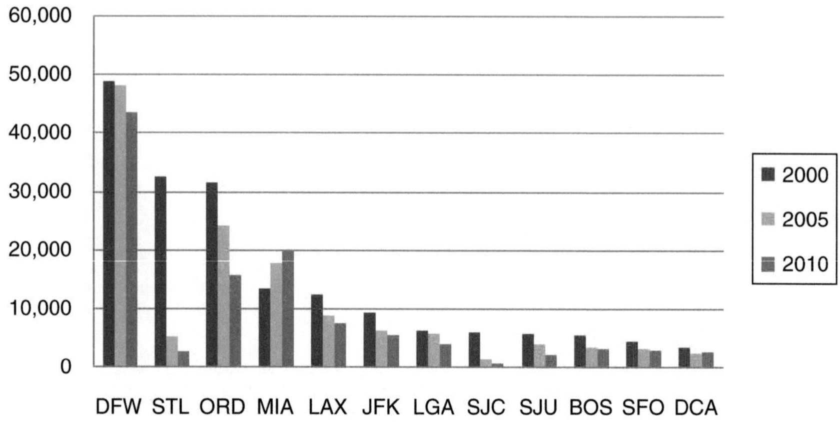

FIGURE E-5 American departures by city.
SOURCE: Data from Bureau of Transportation Statistics (n.d.-a).

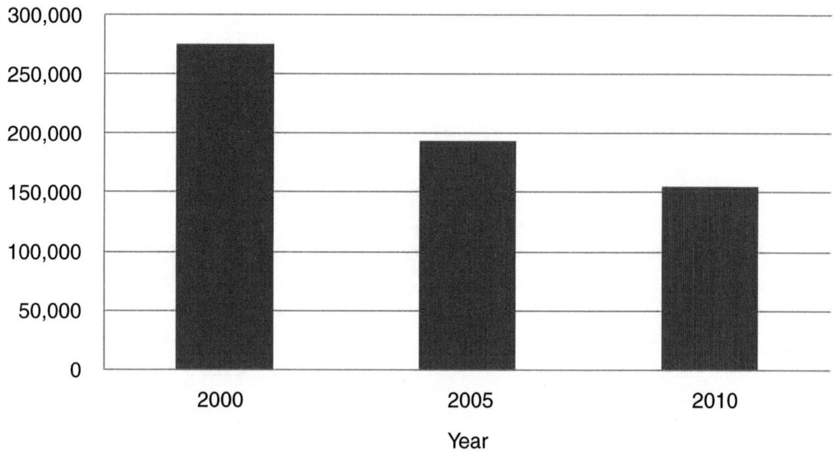

FIGURE E-6 American total departures.
SOURCE: Data from Bureau of Transportation Statistics (n.d.-a).

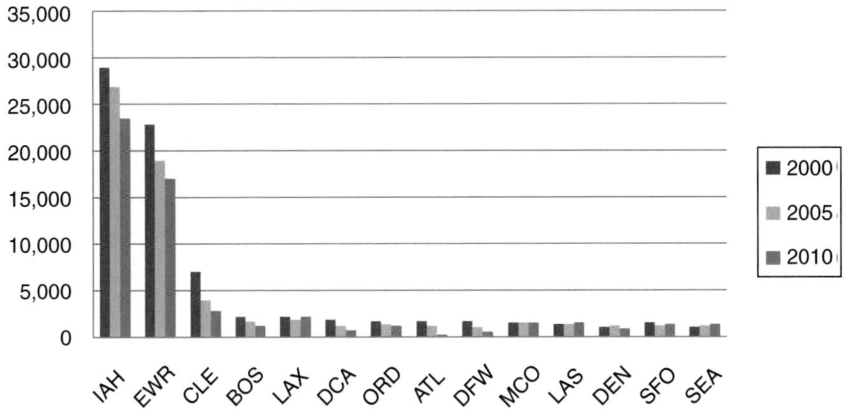

FIGURE E-7 Continental departures by city.
SOURCE: Data from Bureau of Transportation Statistics (n.d.-a).

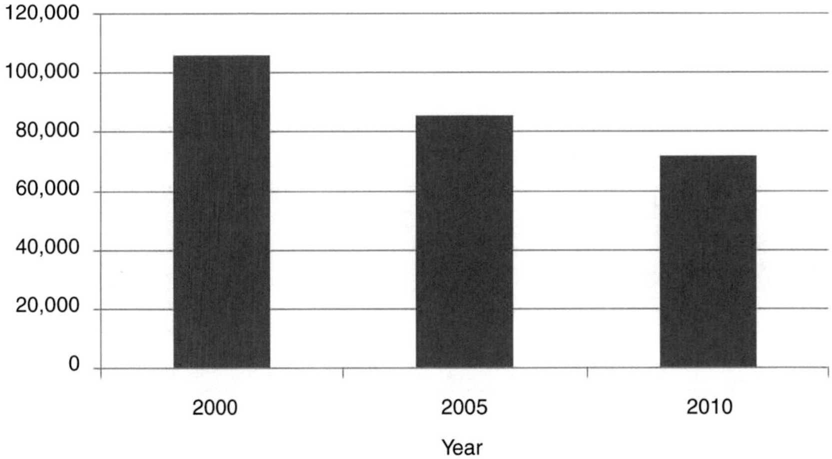

FIGURE E-8 Continental total departures.
SOURCE: Data from Bureau of Transportation Statistics (n.d.-a).

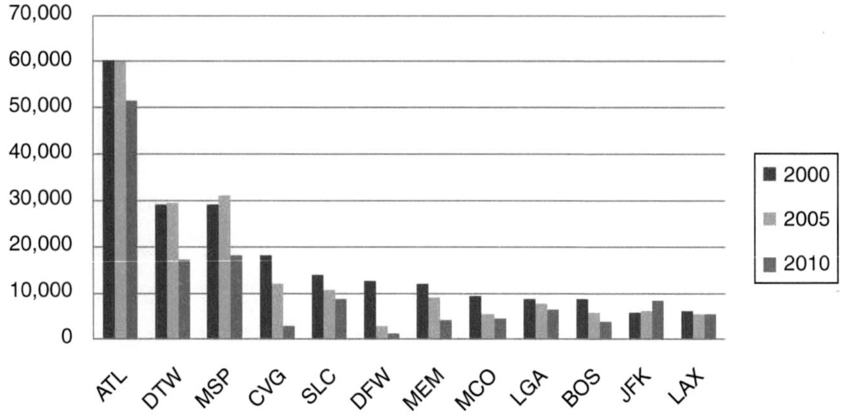

FIGURE E-9 Delta departures by city.
SOURCE: Data from Bureau of Transportation Statistics (n.d.-a).

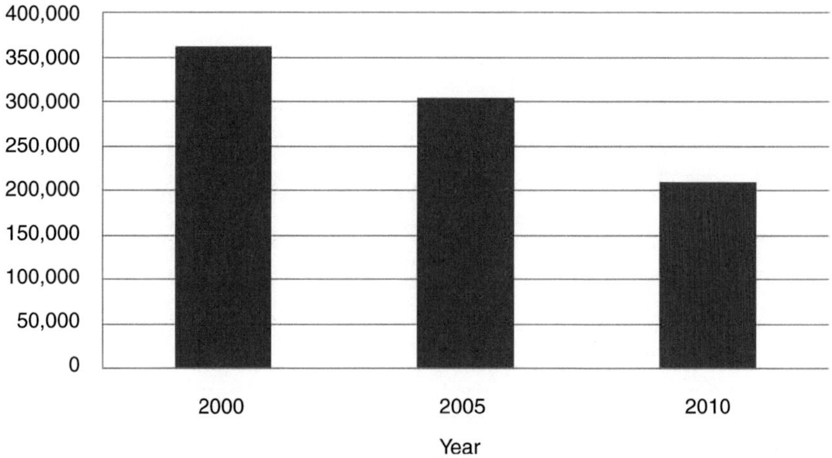

FIGURE E-10 Delta total departures.
SOURCE: Data from Bureau of Transportation Statistics (n.d.-a).

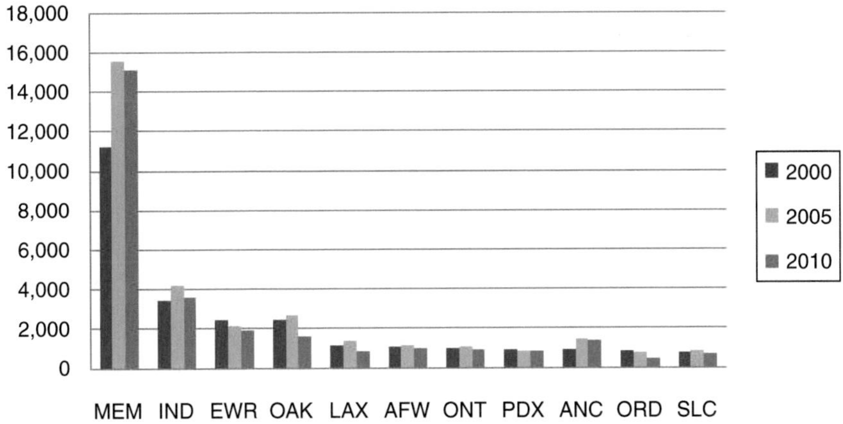

FIGURE E-11 FedEx departures by city.
SOURCE: Data from Bureau of Transportation Statistics (n.d.-a).

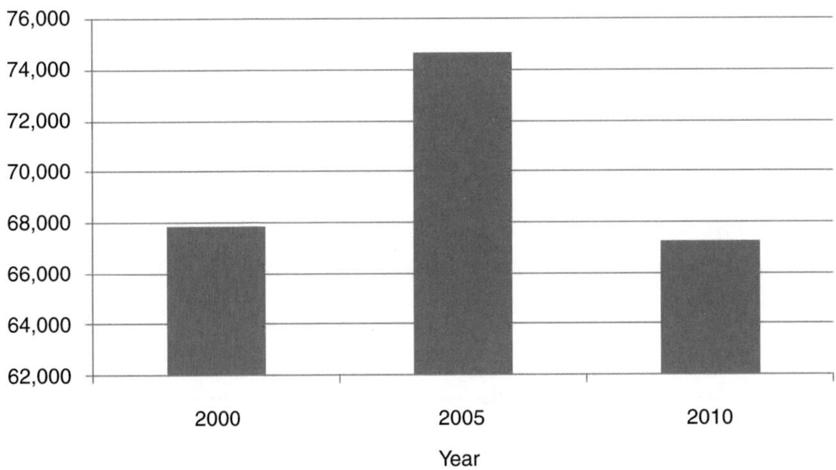

FIGURE E-12 FedEx total departures.
SOURCE: Data from Bureau of Transportation Statistics (n.d.-a).

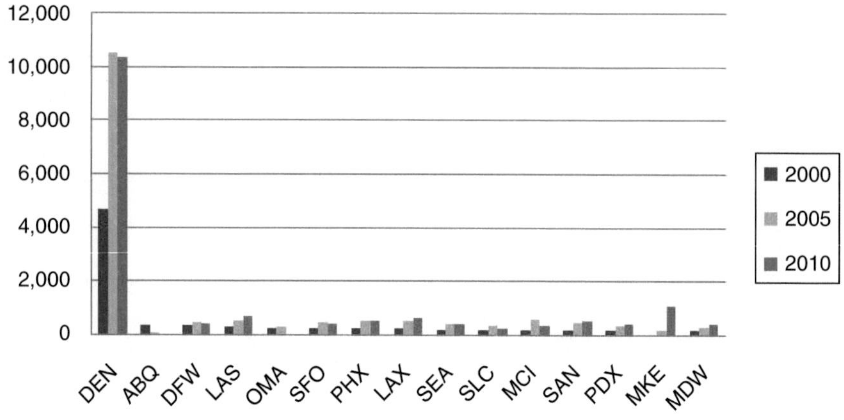

FIGURE E-13 Frontier departures by city.
SOURCE: Data from Bureau of Transportation Statistics (n.d.-a).

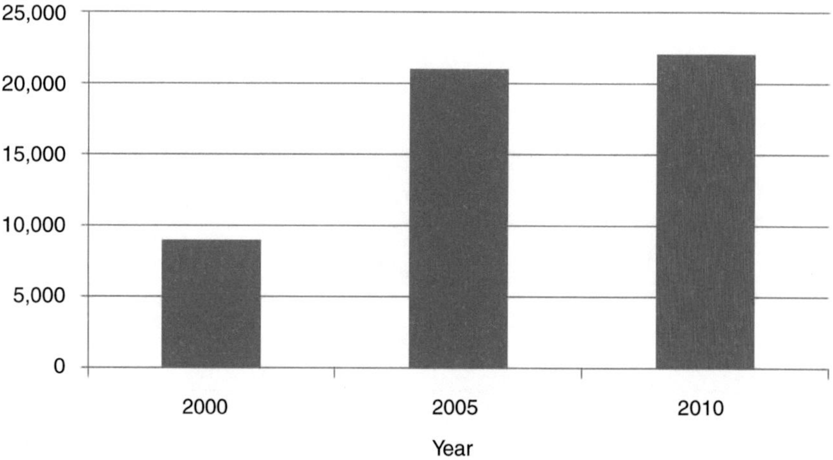

FIGURE E-14 Frontier total departures.
SOURCE: Data from Bureau of Transportation Statistics (n.d.-a).

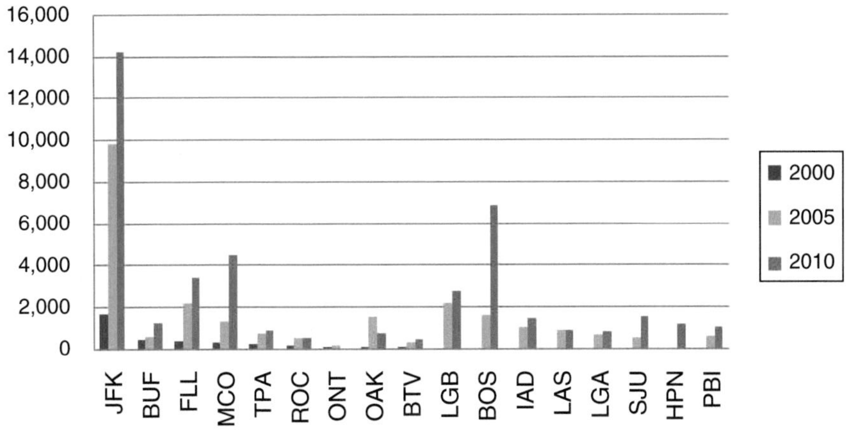

FIGURE E-15 JetBlue departures by city.
SOURCE: Data from Bureau of Transportation Statistics (n.d.-a).

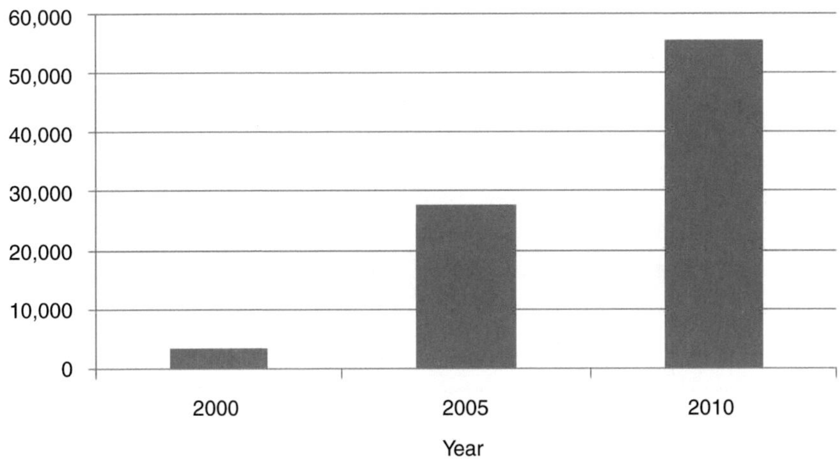

FIGURE E-16 JetBlue total departures.
SOURCE: Data from Bureau of Transportation Statistics (n.d.-a).

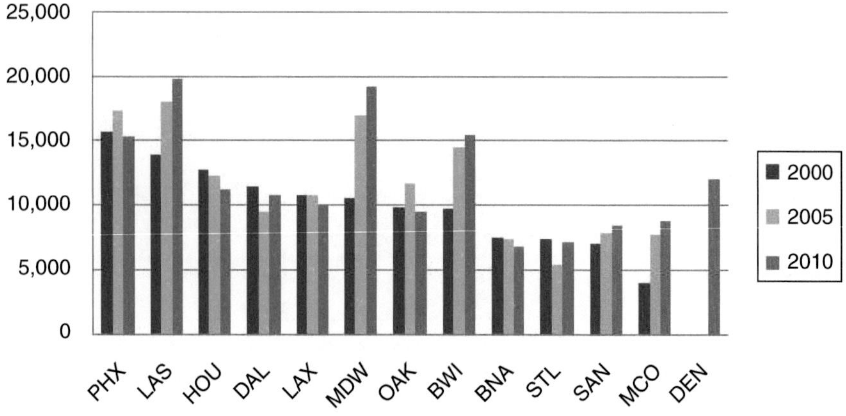

FIGURE E-17 Southwest departures by city.
SOURCE: Data from Bureau of Transportation Statistics (n.d.-a).

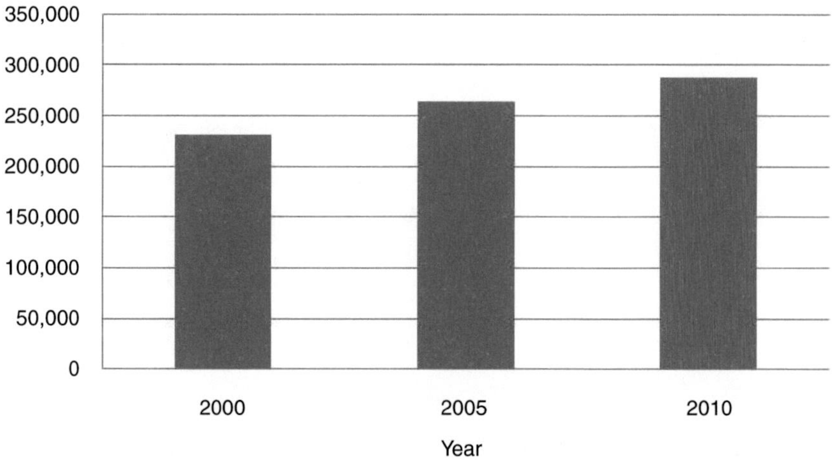

FIGURE E-18 Southwest total departures.
SOURCE: Data from Bureau of Transportation Statistics (n.d.-a).

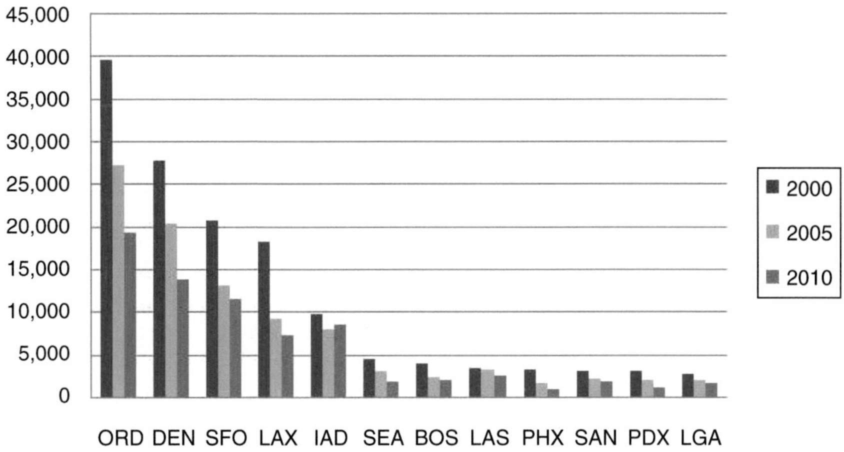

FIGURE E-19 United departures by city.
SOURCE: Data from Bureau of Transportation Statistics (n.d.-a).

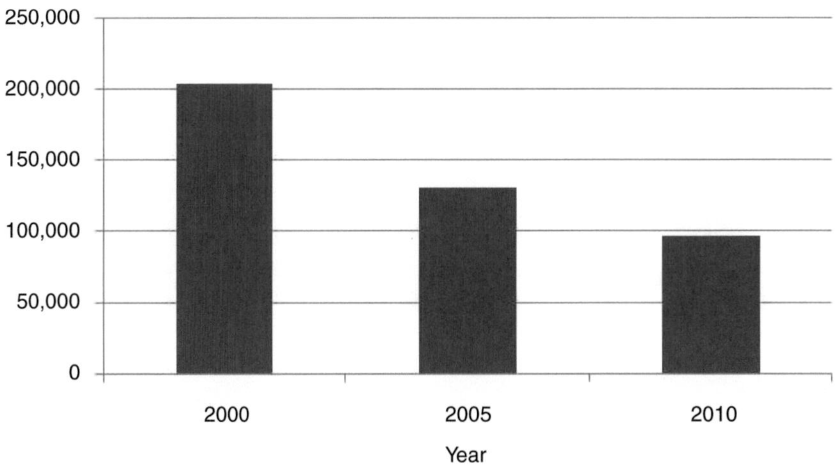

FIGURE E-20 United total departures.
SOURCE: Data from Bureau of Transportation Statistics (n.d.-a).

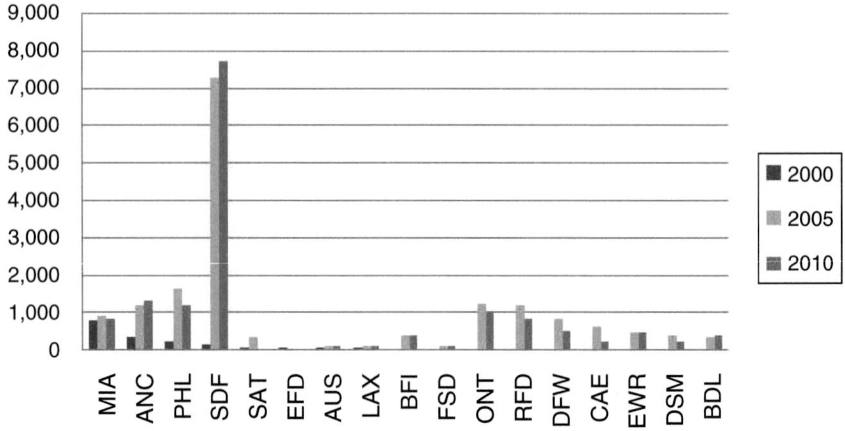

FIGURE E-21 UPS departures by city.
SOURCE: Data from Bureau of Transportation Statistics (n.d.-a).

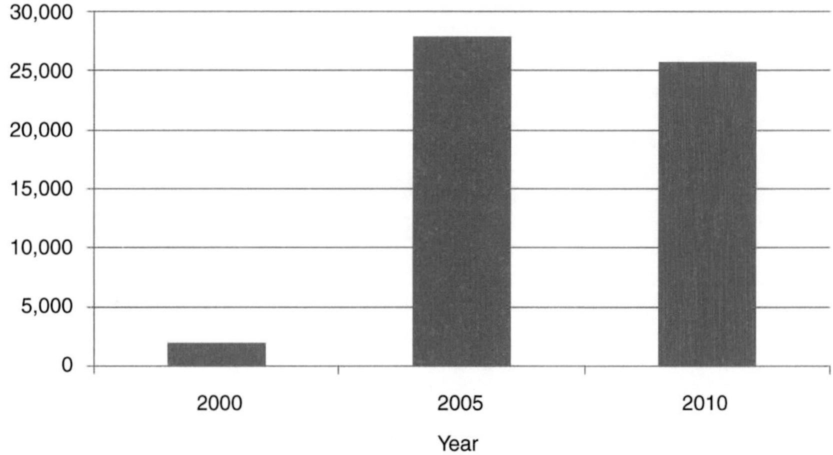

FIGURE E-22 UPS total departures.
SOURCE: Data from Bureau of Transportation Statistics (n.d.-a).

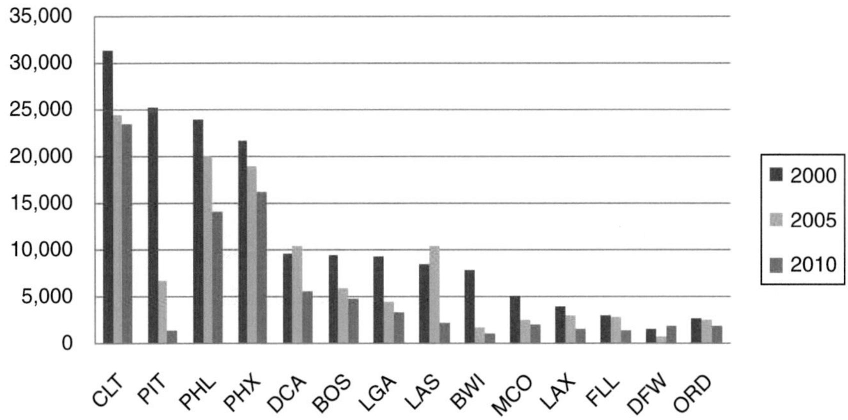

FIGURE E-23 US Airways departures by city.
SOURCE: Data from Bureau of Transportation Statistics (n.d.-a).

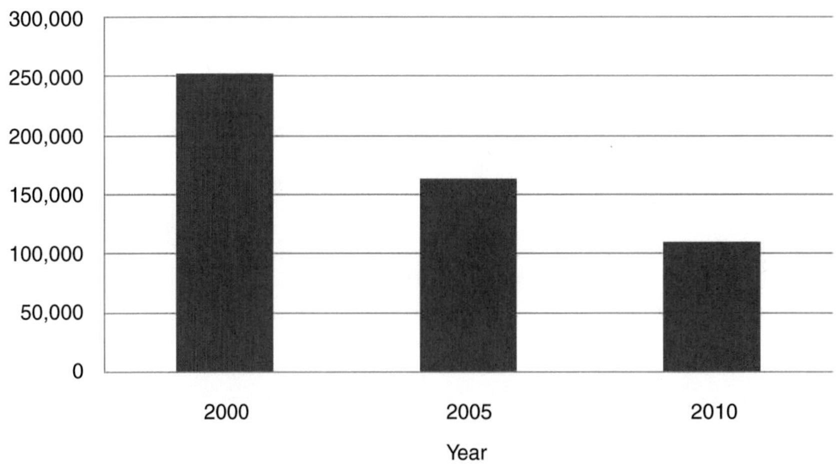

FIGURE E-24 US Airways total departures.
SOURCE: Data from Bureau of Transportation Statistics (n.d.-a).

TABLE E-1 Airport Codes for Airline Departure Analysis

Codes	Airport	City	State
ABE	Lehigh Valley International	Allentown	PA
ABQ	Albuquerque International	Albuquerque	NM
ABR	Municipal	Aberdeen	SD
ACK	Nantucket Memorial	Nantucket	MA
AFW	Fort Worth Alliance	Fort Worth	TX
ALS	Municipal	Alamosa	CO
ANC	Ted Stevens Anchorage International	Anchorage	AK
ASE	Aspen	Aspen	CO
ATL	Hartsfield-Jackson Atlanta International	Atlanta	GA
ATW	Outagamie County	Appleton	WI
AUS	Austin-Bergstrom International	Austin	TX
AVL	Asheville Regional	Fletcher	NC
AZO	Kalamazoo/Battle Creek International	Kalamazoo	MI
BDL	Bradley International	Windsor Locks	CT
BFI	Boeing Field/King County International	Seattle	WA
BHM	Birmingham	Birmingham	AL
BIL	Billings	Billings	MT
BJI	Bemidji	Bemidji	MN
BNA	Nashville International	Nashville	TN
BOI	Boise Air Terminal/Gowen Field	Boise	ID
BOS	Logan International	Boston	MA
BRD	Brainerd Lakes Regional	Brainerd	MN
BTR	Ryan	Baton Rouge	LA
BTV	Burlington International	Burlington	VT
BUF	Buffalo Niagara International	Buffalo	NY
BWI	Baltimore/Washington International Thurgood Marshall	Baltimore	MD
CAE	Metropolitan	Columbia	SC
CAK	Akron/Canton Regional	Akron/Canton	OH
CHA	Lovell Field	Chattanooga	TN
CHO	Albemarle	Charlottesville	VA
CHS	Charleston International	Charleston	SC
CLE	Hopkins International	Cleveland	OH
CLT	Charlotte Douglas	Charlotte	NC
CMH	Port Columbus International	Columbus	OH
COS	Colorado Springs	Colorado Springs	CO
CRP	Corpus Christi International	Corpus Christi	TX
CRW	Yeager	Charleston	WV

TABLE E-1 Continued

Codes	Airport	City	State
CVG	Cincinnati/Northern Kentucky	Covington	KY
CWA	Central Wisconsin	Wausau	WI
DAL	Love Field	Dallas	TX
DAY	James Cox Dayton International	Dayton	OH
DCA	Ronald Reagan Washington National	Washington	DC
DDC	Dodge City Municipal	Dodge City	KS
DEN	Denver International	Denver	CO
DFW	Dallas/Fort Worth International	Dallas	TX
DIK	Dickinson	Dickinson	ND
DSM	Des Moines International	Des Moines	IA
DTW	Detroit Metropolitan Wayne County	Detroit	MI
EFD	Ellington Field	Houston	TX
EUG	Eugene	Eugene	OR
EWB	New Bedford	New Bedford	CT
EWR	Newark Liberty International	Newark	NJ
FAI	Fairbanks International	Fairbanks	AK
FAT	Fresno Air Terminal	Fresno	CA
FLL	Fort Lauderdale/Hollywood International	Fort Lauderdale	FL
FMN	Municipal	Farmington	NM
FSD	Joe Foss Field	Sioux Falls	SD
GCC	Campbell County	Gillette	WY
GEG	Spokane International	Spokane	WA
GJT	Walker Field	Grand Junction	CO
GNV	Gainesville Regional	Gainesville	FL
GPT	Gulfport-Biloxi International	Gulfport	MS
GRR	Gerald R. Ford International	Grand Rapids	MI
GSO	Piedmont Triad International	Greensboro	NC
GSP	Greenville-Spartanburg International	Greenville-Spartanburg	SC
GTR	Golden Triangle Regional	Columbus	OH
HHH	Hilton Head	Hilton Head	SC
HOU	William P. Hobby	Houston	TX
HPN	Westchester County	White Plains	NY
HSV	Huntsville International-Carl T. Jones Field	Huntsville	AL
HYA	Barnstable	Hyannis	MA
IAD	Washington Dulles International	Washington	DC
IAH	George Bush Intercontinental	Houston	TX

continued

TABLE E-1 Continued

Codes	Airport	City	State
IND	Indianapolis International	Indianapolis	IN
ITH	Tompkins County	Ithaca	NY
JAX	Jacksonville	Jacksonville	FL
JFK	John F Kennedy International	New York	NY
JNU	Boundary Bay	Juneau	AK
LAR	General Brees Field	Laramie	WY
LAS	McCarran International	Las Vegas	NV
LAX	Los Angeles International	Los Angeles	CA
LBL	Municipal	Liberal	KS
LGA	LaGuardia	New York	NY
LGB	Long Beach Municipal	Long Beach	CA
LIH	Lihue	Kauai Island	HI
LNK	Lincoln	Lincoln	NE
LWS	Nez Perce County Regional	Lewiston	ID
MBS	MBS International	Saginaw	MI
MCI	Kansas City International	Kansas City	KS
MCO	Orlando International	Orlando	FL
MDT	Harrisburg International	Harrisburg	PA
MDW	Midway	Chicago	IL
MEM	Memphis International	Memphis	TN
MFR	Rogue Valley International-Medford	Medford	OR
MGM	Dannelly Field	Montgomery	AL
MHT	Manchester-Boston Regional	Manchester	NH
MIA	Miami International	Miami	FL
MKE	General Mitchell International	Milwaukee	WI
MLI	Quad-City	Moline	IL
MSN	Dane County Regional	Madison	WI
MSP	Minneapolis-St. Paul International	Minneapolis	MN
MVY	Martha's Vineyard	Vineyard Haven	MA
MYR	Myrtle Beach International	Myrtle Beach	SC
OAK	Oakland International	Oakland	CA
OGG	Kahului	Maui	HI
OKC	Will Rogers World	Oklahoma City	OK
OMA	Eppley Airfield	Omaha	NE
ONT	Ontario International	Ontario	CA
ORD	Chicago O'Hare International	Chicago	IL

TABLE E-1 Continued

Codes	Airport	City	State
ORF	Norfolk International	Norfolk	VA
PBI	Palm Beach International	West Palm Beach	FL
PDX	Portland International	Portland	OR
PFN	Bay County	Panama City	FL
PHL	Philadelphia International	Philadelphia	PA
PHX	Sky Harbor International	Phoenix	AZ
PIT	Pittsburgh International	Pittsburgh	PA
PLN	Emmet County	Pellston	MI
PRC	Prescott	Prescott	AZ
PSC	Tri-Cities	Pasco	WA
PVC	Provincetown	Provincetown	MA
PVD	T.F. Green	Providence	RI
PWM	International Jetport	Portland	ME
RAP	Regional	Rapid City	SD
RDM	Roberts Field	Redmond	OR
RDU	Raleigh-Durham International	Raleigh-Durham	NC
RFD	Greater Rockford	Rockford	IL
RIC	Richmond International	Richmond	VA
RKD	Knox County Regional	Rockland	ME
RKS	Sweetwater County	Rock Springs	WY
RNO	Reno-Tahoe International	Reno	NV
ROA	Roanoke Regional	Roanoke	VA
ROC	Greater Rochester International	Rochester	NY
RSW	Southwest Florida International	Fort Myers	FL
SAN	San Diego International	San Diego	CA
SAT	San Antonio International	San Antonio	TX
SBA	Municipal	Santa Barbara	CA
SBN	South Bend Regional	South Bend	IN
SBY	Wicomico Regional	Salisbury-Ocean City	MD
SCE	University Park	State College	PA
SDF	Louisville International (Standiford Field)	Louisville	KY
SEA	Seattle-Tacoma International	Seattle	WA
SFO	San Francisco International	San Francisco	CA
SHR	Sheridan	Sheridan	WY
SHV	Regional	Shreveport	LA
SJC	Mineta San Jose International	San Jose	CA

continued

TABLE E-1 Continued

Codes	Airport	City	State
SJU	Luis Munoz Marin International	San Juan	PR
SLC	Salt Lake City International	Salt Lake City	UT
SMF	Sacramento International	Sacramento	CA
SNA	John Wayne	Santa Ana	CA
STL	Lambert-St. Louis International	St Louis	MO
STT	Cyril E. King	Charlotte Amalie, St. Thomas	VI
STX	Henry E. Rohlsen	Christiansted, St Croix	VI
SYR	Syracuse Hancock International	Syracuse	NY
TEX	Telluride Regional	Telluride	CO
TLH	Tallahassee Regional	Tallahassee	FL
TPA	Tampa International	Tampa	FL
TUL	Tulsa International	Tulsa	OK
TUS	Tucson International	Tucson	AZ
TYS	McGhee Tyson	Knoxville	TN
VPS	Eglin AFB	Valparaiso	FL
XNA	Northwest Arkansas Regional	Fayetteville	AR
YKM	Yakima Air Terminal	Yakima	WA

Appendix F

Regional Airlines Departures by City

This appendix presents the committee's analysis of changes in the number of aircraft departures discussed in Chapter 2 for regional airlines. Figures F-1 through F-36, ordered alphabetically by airline, show total departures by airport code (refer to Table E-1 in Appendix E for corresponding cities) and by airline, in the cities most frequently served by that airline and thus in the cities most likely to serve as domiciles for pilots. The data used for this analysis were scheduled aircraft departures taken from Air Carrier Summary: T3: U.S. Air Carrier Airport Activity Statistics provided by the Bureau of Transportation Statistics (n.d.-a) of the U.S. Department of Transportation. The data were from the third quarter of 2000, 2005, and 2010. All carriers that reported more than 20,000 aircraft departures in the third quarter of 2010 were examined. This group consisted of 18 regional airlines.

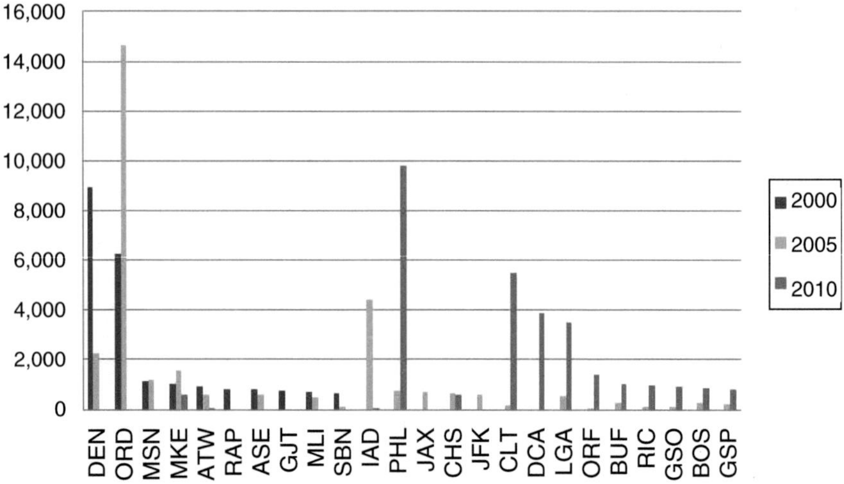

FIGURE F-1 Air Wisconsin departures by city.
SOURCE: Data from Bureau of Transportation Statistics (n.d.-a).

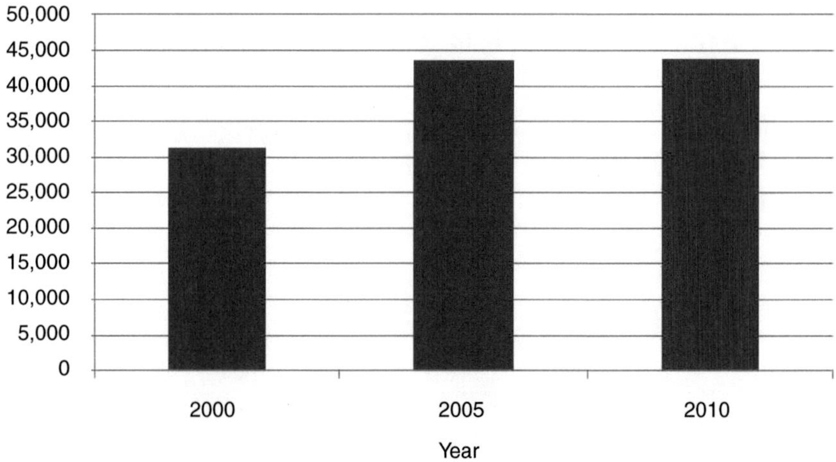

FIGURE F-2 Air Wisconsin total departures.
SOURCE: Data from Bureau of Transportation Statistics (n.d.-a).

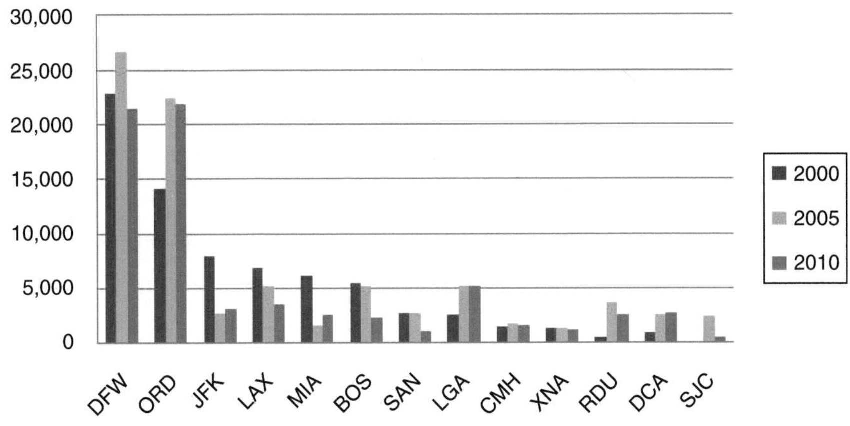

FIGURE F-3 American Eagle departures by city.
SOURCE: Data from Bureau of Transportation Statistics (n.d.-a).

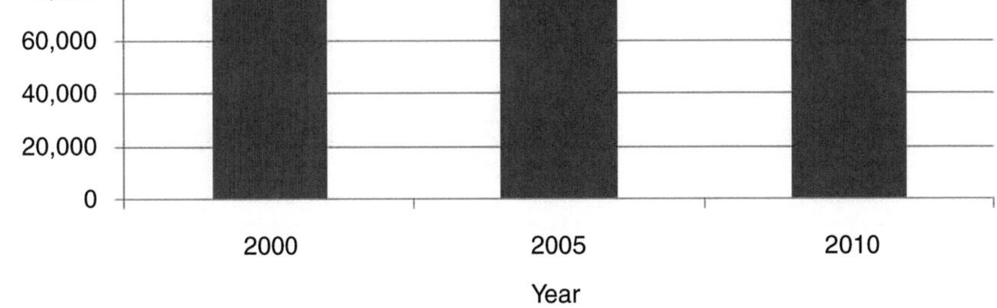

FIGURE F-4 American Eagle total departures.
SOURCE: Data from Bureau of Transportation Statistics (n.d.-a).

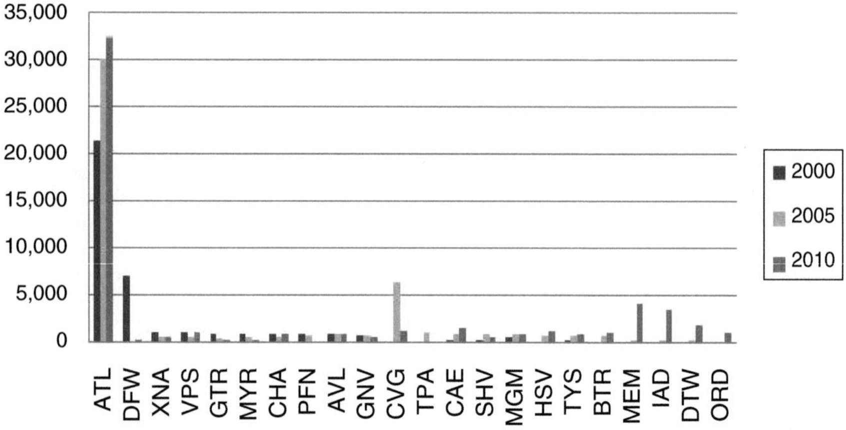

FIGURE F-5 Atlantic SE departures by city.
SOURCE: Data from Bureau of Transportation Statistics (n.d.-a).

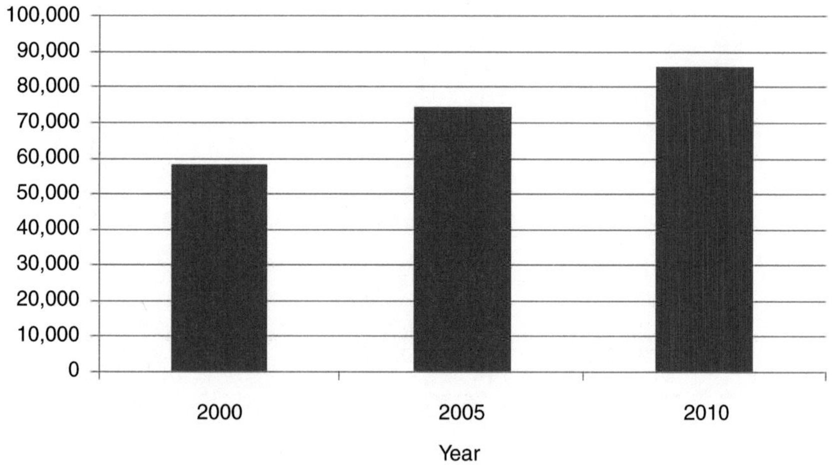

FIGURE F-6 Atlantic SE total departures.
SOURCE: Data from Bureau of Transportation Statistics (n.d.-a).

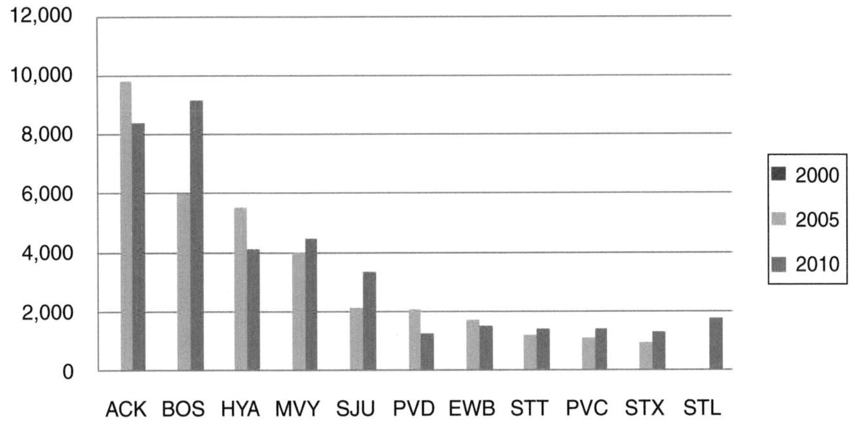

FIGURE F-7 Cape Air departures by city.
SOURCE: Data from Bureau of Transportation Statistics (n.d.-a).

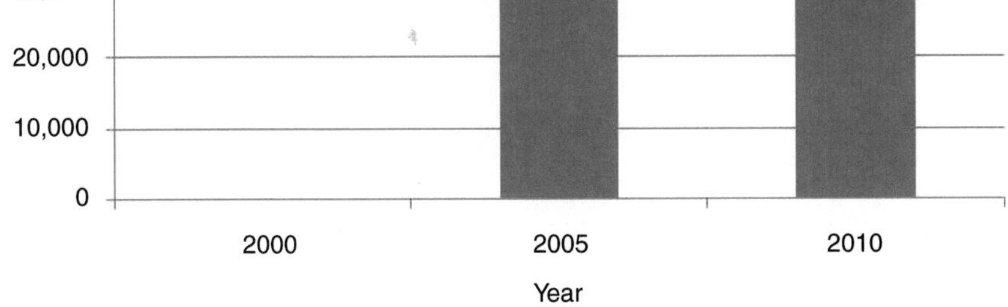

FIGURE F-8 Cape Air total departures.
SOURCE: Data from Bureau of Transportation Statistics (n.d.-a).

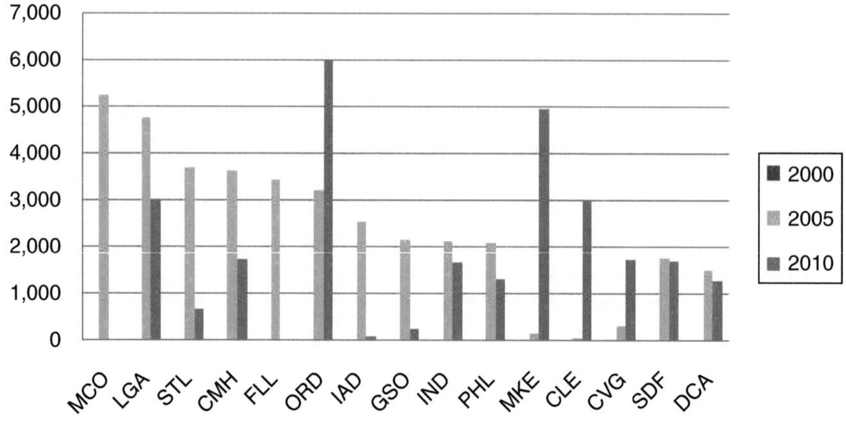

FIGURE F-9 Chautauqua departures by city.
SOURCE: Data from Bureau of Transportation Statistics (n.d.-a).

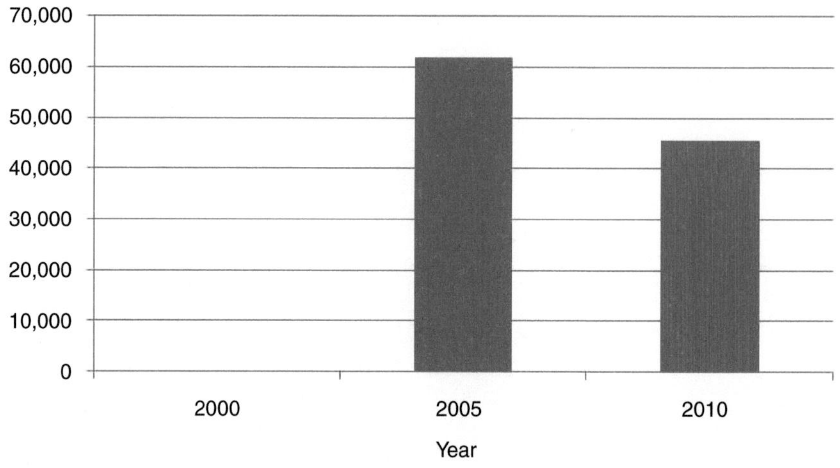

FIGURE F-10 Chautauqua total departures.
SOURCE: Data from Bureau of Transportation Statistics (n.d.-a).

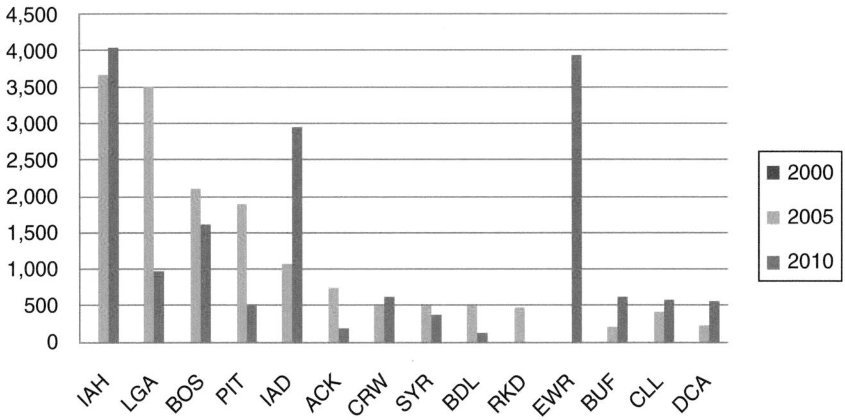

FIGURE F-11 Colgan departures by city.
SOURCE: Data from Bureau of Transportation Statistics (n.d.-a).

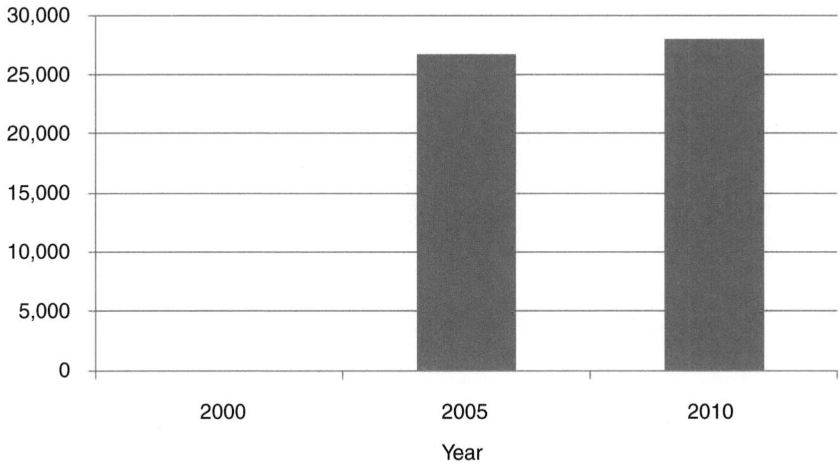

FIGURE F-12 Colgan total departures.
SOURCE: Data from Bureau of Transportation Statistics (n.d.-a).

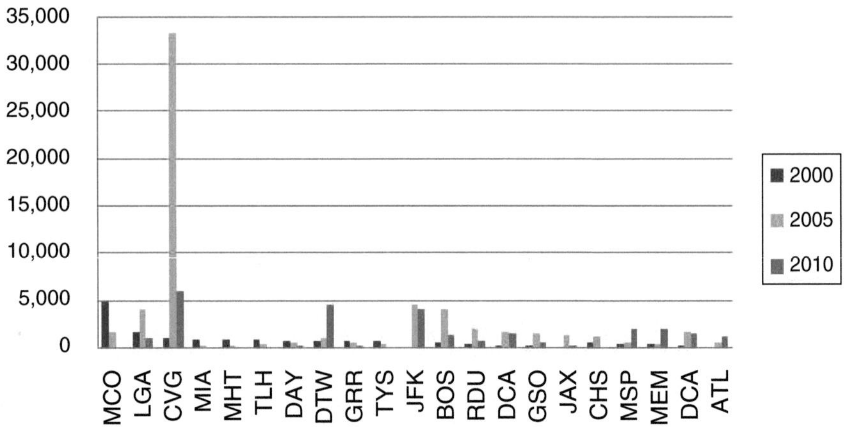

FIGURE F-13 Comair departures by city.
SOURCE: Data from Bureau of Transportation Statistics (n.d.-a).

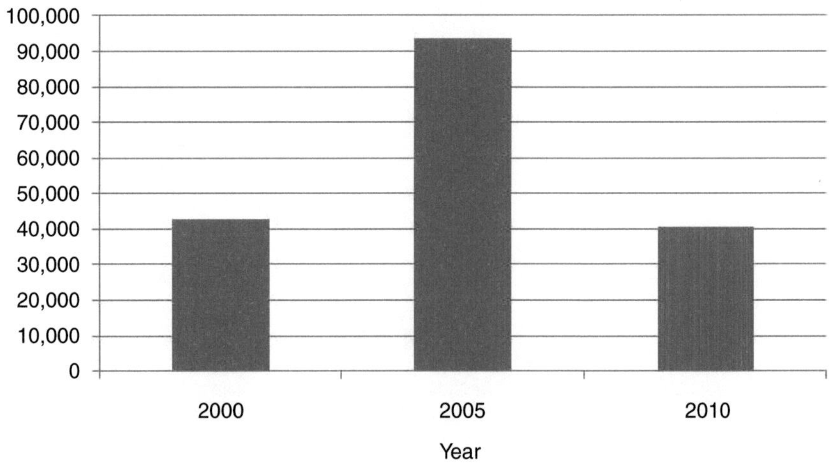

FIGURE F-14 Comair total departures.
SOURCE: Data from Bureau of Transportation Statistics (n.d.-a).

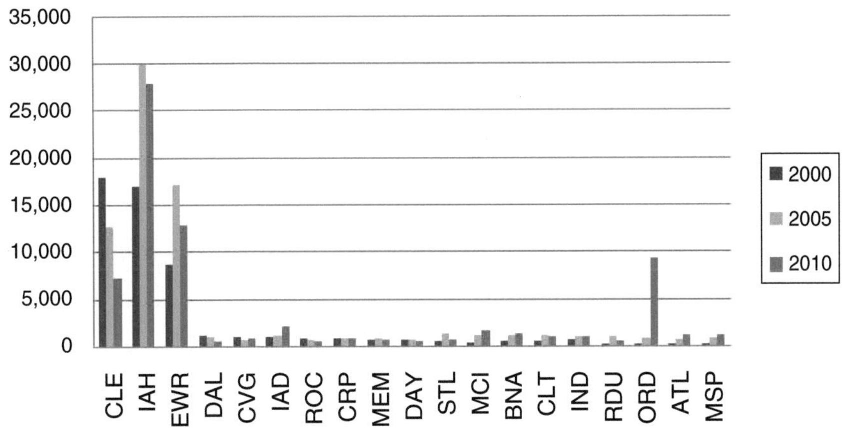

FIGURE F-15 Expressjet departures by city.
SOURCE: Data from Bureau of Transportation Statistics (n.d.-a).

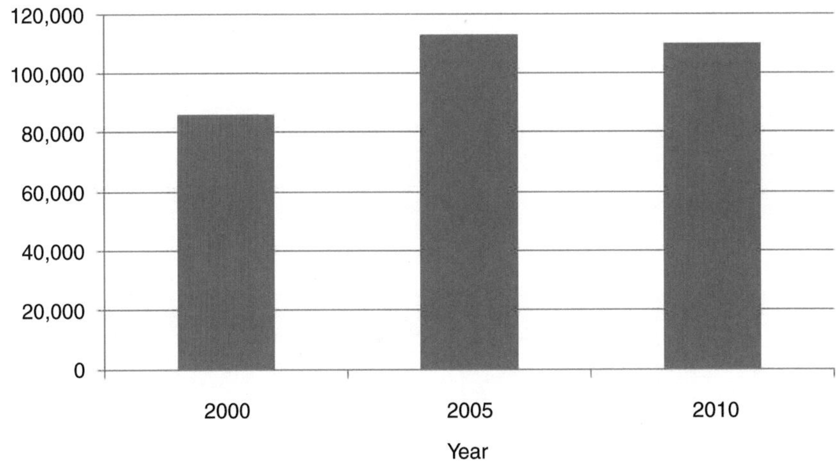

FIGURE F-16 Expressjet total departures.
SOURCE: Data from Bureau of Transportation Statistics (n.d.-a).

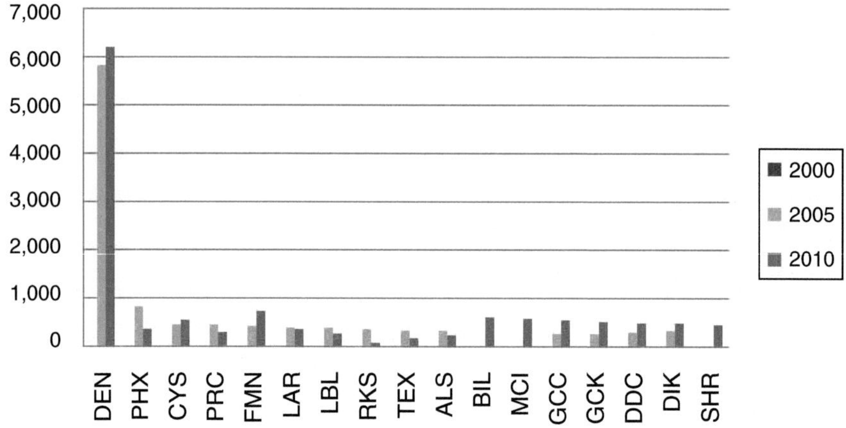

FIGURE F-17 Great Lakes departures by city.
SOURCE: Data from Bureau of Transportation Statistics (n.d.-a).

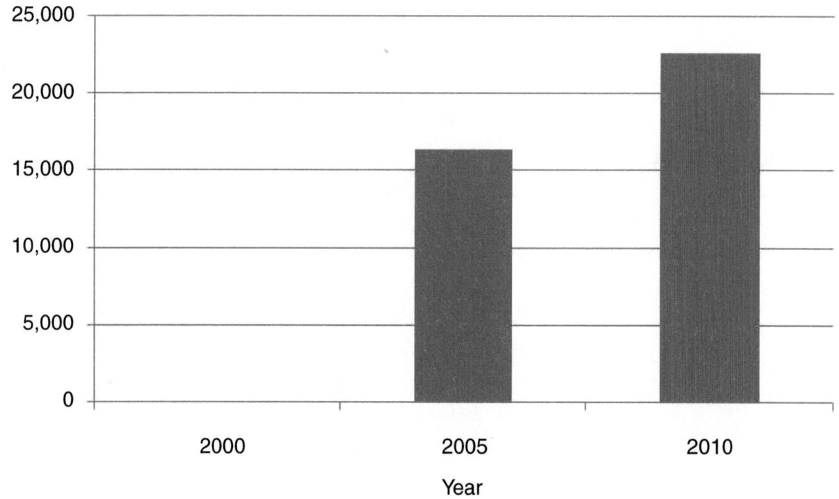

FIGURE F-18 Great Lakes total departures.
SOURCE: Data from Bureau of Transportation Statistics (n.d.-a).

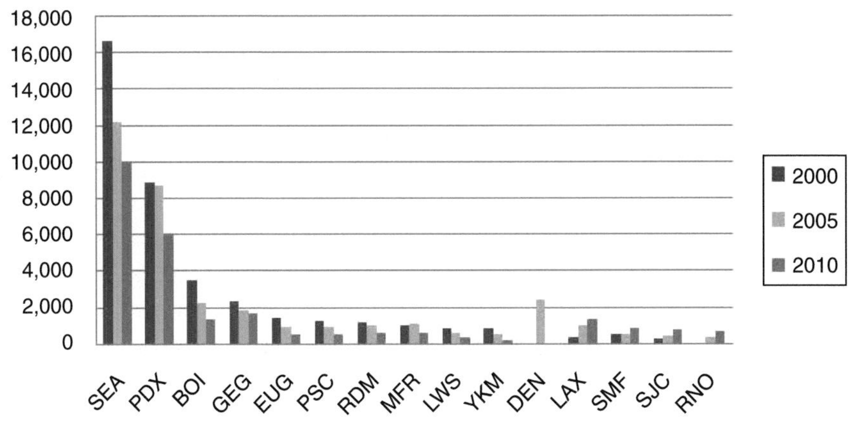

FIGURE F-19 Horizon departures by city.
SOURCE: Data from Bureau of Transportation Statistics (n.d.-a).

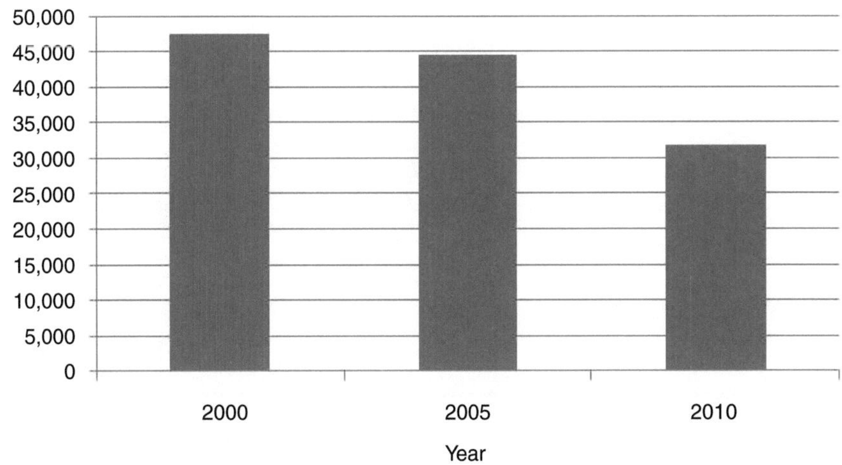

FIGURE F-20 Horizon total departures.
SOURCE: Data from Bureau of Transportation Statistics (n.d.-a).

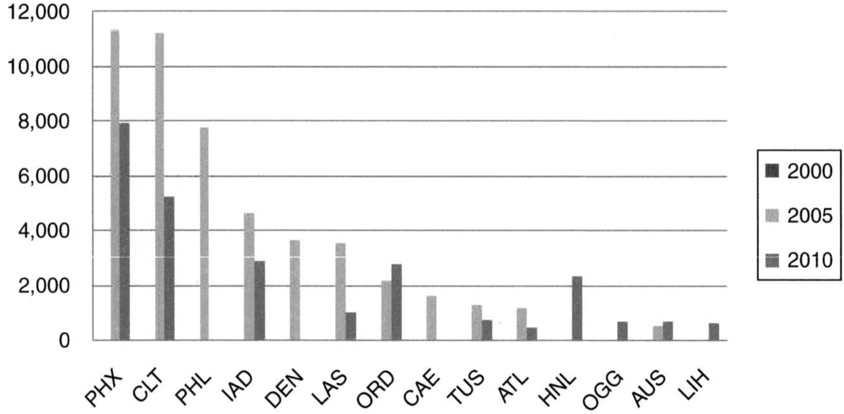

FIGURE F-21 Mesa departures by city.
SOURCE: Data from Bureau of Transportation Statistics (n.d.-a).

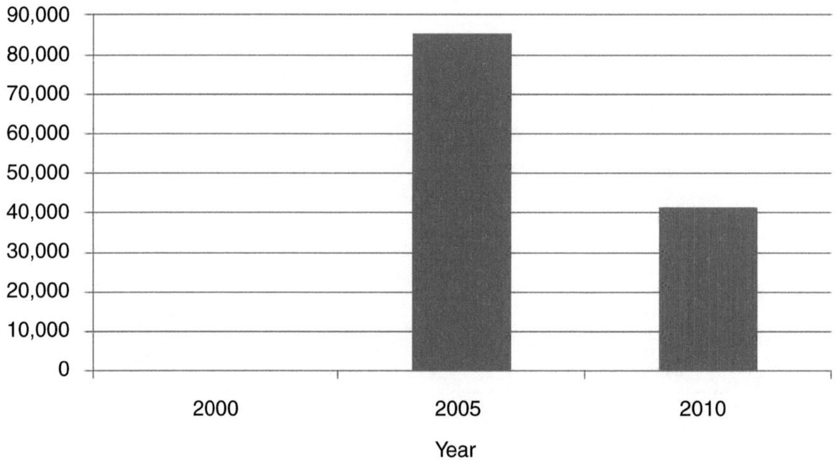

FIGURE F-22 Mesa total departures.
SOURCE: Data from Bureau of Transportation Statistics (n.d.-a).

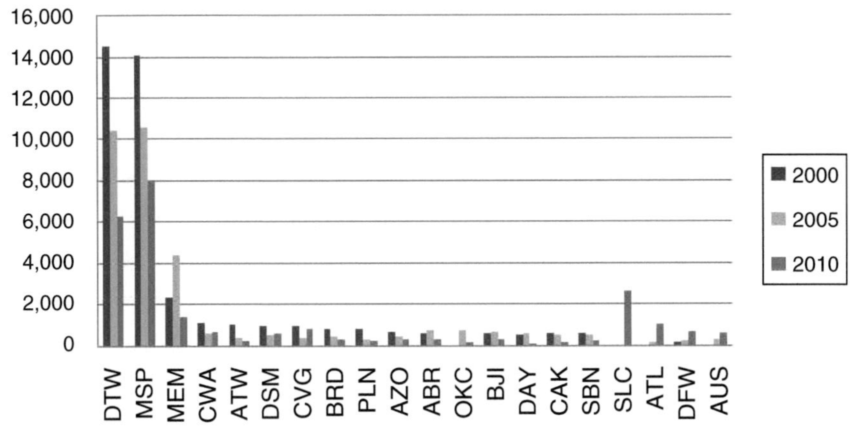

FIGURE F-23 Mesaba departures by city.
SOURCE: Data from Bureau of Transportation Statistics (n.d.-a).

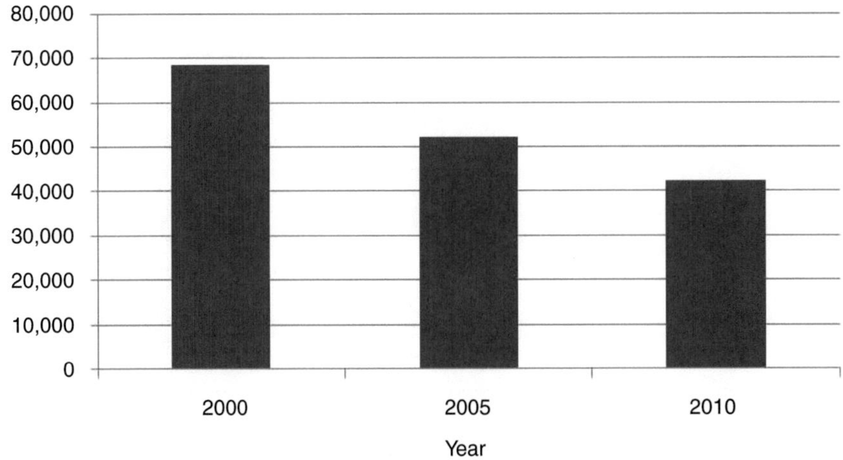

FIGURE F-24 Mesaba total departures.
SOURCE: Data from Bureau of Transportation Statistics (n.d.-a).

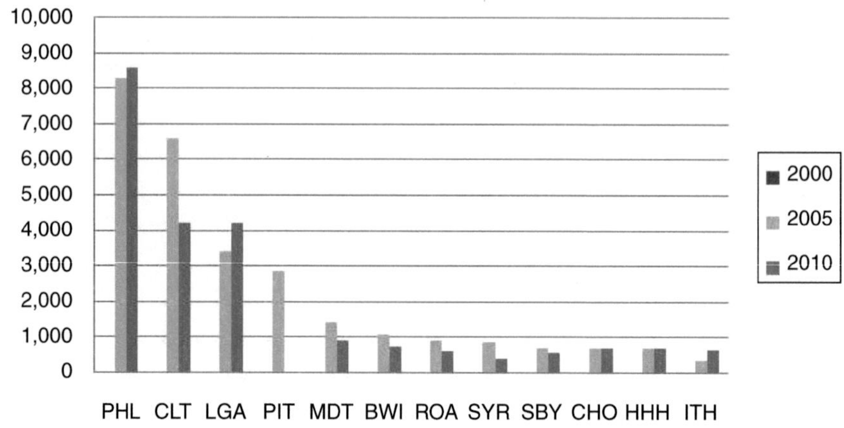

FIGURE F-25 Piedmont departures by city.
SOURCE: Data from Bureau of Transportation Statistics (n.d.-a).

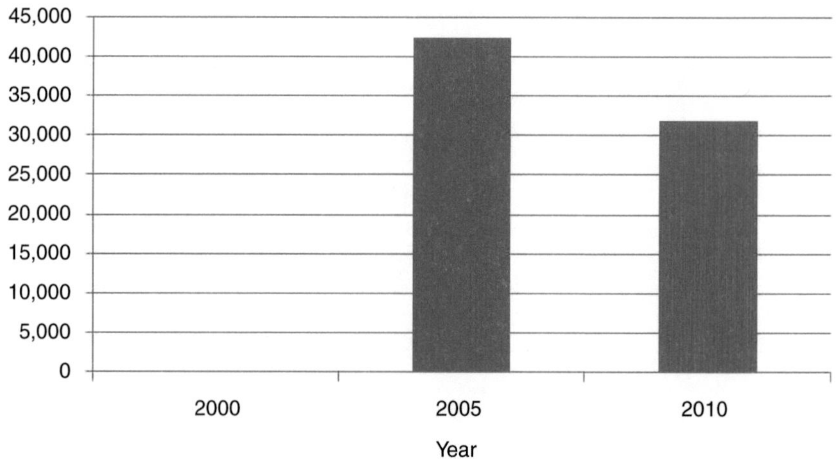

FIGURE F-26 Piedmont total departures.
SOURCE: Data from Bureau of Transportation Statistics (n.d.-a).

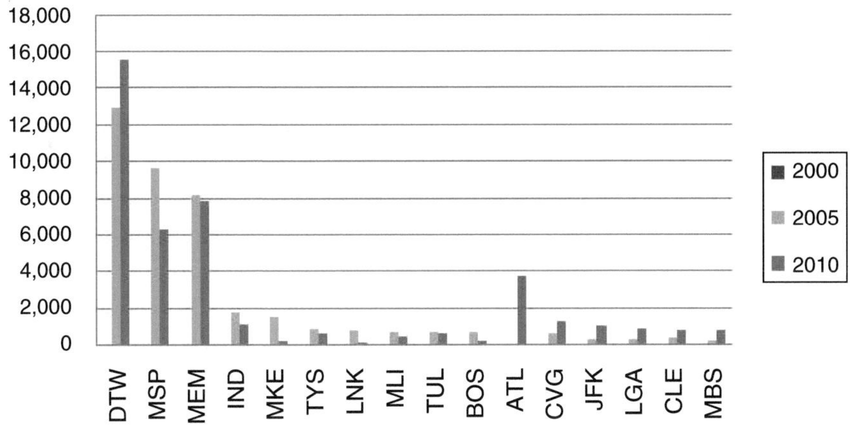

FIGURE F-27 Pinnacle departures by city.
SOURCE: Data from Bureau of Transportation Statistics (n.d.-a).

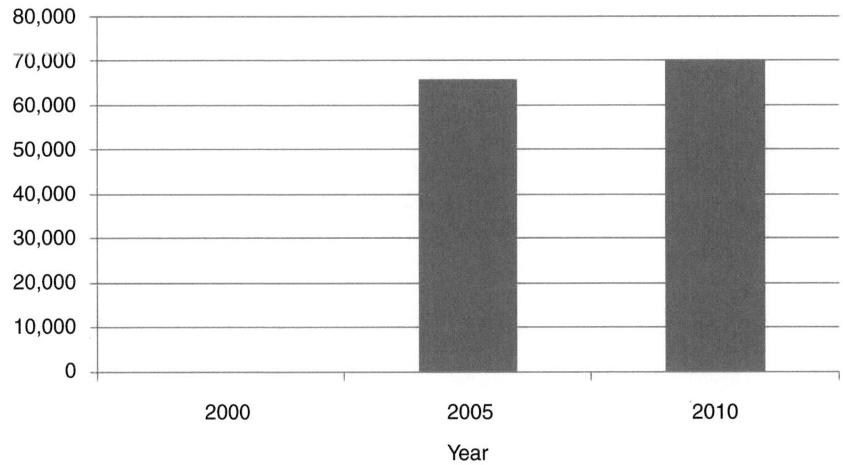

FIGURE F-28 Pinnacle total departures.
SOURCE: Data from Bureau of Transportation Statistics (n.d.-a).

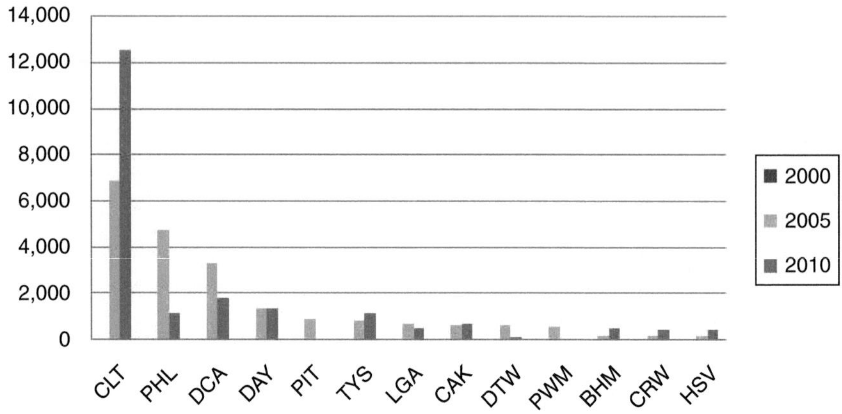

FIGURE F-29 PSA departures by city.
SOURCE: Data from Bureau of Transportation Statistics (n.d.-a).

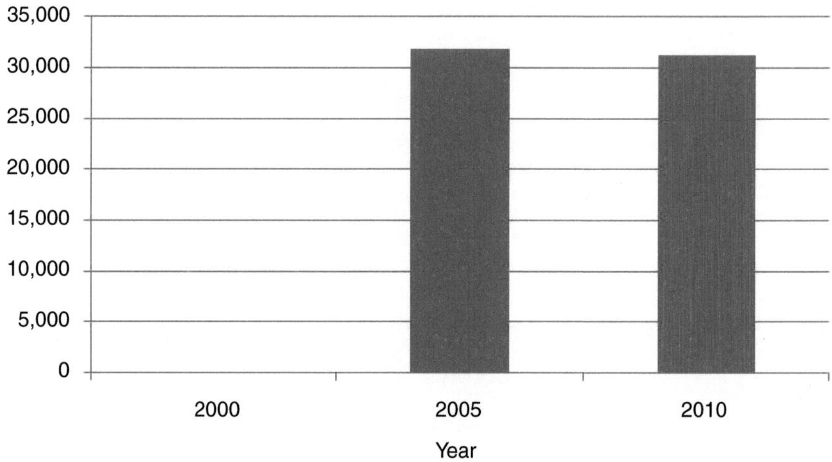

FIGURE F-30 PSA total departures.
SOURCE: Data from Bureau of Transportation Statistics (n.d.-a).

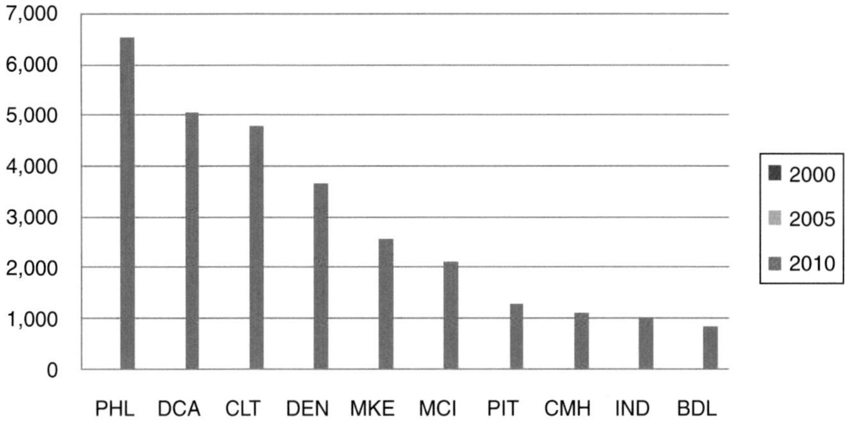

FIGURE F-31 Republic departures by city.
SOURCE: Data from Bureau of Transportation Statistics (n.d.-a).

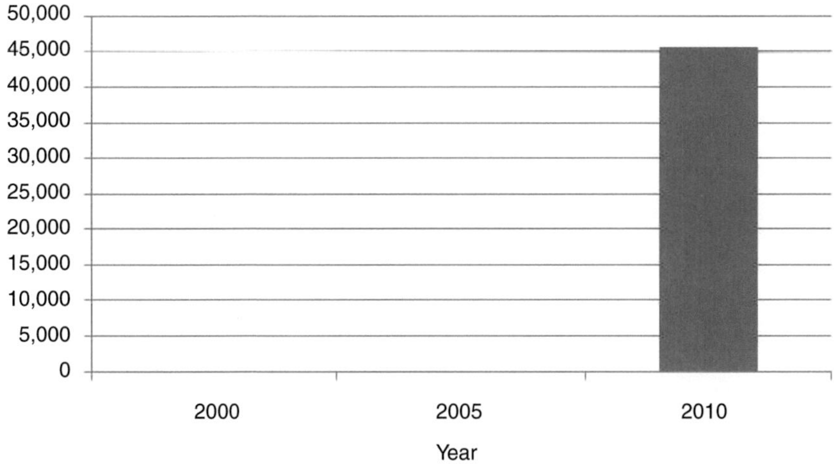

FIGURE F-32 Republic total departures.
SOURCE: Data from Bureau of Transportation Statistics (n.d.-a).

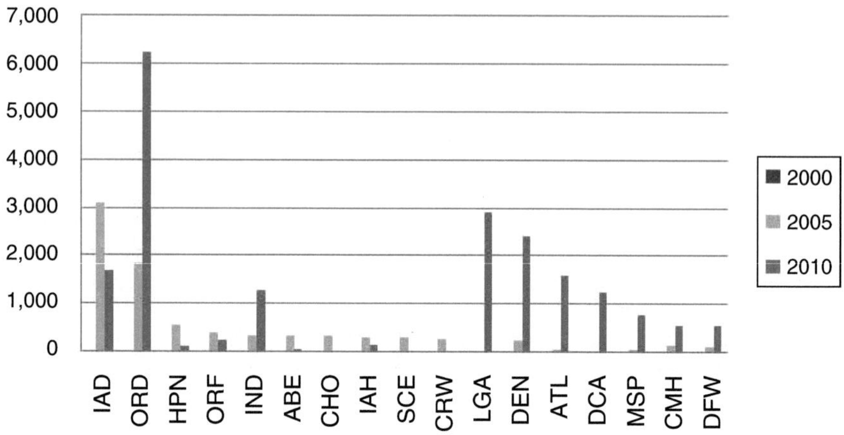

FIGURE F-33 Shuttle America departures by city.
SOURCE: Data from Bureau of Transportation Statistics (n.d.-a).

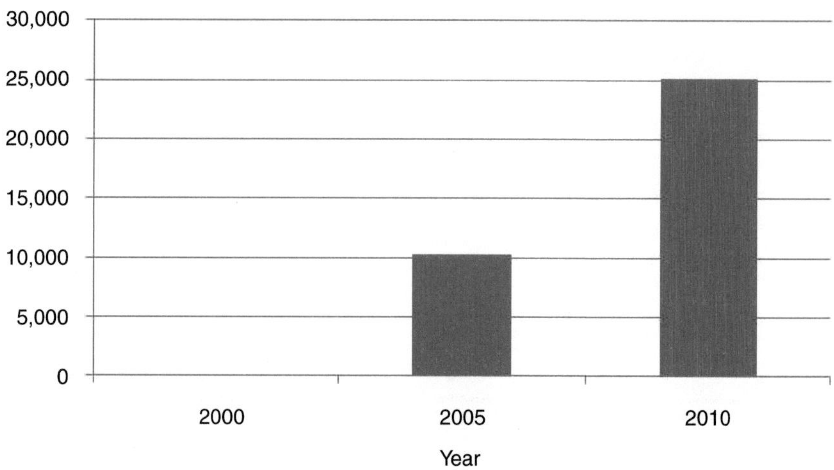

FIGURE F-34 Shuttle America total departures.
SOURCE: Data from Bureau of Transportation Statistics (n.d.-a).

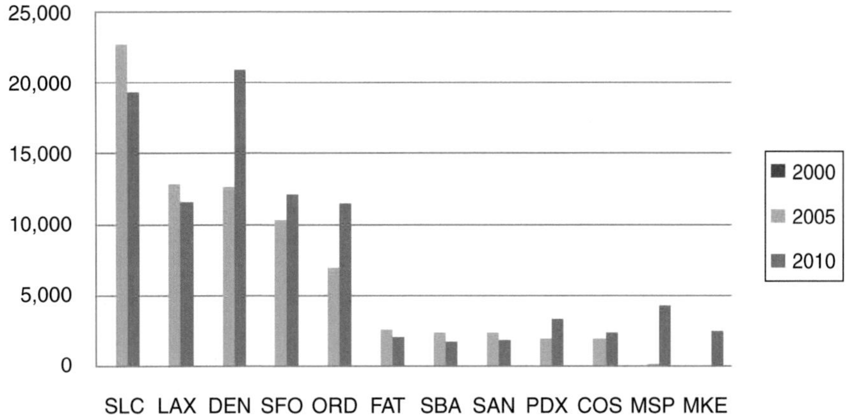

FIGURE F-35 SkyWest departures by city.
SOURCE: Data from Bureau of Transportation Statistics (n.d.-a).

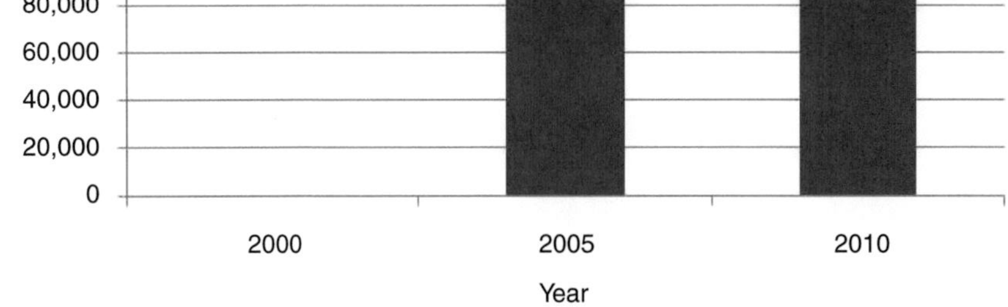

FIGURE F-36 SkyWest total departures.
SOURCE: Data from Bureau of Transportation Statistics (n.d.-a).

Appendix G

Biographical Sketches of Committee Members and Staff

Clinton V. Oster, Jr. (*Chair*) is a professor at the School of Public and Environmental Affairs at Indiana University. Previously, he served as director of the Transportation Research Center and as associate dean at the School of Public and Environmental Affairs at Indiana University. His research focuses on air traffic management and aviation infrastructure, with an emphasis on aviation safety. His research also includes airline economics, airline competition policy, and energy policy. He has been a consultant to the U.S. Department of Transportation, the Federal Aviation Administration, the National Aeronautics and Space Administration (NASA), the European Bank for Reconstruction and Development, state and local governments, and private-sector companies in the United States, Canada, the United Kingdom, Russia, and Australia. He is a member of the National Aviation Advisory Group of the U.S. Government Accountability Office, and he has been an expert witness for the Environment and Natural Resource Division and the Antitrust Division of the U.S. Department of Justice. He received a B.S.E. in chemical engineering from Princeton University, an M.S. in urban and public affairs from Carnegie Mellon University, and a Ph.D. in economics from Harvard University.

Benjamin A. Berman is a senior research associate in the Human Systems Integration Division at the NASA Ames Research Center (affiliated through San Jose State University), and he is a pilot for a major U.S. air carrier with 9,000 hours of flight experience. Before returning to professional flying in 2001, he was on the staff of the National Transportation Safety Board (NTSB), where he served as the chief of the Major Investigations Division and led the Operational Factors Division (responsible for flight operations, air traffic control, and meteorology investigations). At NTSB, he also served as the flight operations investigator for major cases, including the USAir B-737 accident in Pittsburgh and the ValuJet DC-9 accident in the Everglades, and he managed flight crew human factors research projects. He holds an airline transport pilot certificate with type ratings for the Boeing 777, Boeing 737, Embraer 120, and Dornier 228. He received an A.B. summa cum laude in economics from Harvard College.

J. Lynn Caldwell is a senior research psychologist for the U.S. Air Force Research Laboratory, currently stationed at Wright-Patterson Air Force Base in Ohio. Previously, she was with the U.S. Army's Aeromedical Research Laboratory, where she conducted numerous simulator and in-flight investigations on fatigue countermeasures and circadian rhythms in rated military pilots. She has also been a member of the Warfighter Fatigue Countermeasures Program and a distinguished visiting scholar at the U.S. Air Force Academy. She has served as a fatigue consultant for various U.S. Air Force commands and other military and civilian groups. She frequently provides fatigue management workshops, safety briefings, and training courses to aviation personnel, flight surgeons, commanders, and safety officers. She is certified as a sleep specialist by the American Board of Sleep Medicine. She received a Ph.D. in experimental psychology from the University of Southern Mississippi.

David F. Dinges is a professor and chief of the Division of Sleep and Chronobiology and director of the Unit for Experimental Psychiatry in the Department of Psychiatry and associate director of the Center for Sleep and Circadian Neurobiology at the Perelman School of Medicine, University of Pennsylvania. He also leads the neurobehavioral and psychosocial factors team for the National Space Biomedical Research Institute. His research focuses on the physiological, neurobehavioral, and cognitive effects of sleep loss, disturbances of circadian biology, and stress, and the implications of these unmitigated effects on health and safety. He has been president of the U.S. Sleep Research Society and of the World Federation of Sleep Research and Sleep Medicine Societies, and he has served on the board of directors of the American Academy of Sleep Medicine and the National Sleep Foundation. He is currently editor-in-chief of *Sleep*. His awards include the 2004 Decade of Behavior Research Award from the American Psychological Association and the 2007 NASA Distinguished Public Service Medal. He has an A.B. in psychology from Saint Benedict's College, an M.S. in physiological psychology from Saint Louis University, an honorary M.A. from the University of Pennsylvania, and a Ph.D. in physiological psychology from Saint Louis University.

R. Curtis Graeber is the president of The Graeber Group, Ltd. Previously, he served as the chief engineer for human factors and director of regional safety programs at Boeing Commercial Airplanes and in other several management positions in research, airplane design, and safety. He also led Boeing's efforts to improve regional safety, including industry development and implementation of the global aviation safety roadmap. Before joining Boeing, he led the flight crew fatigue research program at NASA's Ames Research Center and served as chief of flight human factors. He also served as the human factors specialist for the Presidential Commission on the Space Shuttle Challenger Accident. He is a fellow of the Royal Aeronautical Society and the Aerospace Medical Association. He has chaired working groups for the Federal Aviation Administration, the Flight Safety Foundation, and the International Civil Aviation Organization. His safety-related awards include the Guild of Air Pilots and Air Navigators' Cumberbatch Trophy and the Aerospace Medical Association's Boothby-Edwards Award. He serves as chair of Air New Zealand's Independent Alertness Advisory Panel, and he is a member of the board of directors of the National Sleep Foundation. He received a Ph.D. in neuropsychology from the University of Virginia.

David E. Meyer is a faculty member of the Cognition and Cognitive Neuroscience Program in the Department of Psychology at the University of Michigan. Previously, he worked in the Human Information Processing Research Department at Bell Telephone Laboratories. His teaching and his research have dealt with fundamental aspects of human perception, attention, learning, memory, language, movement production, reaction time, multitasking, executive mental control, human-computer interaction, personality and cognitive style, cognitive aging, cognitive neuroscience, mathematical models, and computational models. He is a fellow in the Society of Experimental Psychologists, the American Psychological Society, the American Psychological Association, and the American Association for the Advancement of Science. The American Psychological Association has honored him with its Distinguished Scientific Contribution Award. He is a member of the National Academy of Sciences. He received a Ph.D. from the University of Michigan.

Mary Ellen O'Connell (*Senior Staff Officer*) is deputy director for the Board on Human-Systems Integration and the Board on Behavioral, Cognitive, and Sensory Sciences at the National Research Council (NRC). At the NRC, she has served as study director for five major consensus studies: on prevention of mental disorders and substance abuse, international education and foreign languages, ethical considerations for research on housing-related health hazards involving children, reducing underage drinking, and assessing and improving children's health. She also organized workshops on welfare reform and children and gun violence. Previously, she held various positions at the U.S. Department of Health and Human Services (HHS), including serving as director of state and local initiatives in the Office of the Assistant Secretary for Planning and Evaluation. Her previous positions also include work on homeless policy and program design at the U.S. Department of Housing and Urban Development and as director of field services for the Commonwealth of Massachusetts. She has a B.A. with distinction from Cornell University and an M.A. in the management of human services from the Heller School for Social Policy and Management at Brandeis University.

Matthew Rizzo is professor of neurology, engineering, and public policy at the University of Iowa. At the university, he is also vice chair for clinical/translational research and director of the division of neuroergonomics, its visual function laboratory, and its instrumented vehicles in the Department of Neurology, as well as director of the University Aging Mind and Brain Initiative. His clinical interests and activities include behavioral neurology, cognitive neuroscience, and memory disorders. His research interests include behavioral disturbances resulting from central nervous system injury, neural substrates of human vision (including attention and visuomotor control), aging and dementia, driving performance, and driving simulation. He has conducted research on fatigue and truckers for the National Institutes of Health and the Iowa Department of Transportation. He is a member of the American Academy of Neurology, the American Neurological Association, the Human Factors and Ergonomics Society, the Society for Neuroscience, and the Vision Sciences Society. He has an M.D. from Johns Hopkins University School of Medicine.

David J. Schroeder is a private consultant. Previously, he was a manager of the Aerospace Human Factors Research Division at the Civil Aero Medical Institute of the Federal Aviation Administration (FAA), where he also served as supervisor of clinical psychology research and as the long-time administrator of the FAA's Employee Attitude Survey. His research is documented in over 40 Office of Aviation Medicine (OAM) technical reports and in more than 125 presentations in a range of areas, including disorientation, job attitudes, stress, age, shiftwork and fatigue, and color vision. He assisted with the psychological screening of federal air marshals during their post-9/11 hiring increase. He was the Office of Aviation Medicine Manager of the Year in 2005 and led his division to become the OAM Office of the Year in 1999 and 2005. He is past president of the Oklahoma Psychological Association, the Division of Applied Experimental and Engineering Psychology of the American Psychological Association, and the

Aerospace Medical Association. He has a Ph.D. in psychology from the University of Oklahoma.

Toby Warden (*Study Director*) is a program officer with the Board on Human-Systems Integration of the National Research Council (NRC). Previously, she worked as a program officer with the NRC's Board on Atmospheric Sciences and Climate, serving as study director for the projects that published *Climate Stabilization Targets: Emissions, Concentrations, and Impacts Over Decades to Millennia* and *When Weather Matters: Science and Service to Meet Critical Societal Needs*. Prior to joining the NRC staff, she had extensive experience as a program manager and community organizer in the fields of public health and youth advocacy in Boston, Massachusetts. Her doctoral research applied quantitative and qualitative methodologies to examine the rise of the U.S. Mayors Climate Protection Agreement. She has a B.A. in history, magna cum laude, and a Ph.D. in social ecology with an emphasis on environmental analysis and design, both from the University of California, Irvine.

J. Frank Yates is an Arthur F. Thurnau professor, a professor of psychology, a professor of marketing and business administration, and a principal in the Judgment and Decision Laboratory of the Department of Psychology, all at the University of Michigan. He is also the coordinator of the Decision Consortium, which is a University of Michigan-wide association of faculty and students whose scholarship includes significant decision-making elements. The main focus of his research is on decision making at both the theoretical and practical levels. That work has emphasized understanding how people decide in the challenging conditions of real life and developing means of assisting them to decide better in those circumstances. He is a past president of the Society for Judgment and Decision Making and is active in a variety of other efforts to advance decision scholarship, including efforts involving scholarly journals. He has been an active member of many government and other organizations, including the advisory panel of the Decision, Risk, and Management Science Program at the National Science Foundation. He holds a Ph.D. from the University of Michigan.